ISLAM,
THE MIDDLE EAST,
AND THE NEW
GLOBAL HEGEMONY

The Middle East in the International System

ANOUSHIRAVAN EHTESHAMI &
RAYMOND HINNEBUSCH,
SERIES EDITORS

ISLAM,
THE MIDDLE EAST,
AND THE NEW
GLOBAL HEGEMONY

Simon W. Murden

LYNNE
RIENNER
PUBLISHERS

BOULDER
LONDON

Published in the United States of America in 2002 by
Lynne Rienner Publishers, Inc.
1800 30th Street, Boulder, Colorado 80301
www.rienner.com

and in the United Kingdom by
Lynne Rienner Publishers, Inc.
3 Henrietta Street, Covent Garden, London WC2E 8LU

Library of Congress Cataloging-in-Publication Data
Murden, Simon W.
    Islam, the Middle East, and the new global hegemony / Simon W. Murden.
      p. cm.
    Includes bibliographical references and index.
    ISBN 1-58826-059-3 (alk. paper)
    ISBN 1-58826-088-7 (pb.: alk. paper)
    1. Middle East—Politics and government—1945– 2. Islam and politics—Middle
East. 3. Globalization. 4. Liberalism. I. Title.
    DS63.1 M84   2002
    327'.0917'671—dc21

                    2002019700

British Cataloguing in Publication Data
A Cataloguing in Publication record for this book
is available from the British Library.

Printed and bound in the United States of America

The paper used in this publication meets the requirements
of the American National Standard for Permanence of
Paper for Printed Library Materials Z39.48-1984.

5 4 3 2 1

Contents

List of Maps   vii
Acknowledgments   ix

1 Introduction: The Emergence of the West's Global Hegemony
   and Its Final Frontier   1

Part I   Islam in the Global Hegemony

2 Reconstructing the Post–Cold War World: Islam in the
   Cultural Discourse of the West   23

3 The Pax Americana in the Middle East   43

4 The Impact of the Global Economy in Muslim Countries   93

Part 2   Muslim Resistance and Adaptation
        in the Liberal International Order

5 The Islamic Revolt and the Politics of Paralysis   133

6 Islam and the Liberal Idea   155

7 Islam in the International System:
   A Future of Conflict or Cooperation?   185

Appendix 1: The History of the Liberal Idea   211
Appendix 2: The History of the Islamic Faith   213

Bibliography   217
Index   229
About the Book   235

Maps

1.1 The Muslim World in 2001   13

1.2 Muslims in Conflict in the 1990s   15

7.1 The Organization of the Islamic Conference   190

Acknowledgments

I would like to express special thanks to Rosemarie Murden and Trevor Murden for all their help in the production of the final manuscript. Many thanks also to Lynne Rienner's commissioning editor in the UK, Richard Purslow, for all his patience and encouragement during the writing of this book, and to Anoushiravan Ehteshami for his useful advice.

—*S. W. M.*

1

Introduction: The Emergence of the West's Global Hegemony and Its Final Frontier

The twentieth century saw an epic struggle for the modern world. The forces of Western liberalism took on the European alternatives of dynastic absolutism, extremist nationalism, and Marxism-Leninism. Britain, France, Canada, and the United States were to overcome the darkest impulses in European civilization, and individuals were freed from absolute tutelage to the state. With the collapse of the Soviet empire in the late 1980s, Eastern Europe was Westernized, and what Francis Fukuyama called the "liberal idea"—the combination of the rule of law, liberal democracy, and market capitalism—emerged as the basis of a truly global order; it was premised on rationalism, secularism, individualism, and equality and empathy between humans. Liberalism spoke of universal goods, and to the extent that people across the world identified with them, Western civilization transcended the borders of Europe and North America. The West could be found almost everywhere, and although the liberal idea was not universally accepted, it was by far the most important model of what the future world should look like. With Western states and companies behind it, liberalism was the dominant value system of a new global hegemony.

The liberal idea and the world order that stemmed from it had been a long time in the making (see Appendix 1). Liberal ideas originated principally in Britain and France and were transmitted to other parts of Europe and North America. The subsequent development of the West was an incremental process. Liberalism was never applied in an ideal form. Liberal ideas established influential tendencies in the politics and economic systems of Europe and North America, but they always ran alongside other forms of belief and practice. Liberalism was varyingly meshed with Christianity, kingship, class status, nation, and state. The

1

pluralism implicit in liberalism made this kind of normative eclecticism possible. People could aspire to liberal ideals while retaining elements of their preexisting beliefs.

Meshing liberalism with other ideologies sometimes caused tensions within and between societies, but Westerners often lived with these contradictions over long periods. In the nineteenth century, Europeans and Americans alike mixed their liberalism with a concept of civilization that claimed racial and cultural superiority over non-Europeans. In both the British Empire and in the making of the United States, the practices of enslavement, expropriation, and colonial rule were highly illiberal. In Europe, liberalism was inextricably linked to ethnic nationalism, although the two belief systems were not necessarily compatible at all. In Germany and Eastern Europe, liberal ideas never quite managed to emerge from the shadows of authoritarian belief systems. The West and Eastern Europe drifted apart and were only fully reunited at the end of the Cold War. Crucially, for the future of Europe, Germany was thoroughly Westernized after World War II, although Europeans ran their liberalism alongside social democracy in a way that Americans did not.

Liberalism was a flexible belief system, but a dominant model did emerge: an Anglo-American liberalism that owed its preeminence to the geopolitical, economic, and ideational power of Britain and the United States since the eighteenth century. From Woodrow Wilson arguing for a "democratic peace" following World War I, to the planning of the post–World War II order in the Atlantic Charter of 1941, to the capitalist revivalism of Margaret Thatcher and Ronald Reagan in the 1980s, Anglo-American liberalism left great imprints on the history of the twentieth century.

Anglo-American liberalism advocated the idea of limited government but continued to uphold the powers of the nation-state at an international level. Few Britons or Americans wanted world government but instead sought to bring about a constitutional ordering of an international society. The ideal world was a community of democratic states governed by the rule of law, cooperative international institutions, and open markets. To the extent that force was required to police international society, it was to be legitimated through consensual institutions. Powerful actors would remain, but the haphazard violence of the balance of power and great power competition would be a thing of the past. The Anglo-American vision was institutionalized in the founding of the League of Nations and the United Nations, although ideological and geopolitical conflicts stalled its realization until the end of the Cold War. After the Cold War, the UN Security Council became a quasi-legislative body in international society and a significant promoter of Western values and interests in the world.

The Anglo-American preference for freer markets was also immensely influential, especially toward the end of the twentieth century. In the 1980s, Thatcher and Reagan promoted a capitalist revivalism that became the ideological orthodoxy of the West. The interventions of the social democratic state were to be progressively replaced by competitive markets as the principal basis for the socioeconomic order. Revived capitalists were given the lead role in unleashing the power of the technological revolution also taking place in the late twentieth century. Through the mechanisms of world markets, the neoliberal orthodoxy gained great leverage. In Europe, the Anglo-American model was not taken on board wholesale, but the balance between liberalism and social democracy tilted in favor of liberalism.

Liberalism cast an immense, normative shadow across the post–Cold War world. By this time, the West's liberalism had been purged of the worst contradictions and was not overshadowed by its overt association with selfish European nationalisms or U.S. Cold War strategy, although it did still come with the accretions of Western interests. Moreover, the West was by far the most successful group of countries on earth and was both a powerful agent and a role model: it had the material and intersubjective power to socialize the minds of others and to create a mood for some degree of liberalization. What the West said was so influential not only because non-Westerners often believed what the West wanted was probably irresistible but also because liberal ideas did strike various chords in most other states and civil societies. Where this "glocalization" took place, the ideas of the dominant West were liable to crowd out the ideas of the dominated.

The supremacy of the liberal West after the Cold War was all the more significant because it coincided with a technological revolution in communications that greatly increased the tempo of human interactions across distances. The new interconnectedness was summed up in the ubiquitous term *globalization,* and although many of the phenomena associated with it were not new, by the late twentieth century things were reaching a different pitch. What made late-twentieth-century globalization so radical was not the new technology of connectedness by itself but the way in which the technology carried liberal ideas and practices through the multitude of new global networks. Thus, the new globalization was kicked off by the purposeful liberal practices of those Westerners who most benefited from it, although once started, things often took on a life of their own.

In the late twentieth century, then, liberal ideas had a presence and plausibility that enabled them to penetrate and transform non-Western societies in a way not seen before, not even during the age of nineteenth-century European colonialism. Even relatively small amounts of globalized activity, Jan Aart Scholte observed, especially in the less developed parts of the world, could have a disproportionately large impact.[1] Globalization was practically synonymous with the final expansion of a fully realized world liberal order. Indeed, it is difficult to imagine that a single global order—globalization itself—could even exist unless it was founded on the pluralism and cooperative ethos that the liberal hegemony embodied. An old-fashioned state-bound hegemon—operating on the basis of self-interest, power politics, and the balance of power—could not possibly match the ability of Western hegemony to penetrate and integrate almost all other states and societies.

For non-Westerners, the great question was how to go about meshing their local values and interests with those of Western liberalism. The task was often great because the value systems of many local cultures embodied a completely different ontology for understanding and appreciating the world. The integration of global-engaged elites and that of ordinary people was also likely to be at a very different pace. The reproduction of some ideal liberalism could not be expected from non-Western states and societies—although that did not stop the West from sometimes pressing for it—but most did have to face up to the incremental absorption of liberal ideas.

The ideational battleground between the global and the local was bound to embody real tensions. The end of the Cold War itself had released the global phenomenon of localized cultural revivalism, which had been a growing force since the 1970s. Resurgent nationalism and politicized religion could be found almost everywhere. Local peoples had little choice but to deal with Western hegemony, but how they should do it was widely contested. At the beginning of the twenty-first century, the choice between globalized liberalism and cultural revivalism represented the basic alternative in human affairs, as well as Western modernity's last great struggle.

The Architecture of the Western Hegemony

The way the post–Cold War world functioned had its origins in the system of liberal states and institutions that constituted the Western alliance during the Cold War. The Western alliance linked the United States, Western Europe, and Japan, as well as states in other regions that sought shelter around it. The United States was the hegemon of the Western alliance and the key provider of the public international goods that made the alliance what it was. In particular, the United States was the sponsor of a number of local, regional, and global clubs that provided members with increased levels of information, predictability, and support. At the core of the Western alliance was an economic system based on the U.S. dollar as the principal medium of exchange and the gradual opening of markets. The system fostered the postwar reconstruction of Europe and Japan and built an alliance capable of defeating the Soviet threat. The Western system embodied high levels of institutionalization, notably in the form of the International Monetary Fund (IMF), the World Bank, and the General Agreement on Tariffs and Trade (GATT): these institutions survived the end of the Cold War and extended their remit worldwide.

The United States created the Western alliance and remained the principal agent of the international liberal order after the Cold War. In fact, the United States appeared to be a rejuvenated power in the 1990s after two decades of doubt about its future position. The pessimism of "declinists" in the United States—most famously expressed in Paul Kennedy's bestseller, *The Rise and Fall of Great Powers*—had dispersed as the Reagan, Bush, and Clinton administrations successfully reorganized the terms of the Western system.[2] The United States was able to share a number of leadership obligations with Western Europe and Japan, especially in the realm of economics, and this certainly prolonged the life of U.S. primacy. An agreement with Japan brokered at the Plaza Hotel in New York in 1985 began a managed devaluation of the U.S. dollar, and gave the United States a renewed competitive edge.[3] The huge U.S. trade and budget deficits were brought under control, and in the 1990s, the United States economy went on to significantly outperform its European and Japanese partners. The United States experienced a sustained burst of growth in which its superior technologies offered new opportunities for it to lead.

In most geographical regions and functional areas, the United States also remained the West's only global superpower and the indispensable provider of key political and security services for Western hegemony. The United States was an unrivaled military power, massively outspending both partners and rivals alike. At the end of the 1990s, the annual U.S. defense budget was moving toward $300 billion, compared to Japan at approximately $45 billion, France at $40 billion, the United Kingdom at $37 billion, Germany at $33 billion, China at $12 billion, and India at $10 billion.[4] U.S. outspending of all other major countries combined purchased military power that was generations ahead of what anyone else had, although George W. Bush became president in 2001 insisting that the United States must do even more. The memory of the Vietnam War still made Americans cautious about committing land forces abroad, but a new generation of hi-tech weapons platforms and precision-guided munitions made the U.S. Air Force and Navy practically unbeatable. U.S. fighter wings and aircraft carriers cast a shadow around the world.

U.S. military power represented a hegemonic service of definitive importance. For its allies, the umbrella of U.S. conventional and nuclear forces cut the costs of defense and provided great increments of security. U.S. protection encouraged security dependency within the West and, quid pro quo, an acceptance of U.S. leadership, especially through the institution of the North Atlantic Treaty Organization (NATO). The U.S. anti–ballistic missile defense program promoted by the George W. Bush administration, too, was likely to be as useful a dependency-creating hegemonic service as a serious way of actually shooting down ballistic missiles. The United States would lead the Western hegemony as long as the key European states did not mobilize and coordinate their own military potential.

Beyond the West, U.S. military power kept aspirations and practices in check. U.S. forces stabilized local balances of power across the world; it was difficult to imagine that in the Balkans, Middle East, Taiwan Straits, and Korean Peninsula the threat of war could be managed without a U.S. presence or its security guarantees. With its military superiority behind it, the United States was able to articulate the agenda of international security and how the international community should deal with particular issues. As the United States defined the limits of the possible and acceptable, it promoted some causes but silenced and constrained others. In almost every place and every conflict, other actors looked to the United States for security, support, approval, acquiescence, and arbitration.

For all the talk of complex interdependence theorists and critical theorists after the Cold War, military power remained one of the key determinants of who ran the world. Indeed, the neglect of military power in post–Cold War international relations thinking was only possible precisely because the United States was so dominant. Military power did seem less relevant, but only because the U.S. military held the ring everywhere and was likely do so for decades to come. U.S. military power shaped the context of politics across the world and fooled some Western thinkers too.

What is important to understand about the emergence of Western hegemony after the Cold War, though, is that it was far more than just a pax Americana. The United States was primus inter pares, but Western Europeans were also a major force in extending Western hegemony to Eastern Europe, the Mediterranean region, and the rest of the world. The United States was the principal agent of the West by virtue of its unity and size, but it is possible to imagine that the European Union (EU) might one day become a coequal of the United States or even an alternative leader. Moreover, although the respective positions of the United States and Europe might wax or wane, the systemic influence of Western ideas and practices was so entrenched across the post–Cold War world that Western hegemony could exist without a single undisputed leader. Despite appearances, U.S. leadership was no longer as indispensable as it had been during the Cold War.

The other crucial fact about Western hegemony was that it could not be understood simply in terms of old state-centric models. The agency involved in promoting Western hegemony could be rather diffuse. Although Western states remained key, other kinds of economic and social actors were also significant. These "extensive" elements of Western hegemony touched more people around the world than were directly affected by the policies of a few Western states alone.

In a work on the changing geography of hegemony, John Agnew and Stuart Corbridge perceived that a "deterritorialized" world order, which they termed the "hegemony of transnational liberalism," was emerging.[5] Hegemony was no longer an extension of the political and military power of the territorial state but was now rooted in global flows of technology, information, knowledge, and economic growth. Contests over the physical were of decreasing importance; it was in the realm of the hyperreal, cyberspace, and global systems that hegemony was now being made. According to Agnew and Corbridge,

> Economic, cultural and geopolitical power is now embedded in a network of dominant but internally divided countries (including the USA, Germany, and Japan), regional groupings like the European Community, city regions in the so-called Second and Third Worlds, international institutions including the World Bank, GATT, and the United Nations, and the main circuits and institutions of international production and financial capital. What binds these diverse regions and actors together is a shared commitment to an ideology of market eco-

nomics and a growing recognition that territoriality alone is not a
secure basis for economic or geopolitical power.[6]

The kind of people who met under the auspices of the World Economic
Forum in Davos, Switzerland, were those who gave Western hegemony
its global social power: an international elite that was well traveled,
largely Western-educated, English-speaking, and capitalist. The global
economy had its core in the United States, Europe, and Japan, but it
flowed into public and private networks throughout the world, notably
into secondary city regions like Mexico City, São Paulo, Jidda, Kuwait
City, Abu Dhabi and Dubai, Bombay, Kuala Lumpur, Guangzhou,
Singapore, and Seoul. The idea of a simple North-South divide in the
world no longer sufficed. Interdependent networks were the generators
of wealth and power.

Most of those promoting "transnational liberalism" understood the
general direction in which things needed to go, although they were not
always of one mind about the best means of getting there. For many
non-Westerners, contradictory impulses still exerted a powerful influence, and large numbers of people around the world were hostile to the
West. The management and integration task for the Western hegemony
was still a significant one. Western ideas and practices had to be made
plausible to doubters, dissidents marginalized or brought to order, and
markets extended to all potential consumers. The Western hegemony
was good at accomplishing these management and integration tasks.
Crucially, too, the really big states of Russia, China, and India had all
come to accept that engaging with global markets was the only viable
option for long-term development. The Western hegemony was a truly
global presence.

The Social and Cultural
Impact of the Western Hegemony

Western hegemony had profound implications for non-Western states
and societies. The West had already altered the givens of the
Westphalian state system among themselves, but it began to ask questions about public and private practices everywhere after the Cold War.
The West challenged existing locations of identity and authority by
offering, at least in some measure, to privatize and internationalize
some of the most basic of human aspirations: the individual's search for

identity, welfare, and security. Liberalization almost always meant dis-embedding local socioeconomic hegemonies: patron-client networks and bureaucratic states were under pressure to release their grip. States remained the preeminent influence on the lives of most people in the world, but markets and private actors were pressing on the state's control of its social and economic sphere.

The emergence of the new globalization was marked by a deep sense of unease. Even for Westerners, globalization came as a shock as the economic and cultural givens of national life were challenged. The shocks were much greater for non-Westerners, and even though many had long been "globalized" by European colonialism and capitalism, the pace and depth of the changes taking place had quickened markedly. The experience of the globalization often came more as uncontrollable "process" rather than purposeful "practice," and the result was an undercurrent of social instability and discontent.

The new globalization not only came with the liberal politics and economics of the West, but it also brought with it the likelihood of cultural transformation. The cultural milieu of globalization was a complex mix of the global and the local as people of different cultures met each other face-to-face more often, while others created new cosmopolitan communities across global networks that did not meet at all, or only rarely so. Societies were much less bounded, and the new globalization embodied a transformation in the social and cultural horizon for many individuals. The watchword of the new age was "synthesis," with both global and local cultures drawing on each other and producing a myriad of fusions across the different countries of the world.

No one was immune from cultural synthesis, but globalization was, as Peter Beyer observed, a process exogenous to all but the West.[7] The dominant pattern of the global politics and consumer culture was Western, especially American. In fact, the power of cultural images and brands had long been associated with the United States as a hegemonic force, and Hollywood had had a lot to do with hegemony in the world at least since the 1940s. To be really significant, famous, or notorious in the world was to be recognized in the United States. Although some local elites could maneuver around the liberal politics of Western hegemony, it was much more difficult to avoid the ubiquity of globalized capitalism and its cosmopolitan consumer culture. Global capitalists had an impressive capacity to absorb and synthesize in ways that were ultimately political.

Western multinational corporations (MNCs) were at the cutting edge of the new globalization. The never-ending quest of MNCs to entertain and sell did much to further cultural synthesis. Western goods and aspirations were dispatched to the world's consumers directly but were also mediated by local imitators. Benjamin Barber described the advance of this "McWorld" as an inescapable experience of U.S. consumer icons and a landscape of shopping malls, cinemas, sports stadiums, and branded restaurants.[8] Most important, cosmopolitan consumer culture drove the aspiration to work and to consume, and this trend had enormous implications for traditional patriarchal societies by drawing women and youth into the economic system. Giving women and youth wage-earning work, leisure time, and the ability to make consumption decisions was bound to transform local societies.

Cultural identities were bound to become more complex in the new globalization. The resulting tensions were felt even in the West, but the problems were much greater for non-Western societies that were less familiar with the secularism and pluralism that made adaptation easier. The bright colors of globalized modernity were difficult to resist and once introduced into the social cauldron were likely to irreversibly change the appearance of the traditional garb. Thus, the march of late-twentieth-century globalization was closely related to a global cultural counterreaction.

The new globalization set off a multitude of reactions around the world. Cultural imitation and synthesis were commonplace, but so were more regressive reactions. In fact, a revival of traditionalist cultures was one of the most notable phenomena of the late twentieth century. The end of the Soviet empire did much to release a wave of nationalism in Eastern Europe and Central Asia, but the Soviet vacuum was only part of the story. Cultural revivalism was also a reaction to the increasing tempo of globalization. Resurgent nationalism and politicized religion were embedded in much of the politics and conflict that followed the Cold War. If the new globalization presaged an age of openness and free exchange, cultural revivalism was its antithesis.

In the absence of a global-level theory of opposition to the new globalization, resistance was largely parochial, a fact reflected in the religious nature of much cultural revivalism. Religious revivalism represented a stark alternative to the West's hegemony because religious faith was so irrelevant to its ideas and practices. Around the world, some people resisted change by remembering religion. In cases in which religious doctrines were not taken on wholesale, they were often translated into backward-looking moral prescriptions about the role of women, the education of youth, the nature of personal responsibility, the punishment of deviancy, and the definition of the outsider. Religious revivalism was antiliberal.

Religious revivalism was also truly global in its extent. The Islamic revival of the 1970s was one of the great phenomena of the twentieth century. The consequences of the Islamic revival were manifold. The catastrophic airliner attacks on the World Trade Center in New York and the Pentagon in Washington on 11 September 2001 were perhaps the ultimate example of how far some of this Islamic zeal could go. In India, the secular state was challenged by the rise of the Hindu Bharatiya Janata Party, and the Hindu militants who demolished the Ayodhya mosque in late 1992 threatened to drag India into an intercommunal bloodbath. The relaxation of communist totalitarianism in China set off a proliferation of superstitions, most notably the Falun Gong movement. In Southeast Asia, Islamic, Christian, and Buddhist revivalism precipitated more intercommunal conflict. Orthodox and other Christian sects were resurgent in the former communist societies of Eastern Europe, and in the West itself, unusual Christian sects and other more mystical cults—often with some doomsday in mind—occupied the headlines. In the United States, the tone of politics appeared noticeably more conservative and religious, with fundamentalist Christian and right-wing militia groups representing the most extreme angst about some lost dream of community. The violent beginning and end of the siege of the Branch Davidian cult in Waco, Texas, between February and April 1993, and the subsequent bombing of federal offices at the Alfred P. Murrah building in Oklahoma that killed 168 people in April 1995 demonstrated how far some of these extremists were prepared to go.

Cultural conflict was particularly likely where newly religious people looked back to a past ideal and then took fundamentalist direction. Fundamentalists were always bitterly opposed to the perceived "evils" of modernity's secularism, pluralism, social atomization, and moral emptiness. Claiming the legitimacy of God, fundamentalists formulated interpretations of their faith that allowed for political and social violence and sometimes even aspired to reach some final apocalyptic vision. They often sought to purify their society in the most extreme ways. Thus, at the very moment that the Marxist-inspired revolutionaries of the 1950s and 1960s were disappearing, a new breed of religious militants took up the torch of insurgency and terrorism. Violent religious groups sprang up in all the major religions. One thing seemed clear: where fundamentalism lurked in the foreground or background, the chances of successfully meshing local identities with liberal ideas and practices were dramatically reduced.

The Islamic Frontier of the Western Hegemony

Among the cultural revivals taking place in the late twentieth century, that of Islam was the most forceful and extensive. The Islamic revival was a paradigm case for the theorists of culture and cultural conflict and was certainly regarded as such in the seminal post–Cold War works of Francis Fukuyama, Samuel Huntington, and Benjamin Barber.[9] Islam had an influence across large parts of the world that other religions could not match. The Islamic faith (see Appendix 2) had survived as a commentary on political and social life for over 1 billion Muslims; it continued to inform identities, establish boundaries of belonging and exclusion, and motivate behavior. Muslims made up the majority in a swath of countries across Africa and Asia, and a Muslim diaspora was growing rapidly in many other places, notably in the United States and Europe (see Map 1.1).

The rapid expansion of Muslim populations helped drive the Islamic revival and gave it added international tension. Muslim populations in North Africa, the Middle East, and South Asia were exploding: by 2010, Europe could expect 480 million Muslims on its doorstep, of whom over 40 percent would be under the age of fifteen.[10] Muslim economies could not give them things to do, and so many young Muslims sought to move. Muslim immigration into adjoining areas may or may not have been a problem, but it was widely problematized. By the 1990s, for instance, France alone hosted a population of over 4 million Muslims.[11] The liberal's celebration of diversity was liable to stop at Islam. The French government's ban on Islamic headscarves in public schools reflected the unease in Europe about the compatibility of Islamic culture and fears about a Muslim fifth column. Elsewhere, as in the Balkans and Caucasus, the reaction to a perceived Muslim threat was more violent. Muslim migration was an issue that was not going to go away.

The Islamic revival was a consequence of social failure in Muslim societies. In the 1950s and 1960s, Islam was sidelined by nationalist and socialist states, but the political and economic failures of these states opened the way for the return of Islam. Too many Muslims were disillusioned with modernity itself. The Islamic revival from the 1970s

Map 1.1 The Muslim World in 2001

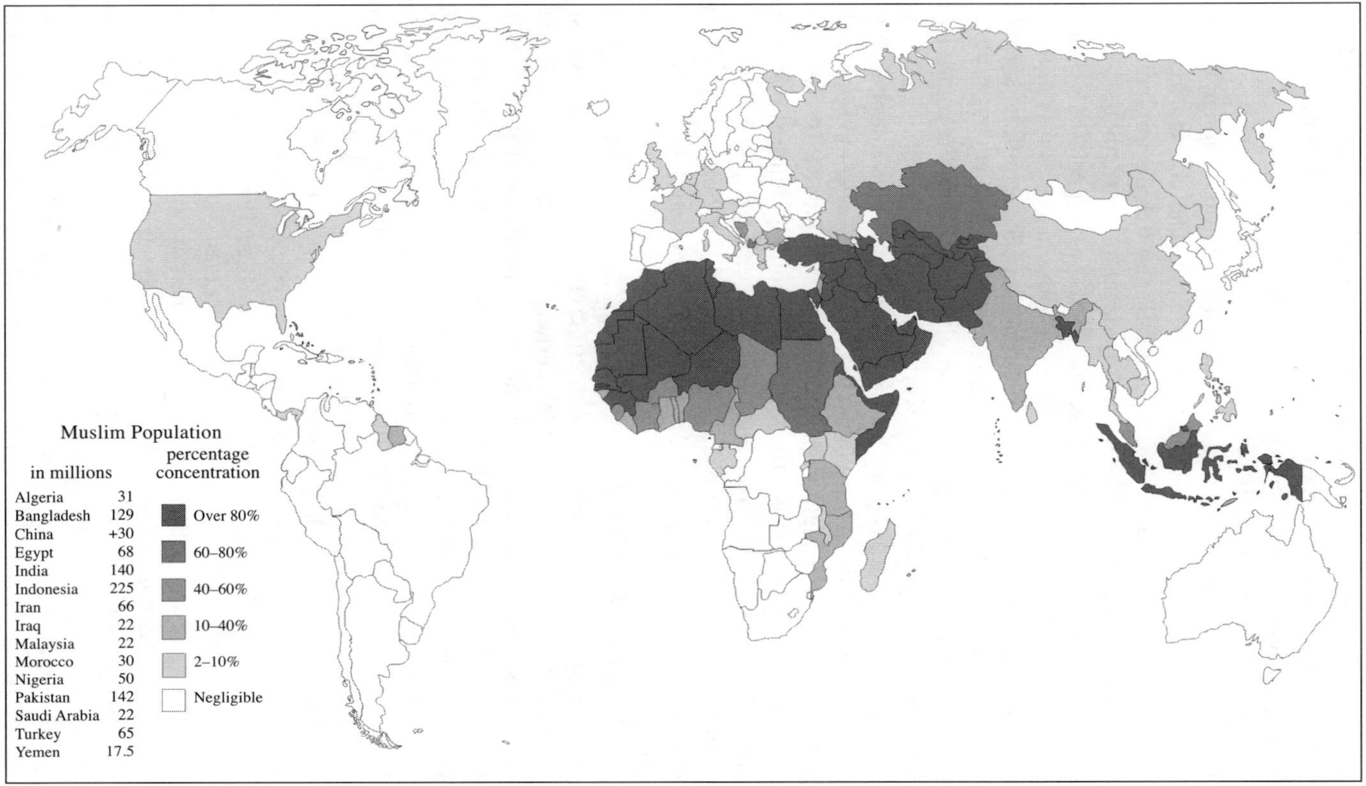

Muslim Population

in millions

Algeria	31
Bangladesh	129
China	+30
Egypt	68
India	140
Indonesia	225
Iran	66
Iraq	22
Malaysia	22
Morocco	30
Nigeria	50
Pakistan	142
Saudi Arabia	22
Turkey	65
Yemen	17.5

percentage
concentration

■ Over 80%
■ 60–80%
■ 40–60%
■ 10–40%
■ 2–10%
□ Negligible

manifested itself in many ways. Ordinary Muslims reaffirmed Islamic rituals and social practices. Muslim intellectuals turned away from overtly European and Western thought and toward Islamic references. The Islamic revival also harbored fundamentalists who sought an Islamic revolution. For the fundamentalists, it was not enough that society was Muslim; the state had to be Islamic. The new militants conspired to return all Muslims to a purer faith through the implementation of *sharia* (Islamic law). The forces of corruption and unbelief—secular Muslims, Islamic modernists, and the West—were declared evil by the fundamentalists, and an Islamic struggle with modernity was initiated.

The Islamic revival led to a multitude of local conflicts across the Muslim world (see Map 1.2). The Iranian Revolution of 1978–1979 was an especially powerful moment, and although Islamic revolutions did not sweep through the Muslim world, Islamic militants haunted many Muslim societies. Muslim politics was prone to violence. Where Muslims lived with non-Muslims, too, violence was common, especially where Islamists sought to promulgate *sharia*. Indeed, Islamic groups were locked in violent conflicts against adjoining cultures and secular states in the Balkans, West and East Africa, Israel and Lebanon, the Caucasus, Central Asia, India, Indonesia, and the Philippines. Muslims certainly became associated with intolerance and violence in the Western mind.

The extent to which the values and practices of the Islamic revival were compatible with those of Western civilization is a sensitive issue. Conflict between Muslims and Westerners is not inevitable, but reconciling their principal systems of thought is not without its difficulties. Islam and Western liberalism do represent different ontologies for understanding and behaving in the world. Islam is about the worship of God. Western thought sold out to humanism and materialism long ago. Islam is a vision of community and social control, whereas liberalism is a vision of individual choice, economic liberation, and the removal of constraints. Islam tends to frown on the idea of individual autonomy and consciousness. Indeed, many Islamists were wedded to the idea of an overarching Islamic state that enforced illiberal injunctions on consumption, criminal law, and the rights of women, youth, and minorities. The reality of the authoritarian state in the Muslim world was also a serious compatibility barrier to engaging with the new globalization. All Muslim states were highly authoritarian and bureaucratic, with centralized and poorly performing economies.

Beyond the rhetoric of incompatibility and cultural conflict, though, there is another story of Muslims in the contemporary world.

Map 1.2 Muslims in Conflict in the 1990s

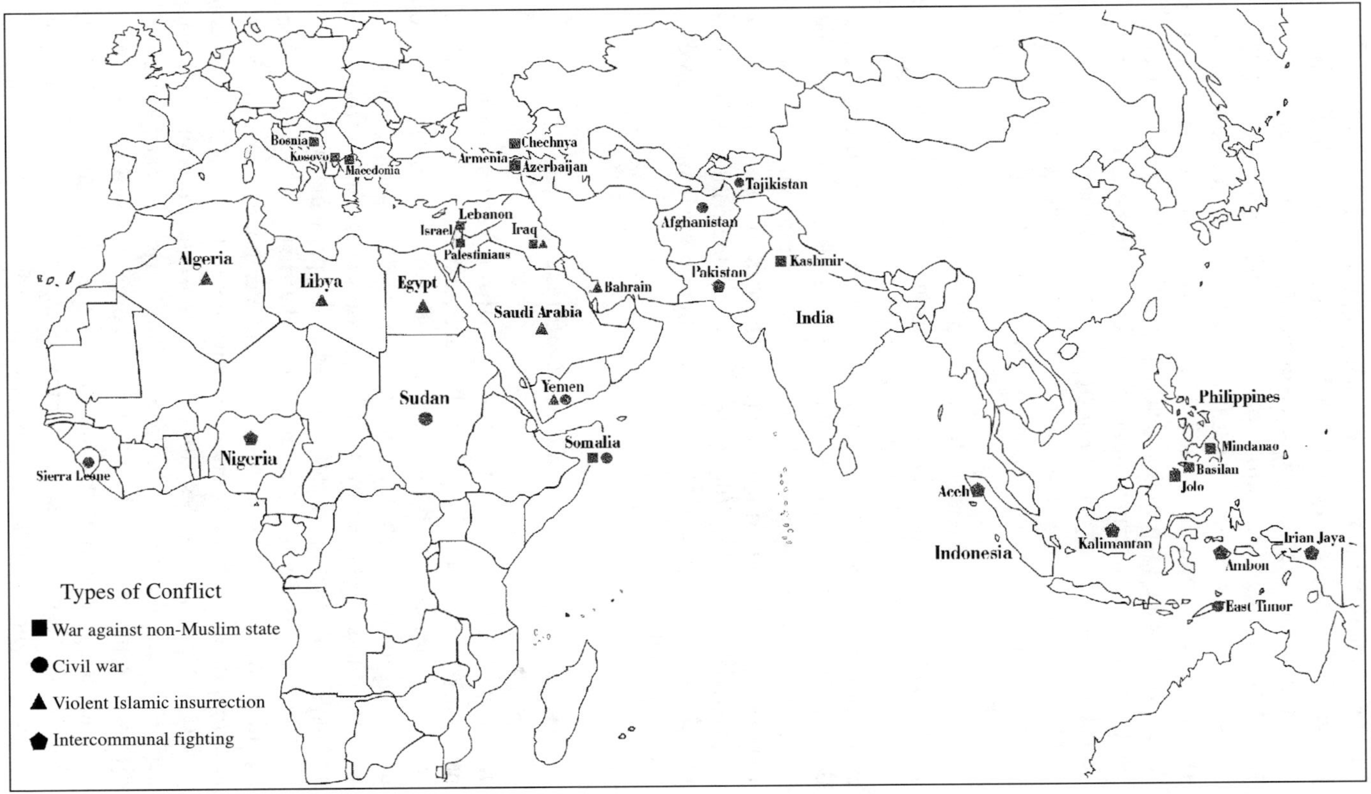

Philippines
Mindanao
Basilan
Jolo
Kalimantan

Irian Jaya
Ambon
East Timor

Indonesia

Aceh

Kashmir
India
Tajikistan
Afghanistan
Pakistan
Chechnya
Armenia Azerbaijan
Bahrain
Saudi Arabia
Yemen
Somalia
Lebanon
Iraq
Israel Palestinians
Egypt
Sudan
Libya
Macedonia
Bosnia Kosovo
Nigeria
Algeria

Sierra Leone

Types of Conflict

■ War against non-Muslim state
● Civil war
▲ Violent Islamic insurrection
⬟ Intercommunal fighting

Muslim values and practices are changing. The debate about the future of Islamic identities is complex. Islam is not a monolithic or unchanging religion and as a political force operates in diverse ways: it is a doctrine both of state legitimization and of resistance to the state; it is social oppressor and oppressed; it is excluder and excluded. Politicized Islam will continue to challenge what it sees as Western, but many Muslims are facing up to the idea of the market economy, as well as to the contemporary international debates about democracy, human rights, and the environment. The majority of Muslims cannot—and do not want to—ignore everything that is modern, Western, or global; they understand that only by engaging with the world can they avoid marginalization.

Of course, the dilemma for Muslims is that although adapting to global realities is a clear interest, engaging with the global opens the door to alien influences and cultural synthesis. Finding an Islamic path to globalized modernity is at the heart of contemporary Muslim politics. The extent to which Muslims can—and desire to—mesh their Islam with liberalism and cosmopolitan consumer culture will be sorted out in the discourse of both Muslims and Westerners, but this path has yet to be properly navigated. What is certain is that the remorseless march of the globalized Western hegemony is changing Muslim peoples and Islamic culture.

Chapter Outline

This book examines the impact of globalized Western hegemony on Muslim societies and how Muslims are adapting to it. The Muslim world is very large and diverse, so the work concentrates on the Muslim heartland of the Middle East, where Islamic values remain influential, where politics is shaped by Islamic discourse, and where the tensions created by the meeting of global and local are particularly stark.

The work is divided into two parts. The first part (Chapters 2 to 4) examines the place that the Muslim world has in the Western hegemony and the pressures being exerted on Muslims to adapt to it. The second part (Chapters 5 to 7) describes the response of Muslims to Western hegemony and the new globalization. Part 2 tries to make sense of the different purposes to which Islam is being put and to what extent Islamic culture is compatible with the values and practices of Western hegemony. What Islam says about contemporary politics, economics, and international relations is the substance of Part 2.

Chapter 2 is an account of the West's cultural discourse about Islam after the Cold War. The ideational software of Western hegemony is outlined, starting with Francis Fukuyama's seminal work on the triumph of the "liberal idea" and his thoughts about Islam. Other Western thinkers were also concerned about Islam, and their interest produced another discourse led by Samuel Huntington's *Clash of Civilizations*. The Muslim world became almost synonymous with cultural conflict, but opinions in the West differed over the nature and scale of the "Islamic threat." In Chapter 2, I assess whether the post–Cold War discourse has reinforced the exclusion and marginalization of Muslims in the world.

In Chapter 3, I examine the geopolitics of the post–Cold War international order, specifically, how and why a pax Americana is enforced in the Middle East. I describe how the United States and its allies have met challengers in the Middle East and the way in which global-level institutions are used to support the projection of U.S. power. The varying responses of Muslim states and Islamic activists to Western policy are outlined. The Islamic militants who attacked the United States on 11 September 2001 represented the most extreme response to the dominating presence of the United States in the Middle East. At the time of this writing, the attacks had only recently occurred, and the many consequences that were bound to follow were yet to fully unfold, but I do try to highlight the key issues in the conflict between the United States and the Bin Laden militants as well as some of the broader implications of the new war on terrorism.

The problems that Muslims face in engaging with the global economy are set out in Chapter 4. Whether Muslims can sensibly pursue distinctively Islamic normative goals in the context of the global market economy is assessed. The sociocultural impact of the new globalization is also examined, especially the way that markets and cosmopolitan consumerism may be undermining existing patterns of culture and social order in the Muslim world. Islamists continue to make Islam relevant, but global forces promote an alternative system of aspiration and welfare that is powerful. A debate exists within Muslim societies between those who seek to create a new plausibility for Islam and those determined to make Islam compelling in more traditional ways.

In Chapter 5, I reflect on the state of contemporary Muslim politics. The contest between the authoritarian secular state and Islamic revivalists has resulted in deadlock. I examine the origin of the Islamic revolt, the resulting conflict, the absence of a decisive outcome, and the paralyzed politics that bedevil the contemporary Muslim world. Some

Muslim countries have been more innovative than others in moving forward, but until a viable accommodation can be reached between the state and the Islamists, most Muslim societies will struggle to successfully adapt to the challenges that they face.

Chapter 6 turns to the shadow that the "liberal idea" casts on Muslim societies and how Muslims have responded to the global mood for democracy and human rights. Muslim countries are almost all authoritarian and undemocratic, and the Islamic opposition has never really pressed for democracy. The reasons for authoritarianism are deeply entrenched in Muslim societies and Islamic culture, but significant developments in thought and practice are under way across the Middle East. A number of comparisons between Middle Eastern states are made, but special attention is given to the attempt in the latter 1990s to democratize the Islamic Republic of Iran.

In the final chapter, I examine how Muslim countries relate to the international system and whether Islam has any meaningful role in the contemporary world. Modern Muslim states have rarely pushed Islamic theory in the international system, although Islam is important because it establishes common preferences among Muslim states. Islamic commonality is the basis of an alliance system, but as an examination of Muslim states and the Organization of the Islamic Conference (OIC) shows, this possibility is distinctly limited. Islamic countries are too divided to represent a coherent force—much less a counterhegemonic one—although Islam does act to resist some of the ideas and practices of Western hegemony.

The global hegemony that emerged at the end of the Cold War has become an essential reference point for almost everyone on Earth. In the Muslim world, the tensions between the global and local were pronounced. Muslim peoples had to decide—and are still deciding—what in their cultures could be saved, what would be lost, and how they were going to interact with the West's hegemony. Whether Islamic countries can successfully adapt to liberal ideas and global markets will substantially define their future role in the international system, as well as political and social conditions across large parts of the world. The relationship between the Muslim, Islamic, and global is an important matter for the future of the entire world.

Notes

1. Scholte, "Global Capitalism and the State," *International Affairs* 73, no. 3, July 1997, 441.

2. Kennedy, *The Rise and Fall of Great Powers*, 1989.

3. Cumings, "Still the American Century?" *Review of International Studies* 25, Special Issue, December 1999, 284.

4. Figures for Russia are not available. The figures for China are probably a significant underestimate. *CIA World FactBook*, http://www.cia.gov.publications/factbook/indexgo.html.

5. Agnew and Corbridge, *Mastering Space*, 1995, chap. 7.

6. Ibid., 205, 207.

7. Beyer, *Religion and Globalization*, 1994, 8–9.

8. Barber, *Jihad vs. McWorld*, 1996.

9. Fukuyama, *The End of History and the Last Man*, 1992; Huntington, *The Clash of Civilizations and the Remaking of the World Order*, 1996; Barber, *Jihad vs. McWorld*.

10. Dervis and Shafik, "The Middle East and North Africa: A Tale of Two Futures," *Middle East Journal* 52, no. 4, Autumn 1998, 507.

11. John Esposito, "Clash of Civilizations? Contemporary Images of Islam in the West," in Gema Martin Munoz, ed., *Islam, Modernism, and the West*, 1999, 96.

PART ONE

ISLAM IN THE GLOBAL HEGEMONY

2

Reconstructing the Post–Cold War World: Islam in the Cultural Discourse of the West

For forty years following World War II, the international system was dominated by the bipolar divisions of the Cold War and understood principally by means of realist and neorealist theories. The many differences between the peoples and states of the world were subsumed into the global geopolitical struggle between the United States and the Soviet Union. Differences were defined in ideological terms and were superimposed over other cultural and political characteristics. The superpowers offered their models to the world for imitation, and alignment to one of the two great blocs defined the "Other." The end of the Cold War not only put an end to bipolar organization of international politics but also challenged the familiar understandings about it.

In the rethinking of international relations that took place after the Cold War, a number of themes assumed new significance for both academics and practitioners. If the world seemed to be coming together in some ways, in others it seemed to be coming apart. The new globalization was the dominant feature of the post–Cold War world, but it met its antithesis in the assertion of local cultures, specifically in the form of nationalism and religion. Culture did seem more important because in a rapidly changing world, so many people were asking questions about who they were, who they wanted to be, and where the societies in which they lived were going. Thinking about culture also offered a way of understanding the similarities and differences of the new age and of reorganizing understandings about "them" and "us." Cultures define internal and external boundaries by encouraging belief in the value of cultural tradition and its distinctiveness.

The reformulation of boundaries along religious lines was one of the most significant cultural phenomena of the post–Cold War world.

23

Even at the end of the twentieth century, when references were made to cultural authenticity, they were most often about religious values and were made by those priests, mullahs, and gurus who claimed to be qualified to transmit them. The collapse of Soviet power did much to release this religious assertiveness from Yugoslavia to Tajikistan, but religious revivalism actually predated the end of the Cold War. Across the Muslim world, for instance, a crisis in modernization since the 1970s had had much to do with an Islamic revival that was notable for its duration and global extent.

During the Cold War, the Islamic revival was a sideshow in the geopolitics of the Soviet-U.S. confrontation. Western policymakers recognized a "crescent of crisis" in the Middle East and southwestern Asia—notably in the "northern tier" of Turkey, Iran, Pakistan, and Afghanistan—but reduced its significance to the opportunity it gave to the Soviets. After the Cold War, the meaning of the Islamic revival had to be reassessed. Cultural revivalism now provided the principal resistance to the universalizing liberal order and so assumed an independent significance. Islam was the biggest of the cultural locals, with over 1 billion Muslims stretching from West Africa through the Eurasian continent and on to the Philippines. Islam was also the most forceful of the cultural revivals at play in the world, and it provided a completely different moral and political vision from that offered by the globally dominant West.

Many of the Western writers leading the discourse about culture tended to see Islam as a source of backwardness and insecurity. The urge to identify the next threat to the West was a particular need in some quarters. The representation of Islam in the emerging discourse was important because it established a priori understandings about Muslims and their attitude toward the West. Perceiving Muslims as a problem was liable, as John Agnew and Stuart Corbridge have argued more generally, to turn them into "security commodities, readily subject to invasion, control or bombing."[1] The West has had a long tradition of designating others as backward and itself as *the* model of progress. Between Western arrogance and Islamic assertiveness in the discourse, the potential for trust and cooperation was diminished. Relations between the West and the Muslim world faced an uphill struggle right from the very beginning of the post–Cold War era.

The Triumph of the Liberal Idea

Winning the Cold War occasioned a wave of confidence in the West. The moment of euphoria was perhaps best expressed in Francis

Fukuyama's "end of history" thesis, first published in the *National Interest* in 1989 and then in his subsequent book, *The End of History and the Last Man*.[2] According to Fukuyama, the end of the Cold War had not only left the liberal idea as the unrivaled global model but had also revealed it to be the ultimate form of political and social development. Liberalism had taken human society as far as it could progress, and "history," in that sense, was at an end.[3]

Fukuyama recognized that the liberal idea had its problems, but they were minor and solvable compared to the alternatives. For most of the people, most of the time, liberalism outlined the system best capable of fulfilling humanity's deepest longings for material betterment and an equality of recognition. The forms of community governed by moral imperatives were inferior to those in which individuals contracted with each other to be "participant, rational, secular, mobile, empathetic, and tolerant."[4] The liberal society elevated the rights of the individual to a hitherto unknown significance. Liberalism was also represented as the historic triumph of the "mechanism of modern natural science"[5] and was the system that could best manage economic and technological progress: it was no accident that liberal democracies won the great combats of the twentieth century. Globalization reinforced the advantages of liberal societies because only they could properly manage the information exchange and technological innovation required in the complex postindustrial economy. Dictators and bureaucracies simply could not compete in the long run.

All of history may have been leading to the liberal moment, but Fukuyama conceded that liberals still faced obstacles and specifically pointed to renewed religious and nationalist appeals. In fact, Fukuyama perceived a new global dividing line between the "historical" and "posthistorical" worlds: in other words, between those that had reached liberal modernity and those that had not. The two worlds led parallel but separate existences, each living by a different set of rules and only really meeting over global security issues such as oil, terrorism, and refugees. Economic interactions dominated the posthistorical world, but a number of posthistorical states, such as the United States and Britain, had to play the game of power politics in order to manage the problems emanating from the historical world.[6] Fukuyama thought the Middle East was a paradigm case of a "historical" region bypassed by the global tide of liberal reform.[7] Middle Eastern oil wealth had eased the pressures to change.

Islamic culture was another block to progress for Fukuyama. Islam and liberalism basically could not be meshed together. Islamists did not want to adapt but to conquer modernity, and Fukuyama perceived that

Islamic fundamentalism bears a more than superficial resemblance to European fascism. As in the case of European fascism, it is no surprise that the fundamentalist revival hit the most apparently modern countries the hardest, for it was they whose traditional cultures had been most thoroughly threatened by the import of Western values. The strength of the Islamic revival can only be understood if one understands how deeply the dignity of Islamic society had been wounded in its double failure to maintain the coherence of its traditional society and to successfully assimilate the techniques and values of the West![8]

A serious Islamic threat was there, but Fukuyama was optimistic about the ultimate outcome of the struggle for liberal modernity in the Muslim world, arguing that

Islam has . . . defeated liberal democracy in many parts of the Islamic world, posing a grave threat to liberal practices even in countries where it has not achieved political power directly. . . . Despite the power demonstrated by Islam in its current revival, however, it remains the case that this religion has virtually no appeal outside those areas that were culturally Islamic to begin with. The days of Islam's cultural conquests, it would seem, are over: it can win back lapsed adherents, but has no resonance for young people in Berlin, Tokyo, or Moscow. And while nearly a billion people are culturally Islamic—one-fifth of the world's population—they cannot challenge liberal democracy on its own territory or on the level of ideas. Indeed, the Islamic world would seem more vulnerable to liberal ideas in the long run than the reverse, and such liberalism has attracted numerous and powerful Muslim adherents over the past century and a half. Part of the reason for the current, fundamentalist revival is the strength of the perceived threat from liberal Western values to traditional Islamic societies.[9]

Muslim states had already taken on board many of the intellectual, organizational, and physical forms of modernity, such as "rational" education, modern bureaucracy, and urbanization, and these adaptations were bound to undermine the traditional social base of Islam. Fukuyama also reassured liberals that there were "no true barbarians at the gates, unaware of the power of modern natural science."[10] The liberal idea had the force of history behind it, and would eventually overwhelm its "historical" competitors, for there was

not a single branch of mankind that has not been touched by the Mechanism, and which has not become linked to the rest of mankind through the universal economic nexus of modern consumerism. It is not the mark of provincialism but of cosmopolitanism to recognize that there has emerged in the last few centuries something like a true global culture, centring around technologically driven economic growth and the capitalist social relations necessary to produce and sustain it. Societies which have sought to resist this unification, from Tokugama Japan and the Sublime Porte, to the Soviet Union, the People's Republic of China, Burma, and Iran, have managed to fight rearguard actions that have lasted for only a generation or two. Those who were not defeated by superior military technology were seduced by the glittering material world that modern natural science has created. While not every country is capable of becoming a consumer society in the near future, there is hardly a society in the world that does not embrace the goal itself.[11]

In essence, then, the struggle for modernity had been resolved in favor of Western liberalism, and all that there was left to do was to mop up the stragglers of yesterday. Human societies would come to resemble each other. After centuries of conflict between religious, monarchical, nationalist, communist, and liberal social systems, the big struggles for the future of history were over. Quite simply, what had emerged victorious was

not so much liberal practice, as the liberal *idea*. That is to say, for a very large part of the world there is no ideology with pretensions to universality that [was] in a position to challenge liberal-democracy, and no universal principle of legitimacy other than the sovereignty of the people.[12]

The liberal idea represented a universal civilization to which all should — and ultimately had no choice but to — aspire.

Fukuyama was important. A thesis that so brashly proclaimed the end of history was easy to criticize, and it was widely misrepresented. Despite the distractions in the argument, Fukuyama remains the best account of the philosophical underpinnings of the global liberal order. What Fukuyama had done so early in the post–Cold War period was to provide the definitive account of why the liberal idea was good, why the West and its values had triumphed, and why it would continue to prove irresistible. What Fukuyama had also done, though, was essentially proclaim the closure of any real discourse between civilizations; the West was the true universal civilization, and in the last analysis, it could learn little from the others. The West must teach the others.

In the political and intellectual circles of the West, especially in the United States, many knew what Fukuyama had done. Many more subscribed to the idea that liberal politics and open markets were best and that the direction of the new globalization project would be as Fukuyama suggested. For those Americans who believed that the

United States must be engaged in the world, Fukuyama showed them why. Fukuyama was the intellectual voice of a U.S. mission to take the liberal idea to the unconverted world: a mission accepted by the Bush and Clinton administrations. In short, the liberal idea was the ideological software of the new Western hegemony and a weapon in the emerging global battle for politics and culture.

The End of Euphoria

Fukuyama himself recognized that the liberal idea represented a kind of leveling-down banality and an obsession with the material that left an opening for less rational forms of striving. Many human longings were satisfied by the liberal idea, but humanity's search for the spiritual and love of the epic were not. Liberal democratic life could be dull and might not always satisfy "man as man." In fact, many peoples came out of the Cold War not looking forward to a liberal future but looking back to rediscover a past that communism had taken from them. National and religious revivals took hold in many locations. The "parochial revolt" reflected the continuing power of the alternatives to liberalism, as well as a direct hostility to the West itself. Western liberalism was widely stereotyped for its arrogance, irresponsible individualism, and permissive sexual practices, and its model of capitalism was denounced as exploitative and morally bankrupt. The forces of parochialism sought to turn back the tide of secularism, pluralism, and amorality inherent in liberalism. The Western hegemony had a great deal of unfinished—and perhaps unfinishable—business to do with the parochial before it could homogenize the world and finally end history.

An emerging pessimism in the post–Cold War discourse was soon to be born amid a number of real conflicts in the former Soviet Union, Yugoslavia, and the Middle East. In many other respects, it also became clear that the new order was going to be much more chaotic than had at first been touted. The West and its global system, Barrie Axford perceived, was now faced by "new demons in the shape of fundamentalist mullahs, or warlords and drug barons straight out of the script of Mad Max, [that] have come to challenge the 'peace dividends' purchased so dearly."[13] The new era soon invited comparisons with another period of chaos in the Western mind: that of the medieval world, where power and authority were diffuse and where religious solidarity, parochial cults, and barbarians at the gates were recurrent facts of life. Similarly, the universal civilization propounded a genuine ideal but also faced its enemies with the pursuit of self-interest and the practice of violence masked as crusading. The proposition that the universal civilization could unite humanity in harmony after the Cold War quickly seemed an illusion. The heady days of 1989 soon faded, and although Fukuyama's message about the "liberal idea" continued to be influential, his end of history terminology seemed less relevant. The world was not about to give up its history, and a new discourse seemed appropriate. Fukuyama was to be tempered by Samuel Huntington.

The new pessimism was best and most influentially reflected in the discourse fired by Harvard professor Samuel Huntington. In a 1993 article in *Foreign Affairs* and in a subsequent book, *The Clash of Civilizations and the Remaking of the World Order,* Huntington offered a paradigm of world politics in which patterns of conflict and cooperation were dominated by cultural references and ultimately by civilizations.[14] Huntington insisted that it was a mistake to regard the liberal order as anything more than an extension of Western power and suggested that cultural and civilizational differences would come to dominate world politics. The civilizations that mattered were the Sinic, Japanese, Hindu, Islamic, Orthodox, Western, Latin American, and, possibly, African.

For Huntington, the end of the Cold War had inaugurated a new phase in history. Thus far, the history of the international system had been essentially about the struggles between monarchs, nations, and ideologies within Western civilization. The post–Cold War world was now taking on a Western and non-Western dynamic because of four intersecting trends at play. The first of the trends was the relative decline of the West. The second was the rise of the Asian economy and its associated "cultural affirmation," with China poised to become the greatest power in human history. Third, the Muslim world was undergoing a population explosion and its associated Islamic revival. The fourth trend was globalization, including the expansion of transnational flows of commerce, information, and people. Economic change was detaching people from local loyalties and weakening the state. The coincidence of all four factors in the post–Cold War world was forging a world of civilizations and that required a new intellectual paradigm.

The new cultural politics worked at the level of motivation. The behavior of actors was shaped by the immanent beliefs and preferences that they held, and these beliefs were influenced by resurgent cultures. States remained key actors, but civilizational politics became real when states and peoples identified with each other's cultural concerns or rallied around the "core state" of a civilization. The Orthodox, Hindu,

Sinic, and Japanese civilizations were clearly centered on powerful unitary states. The West had a closely linked core that included the United States, Germany, France, and Britain. Islam was without a clear core state and for this reason experienced much more intracivilizational conflict as a number of contenders—Turkey, Iran, Iraq, Egypt, and Saudi Arabia—competed for influence. The fact that Islam was divided, however, did not refute the idea that a pan-Islamic consciousness existed.

Huntington's thesis pointed to a world of heightened conflict. Cultural conflict could be found at "micro" and "macro" levels. At the microlevel, groups from different civilizations were prone to conflict across local "fault lines" over people and territory and, by means of a "kin-country syndrome," were liable to bring in their wider brethren. Huntington noted that

> once started, fault line wars, like other communal conflicts, tend to take on a life of their own and to develop in an action-reaction pattern. Identities which had previously been multiple and casual become focused and hardened; communal conflicts are appropriately termed "identity wars." As violence increases, the initial issues at stake tend to get redefined more exclusively as "us" against "them" and group cohesion and commitment are enhanced. Political leaders expand and deepen their appeals to ethnic and religious loyalties, and civilizational consciousness strengthens in relation to other identities. A "hate dynamic" emerges, comparable to the "security dilemma" in international relations, in which mutual fears, distrust, and hatred feed on each other.[15]

Huntington thought Islam particularly problematic: "Islam's borders are bloody, and so are its innards. . . . Muslim bellicosity and violence are late twentieth century facts which neither Muslims nor non-Muslims can deny."[16] According to Huntington, Islam was so prone to conflict because it esteemed the military; others were encroaching on it; it was an absolute faith regarded as superior; Muslims were weak and under attack; there was no core Islamic state to protect the faith; and Muslim populations were exploding and expanding. With Islamic peoples in conflict with adjoining groups in West Africa, Sudan, Bosnia, Kosovo, Cyprus, the Middle East, Chechnya, Tajikistan, Kashmir, India, Indonesia, and the Philippines, Huntington could certainly point to a body of empirical evidence suggesting that Muslims and their neighbors did find it difficult to live with each other.

At the macrolevel, a general competition for capabilities and influence seemed evident to Huntington, with the principal division between the "West" and, to varying degrees, the "rest." Western hegemony was most contested by the two most dynamic non-Western civilizations, the Sinic and Islamic. The Western effort to spread its liberalism to others was widely regarded as a form of imperialism.[17] The West said its liberal values were universal, but Western individualism, secularism, pluralism, democracy, and human rights had only superficial resonance in Islamic, Sinic, Hindu, Buddhist, and Orthodox cultures. In reality, the differences between civilizations ran very deep: they were about man and God; man and woman; the individual and the state; and notions of rights, authority, obligation, and justice. Cultural references had been socially constructed over centuries and were too powerful to be easily overcome; they spoke to most of the people on Earth in a way that liberalism did not. Huntington rejected the idea of universal liberal human rights and went on to call for noninterference between cultural groups, a position that critics found outrageous. In fact, Huntington thought that as the West continued its relative decline, so would the appeal of its liberal values.

Huntington was important in the post–Cold War discourse not only because he offered a vision of the future that did not foresee the triumph of a global liberal order but also because he represented the reformulation of conservative tendencies in Western thought. *The Clash of Civilizations* was pessimistic about human nature, predicted an international system beset by conflict, and argued for a new communal solidarity in the form of a Western nationalism. Huntington was as much concerned with how the West should see itself as about outlining intercultural divisions. He rejected the idea that Western civilization was the universal civilization as not only a manifestation of Western arrogance but also as dangerously unreal. Unless Americans and Europeans appreciated their distinctiveness and purposefully stuck together, it was possible to foresee that one day, the West might cease to exist altogether. In many ways, Huntington sought to take Western liberalism back in time and to run it alongside an overtly communitarian philosophy; it had taken much of the twentieth century to purge liberalism of the more obvious accretions of nationalism and realism, with all the exclusionary principles and practices that those traditions embodied.

The "Islamic Threat"?

In much of the clash of civilizations thesis, Islam came into the frame, with Huntington reaffirming some very well established notions about it in the West. The idea that Islam was a threat to European and Western civilizations was almost as old as Islam itself. In recent years, Western concerns were heightened by the Iranian Revolution of 1978–1979. The experience of the Reagan administration in relation to Iran, Libya, Syria, and Lebanon also raised the specter of an Arab and Islamic bloc that was fiercely resistant to the West. The Iranian Revolution itself saw the Shah's show of modernity overwhelmed by Islamists who spoke of the United States as the Great Satan. A pan-Islamic revolution did not sweep through Muslim lands after Iran, but the stability of the Middle East was rocked. In a chronicle of the time, Elie Kedourie perceived, the Islamic resurgence was potentially so dangerous because of the points of similarity with Bolshevism, and

> like the Marxists, Khomeini and Qadaffi denounce the West as exploitative and imperialist. . . . The Marxist notion that Western imperialism is the inevitable outcome of capitalist processes is now extremely widespread, and this idea is being used to articulate and rationalize the ancient Islamic hostility.[18]

According to Kedourie, a new Western-Muslim iron curtain was going up, and it was of concern because Islam was a potential surrogate for Soviet expansionism. In fact, the picture was more complicated. The United States was not inherently hostile to all Islamic forces, no matter how backward looking. The Soviet invasion of Afghanistan in 1979 gave the United States common cause with the Afghan mujahidin and occasioned a major U.S. effort to support the war against Soviet forces; of course, this relationship with some mujahidin groups was to be reestablished following the 11 September 2001 attacks on New York and Washington and the initiation of the United States' own war in Afghanistan. Nevertheless, even as Westerners continued to think about Islam in the Cold War context, it was clear that there was a new force out there.

The end of the Cold War meant that the Islamic threat was no longer a subsidiary of another conflict, and it began to attract much more interest in the West. At a popular level, Hollywood needed new villains, and few moviegoers can have failed to notice that Muslim maniacs were a serious problem, or at least they were in mainstream motion pictures like *Naked Gun* (1988), *Navy Seals* (1990), *True Lies* (1994), *Executive Decision* (1996), and *G.I. Jane* (1997). At an intellectual level, a body of writing also emerged—some predating the *Clash of Civilizations*—foretelling a future of heightened conflict between the West and Islam.[19] For Westerners, the issues of nuclear proliferation, terrorism, and Muslim population growth and movement were real security problems with a geopolitical dimension. The prospect of nuclear weapons proliferation looked particularly dangerous. According to Huntington, having forged an alliance with China, some Muslim states were in danger of playing Russian roulette with the West, India, and Israel.[20]

Huntington's pessimism about the incompatibility of the West and Islam was reinforced by a number of U.S. advocates, including Steven David, Anthony Lake, Charles Krauthammer, Martin Kramer, Daniel Pipes, Judith Miller, and Peter Rodman, with British support from Bernard Lewis and Barry Buzan.[21] These pessimists did not have to look very far to see Islamic peoples in conflict or to find prominent Islamic personalities who embraced the idea of a clash of civilizations. Few of these writers viewed Islam as a monolith, but all perceived Islamic hostility to the West and its values. Islam and liberal democracy were said to be fundamentally incompatible, and they believed that this conflict ought to count in U.S. policymaking. The United States needed to reorient its policy thinking and security apparatus to meet these threats head on. Appeasement was not an option.

Writing in *Foreign Affairs,* for instance, Judith Miller rejected the idea of a monolithic "green menace" but highlighted how Islam in practice worked against democracy, pluralism, and human rights and how Islamic militants were prone to gross intolerance and violence.[22] Muslims in general tended not to "embrace the truths that most Americans held to be self-evident." The policy prescriptions followed, and Miller advised that "in any new world order, Americans should not be ashamed to say that they favor pluralism, tolerance and diversity, and that they reject the notion that God is on anyone's side."[23] The United States had to be skeptical of those who used Islam to democratize or liberate and had to adopt a policy that essentially meant saving Muslims from themselves. The United States should not support democratic reforms or Islamic movements, no matter how popular, if that might mean "one person, one vote, one time."[24] Islamists had to measure up to the Universal Declaration on Human Rights before they could be recognized, although no U.S. ally in the Middle East met these standards either. The new world order, it seemed, had democratic imperatives without actually having to be democratic.

Not to be deemed genuinely democratic was to be accorded an unequal status in much U.S. thinking. Of course, one of the principal purposes of this kind of anti-Islamic approach was to maintain the difference between the way Westerners regarded Muslims and the way they should regard "democratic Israel." The basic advice was that Muslims were different and dangerous, whereas Israelis must be supported. Israel remained a strategic asset of the West in the heart of Muslim lands, which ultimately made Israel good and turning a blind eye to its transgressions in international law acceptable. Yet again, some Westerners were seeking to run their liberalism alongside self-interest and communitarian prejudice.

The Islamic threat literature was significant because it came at a time when Americans were thinking about who the next enemy might be, as well as who might next occupy the time of their armed forces. The plausibility of the Islamic threat was underscored by the activities of Islamists in the Middle East and in the West itself. The bombing of the World Trade Center in New York in 1993 was the most startling demonstration of the Islamic threat: Maria Pinto perceived that ordinary Americans suddenly understood that Middle Eastern violence was creeping inexorably across borders and that Shaikh Omar Abdel Rahman, the blind Muslim cleric behind the bombing, "seemed the emissary of a global threat to America and its way of life."[25] Whether acts of Islamic insurgency represented a significant international Islamic conspiracy was debatable, but there were those in the United States arguing that it did and that a "Tehran-Khartoum axis" was at the center of the threat.

Criticisms of The Clash

The pessimistic thinking about Western-Islamic relations led by Huntington was very widely read in both the West and the Muslim world and undoubtedly shaped the academic and policy discourse. The pessimism was contested. Huntington himself came in for vehement criticism. A varied group of "progressive" theorists and constructivists, including Ken Booth, Stephen Chan, Fred Halliday, Jacinta O'Hagan, Adam Tarock, and David Welch, were particularly hostile to Huntington.[26] Huntington challenged critical theorists not only by threatening to put explanatory power into the hands of area specialists but also by synthesizing constructivism and realism. Huntington's thesis was not realist or neorealist in the strict sense—he did not refer to some timeless human nature or to undifferentiated *raison d'état*—but he did suggest that humans were prone to violence and that human history had been about different kinds of conflict. Huntington presented a world of constructions, but as Robert Jervis observed, he did not share most constructivists' hopes for peace, equality, and cooperation between humans.[27]

Much of the criticism of Huntington parodied his work, but his treatment of culture and civilization did lack depth. *The Clash of Civilizations* pushed the coherence of civilizational politics too far and failed to reflect how cultures interact with others. Jacinta O'Hagan believed that he had ignored the extent to which cultures could "selectively synthesise certain elements of another culture into its own, while weeding out those elements seen as undesirable or inappropriate."[28] Part of the criticism, as William Pfaff highlighted, stemmed from the fact that *The Clash of Civilizations* was not really an anthropological or sociological study of culture and civilization.[29] Rather, it was a descriptive analysis of the language and purpose of new patterns of conflict in the post–Cold War world. *The Clash* was about conflict, not cooperation, although this focus inevitably gave a distorted impression of civilizations. Another story of Islam could be told, for instance, although part of Islam's contemporary importance to Huntington was that there were Islamists who had wholeheartedly adopted the language of civilizational conflict.

Another criticism that could be leveled at Huntington was that he did not sufficiently consider the factors restraining cultural conflict. Actual behavior clearly results from a combination of things, including culture but also national, state-centered, and economic impulses. Huntington passed over the power of the state and the force of global capitalism; in most places, cultural politics operate within the framework of these two great structures and only rarely break free of their restraints. Shortly after the Huntington's 1993 article, Fouad Ajami set out the neorealist counter. For Ajami, a certain amount of "tradition mongering" and a few Muslim "stragglers" in such places as Bosnia did not prove the thesis.[30] Ajami insisted that

> civilizations do not control states, states control civilizations. States avert their gaze from blood ties when they need to; they see brotherhood and faith and kin when it is in their interest to do so. We remain in a world of self-help. The solitude of states continues.[31]

Ajami's criticism could be supported by evidence, although visualizing a simple dichotomy between *raison d'état* and cultural preferences was problematic. Nevertheless, Huntington did underestimate the extent to which the state is still an autonomous generator of behavior. When *raison d'état* contradicts civilizational impulses, the immediacy of the state tends to win out, and the behavior of many Muslim states seems to demonstrate this tendency.

The biggest omission in *The Clash of Civilizations,* though, was a proper analysis of the influence of global capitalism and the cultural baggage that went with it. Huntington dismissed the power of Western culture and consumerism in little more than one page of *The Clash*.[32] In reality, engaging with global markets counteracts the urges of even the most belligerent of civilizational warriors. A reading of Benjamin Barber's *Jihad vs. McWorld* is perhaps the best antidote to Huntington's downplaying of capitalism and consumerism. For Barber, the encroachment of McWorld had precipitated culture revivalism and the outbreak of cultural struggles (jihad) in the first place. The world was caught between "Babel and Disneyland" rather than between competing Babels.[33] Jihad and McWorld were intimately related—"locked together in a kind of Freudian moment of the ongoing culture struggle"—but although the struggle would not end quickly, Barber thought that the forces of McWorld would prove stronger.[34] The weight and glitter of global capitalism would eventually subdue jihad's microwars. If Barber was right, Huntington was merely describing a series of "glocal" moments that were significant at the microlevel but not at the macrolevel. The politics of civilizations would be subdued as long as the world economy continued to offer material advantages to enough states and peoples.

The heat in the debate about Huntington partly stemmed from the fear of his critics that cultural pessimism might become a self-fulfilling prophecy, that it would needlessly construct new divisions and conflicts where none really existed. Ken Booth thought that Huntington's "bumper-sticker version of world politics" was "deeply flawed and politically pernicious; but . . . powerful."[35] In fact, in the years since the 1993 article, David Welch observed, there is little evidence that Western policymakers have taken *The Clash of Civilizations* on board. Welch noted, though, that Huntington had retained a curious influence on academic discourse.[36] The stark choices that Huntington posed had afforded the chance for some "intellectual swordplay," but, more significant, he had struck at a moment when Westerners were thinking about the future world and the next Other.[37] Michael Hudson agreed that governments had purposefully steered clear of *The Clash* but was less sanguine about the consequences, in that

> the Islamic threat like its big brother "the clash of civilizations," could well turn out to be a self-confirming hypothesis. While academic discussion of political Islam, generally, has been enlightening, the public debate all too often has been marred by stereotypes and reductionist analysis. . . . Department of State spokesmen have consistently tried to take a nuanced position even while their political superiors conflate Islamism and terrorism.[38]

For U.S. policymakers, vital interests in the Muslim world required a more sophisticated analysis. To take notice of Huntington was to risk creating needless divisions with important states like Turkey, Egypt, Pakistan, Malaysia, Indonesia, and above all Saudi Arabia; U.S. policymakers were too effective to do this. In a speech in June 1992, U.S. assistant secretary of state for Near Eastern and South Asian affairs, Edward Djerejian, set out the position that was to be followed by successive administrations.[39] Djerejian perceived that Islam was one of the world's great faiths and the United States did not regard it as the next "ism" to confront the West. Islam was not the problem; misinterpretations of the faith that produced extremism were. The United States realized that Islam was a complex phenomenon and would only seek to resist those extremists on a case-by-case basis. U.S. policy did not threaten the vast majority of Muslims, but those that the U.S. identified as extremists would be resisted, even if that meant turning a blind eye to the promotion of democracy in certain Muslim countries.

For all the criticisms of Huntington, though, he did describe some important things about the post–Cold War world: that people from different cultures hold immanent preferences that shape their behavior seems difficult to deny. The way humans view the world through their beliefs — through their Western liberalism or Islamism — is clearly important, although the link between immanent cultural preference and geopolitical outcome remains far from straightforward.

Moreover, Huntington's direct influence on Western policymakers may have been limited, but there can be little doubt that *The Clash of Civilizations* was a key reference point in post–Cold War discourse. When talking about the relationship between Islam and the West, Huntington almost had to be either cited or debunked. He also reinforced some very widely held beliefs in the West that Islam was not entirely compatible with Western values. Although many Western academics and politicians were repelled by Huntington's stridency, most Western liberals were ultimately hostile to Islam. Islam supported social systems that were resistant to liberal democracy and human rights and practiced unacceptable forms of discrimination, especially the subordination of women. Westerners did not need to go all the way toward advocating a "clash of civilizations" to believe that Islam was a force that had to be managed and in some cases opposed.

In the Islamic world, too, *The Clash of Civilizations* had an enormous influence on political discourse. Islamic fundamentalists were the strange bedfellows of Huntington and, as Fred Halliday pointed out, were all too happy to see Islam defined as a separate and immutable moral and cultural system.[40] Islamic militants were not the only ones who felt empowered by a discourse on civilizations. The elites who ran Muslim states also referred to *The Clash* as a way of enhancing their international bargaining power, although most wanted to avoid confirming conflict lines. Muslim leaders were quick to point out the West's proclivity for defining the Other and its apparent need to find an enemy for the post–Cold War world.

In the later 1990s, the Islamic Republic of Iran's president, Mohammad Khatami, initiated the "dialogue amongst the civilizations," and this agenda was taken up by the Organization of the Islamic Conference (OIC). The Tehran Declaration on Dialogue Among Civilizations, produced at the OIC summit in Tehran in May 1999, explicitly rejected the idea of a clash of civilizations but defined the principles and measures by which civilizations could exist in peace and cooperation. Of course, many of the recommendations that the OIC voiced were really about getting the West to respect Islamic culture and the physical integrity of Muslim countries.[41]

What Muslim states wanted to do was establish the terms for inter-subjective understandings at a global level that were based on references to civilizations. Feeding the idea of civilizations into the global discourse about the future of humankind was synonymous with feeding in Islamic ideas. Muslims liked the idea of civilizations in global politics partly because it was a response to the West's liberal universalism. The idea of civilizations came to the attention of everyone when Islamic states successfully lobbied the UN General Assembly to make 2001 the UN Year of Dialogue Among Civilizations.[42] Perhaps some of Huntington's critics ought to reflect that to the extent that a global discourse about civilizations existed, it tended to empower the dominated, although that did not necessarily make the idea enlightened.

Western leaders did not really want to have to deal with the idea of different civilizations when they had the liberal idea. For the West, it was much better to define civilization according to some universal standard of good: of course, that really meant defining civilization according to the universal standards of liberalism, but it was important not to too explicitly equate this definition with the West. The dynamic in the discourse really came to the fore in the aftermath of the 11 September 2001 attacks by Islamic militants on the United States. Western leaders constantly rammed home the point that the West had no fundamental difference or quarrel with Islam or the Muslim world. Indeed, when Italian prime minister Silvio Berlusconi inadvertently broke ranks and made the mistake of highlighting differences between Western and

Islamic standards of civilization at a press conference in Germany on 26 September 2001, he was roundly condemned across both the Western and Muslim worlds, although for different reasons.[43]

Finding the Middle Way in the Discourse

Fukuyama and Huntington were both seminal figures in post–Cold War thought who represented poles in the culture discourse, although neither managed to establish his thesis as the new paradigm. In fact, where the world was going after the Cold War was unclear. Thinking in the West was broadly neither as optimistic as Fukuyama's nor as pessimistic as Huntington's. By the end of the 1990s, something of a synthesis of Fukuyama and Huntington had emerged. A new age of global cooperation might or might not be possible, but in the foreseeable future, the world seemed likely be one of "zones." Echoing Fukuyama's darker moments, Barry Buzan and Richard Little reiterated the idea of zones of peace and zones of conflict, observing in 1999 a future in which

> one world (call it the zone of peace or the post-historical world) is defined by a postmodern security community of powerful advanced capitalist industrial democracies, and international relations within this world no longer operate according to old Westphalian/realist rules. In the zone of peace, states do not expect or prepare for war against each other, and since this zone contains most of the great powers this is a very significant development for the whole of the international system. Reflecting the character of postmodern states, highly developed capitalist economies and societies are exceptionally open and interdependent, transnational players are numerous and strong, and international society is well developed. . . . The other world (call it the zone of conflict or the historical world) is comprised of a mixture of modern and premodern states. In relations amongst (and within) these states classical realist rules still obtain, and war is a useable and used instrument of policy. In this zone, international relations operate by the Westphalian/realist rules of power politics that prevailed all over the world up to 1945. States expect and prepare for the possibility of serious tension with their neighbours.[44]

Buzan and Little went on to specify that there were fundamental qualitative differences between the way in which states and societies in the Western system related to each other and the way that things happened in the Middle East, South Asia, and many other places; these differences were rooted in history and in the shape of the international political and economic system. Non-Westerners were still to have their values transformed, and until they did, the tense relationship between the different zones would be one of the most important features of international politics. Buzan and Little wondered,

> will the weaker, but perhaps more aggressive, zone of conflict begin to penetrate and impinge upon the zone of peace through threats of terrorism, long-range weapons of mass destruction, migration, disease, debt repudiation, and suchlike? Will the unquestionably more powerful zone of peace seek to penetrate and influence the zone of conflict, using the levers of geo-economics, and occasionally more robust forms of intervention, to manipulate state-making in the zone of conflict? Will the postmodern world try to insulate itself by constructing buffer zones in Mexico, Central Europe, Turkey and North Africa, and trying to stay out of the more chaotic parts of the zone of conflict? Or will it try to engage with the whole, pushing towards a new world order in its own image?[45]

What was common to much post–Cold War Western discourse was that it continued to pigeonhole places as advanced or backward; this was the language of hegemony. Western thought was continuing to do what it had done for centuries: to designate certain parts of the world as different and aspire to incorporate or contain them on its own terms. In the age of Western hegemony and the new globalization, incorporation implied an unprecedented degree of penetration and reform for other cultures. Although there was awareness in the West about oversimplifying their perceptions of other cultures, most Westerners regarded Islam and the nature of most Muslim societies as problematic. The Muslims were widely regarded to be too different and potentially dangerous; from there, it was not a great jump to condone the imperative of controlling the Muslim world and, if necessary, to do so with extraordinary means.

Notes

1. Agnew and Corbridge, *Mastering Space,* 1995, 48–49.
2. Fukuyama, *The End of History and the Last Man,* 1992.
3. Fukuyama observed that "we cannot picture ourselves a world that is essentially different from the present one, and at the same time better. Other, less reflective ages also thought of themselves as the best, but we arrive at this conclusion exhausted, as it were, from the pursuit of alternatives we felt *had* to be better than liberal democracy." Ibid., 46.
4. Ibid., 214–215.
5. Ibid., Introduction, xv; see also chap. 10.

6. Ibid., 277.

7. Ibid., 43–44.

8. Ibid., 237.

9. Ibid., 46.

10. Ibid., 88.

11. Ibid., 126.

12. Ibid., 45.

13. Axford, *The Global System,* 1995, 180.

14. Huntington, "The Clash of Civilizations," *Foreign Affairs* 72, no. 3, Summer 1993, 22–49; Huntington, *The Clash of Civilizations and the Remaking of the World Order,* 1996.

15. Huntington, *The Clash of Civilizations and the Remaking of the World Order,* 266.

16. Ibid., 258.

17. Huntington observed that "at the end of the twentieth century the concept of a universal civilization helps justify Western cultural dominance over other societies and the need for those societies to ape Western practices and institutions. Universalism is the ideology of the West for confrontations with non-Western cultures. . . . The non-Wests see as Western what the West sees as universal. . . . To the extent that non-Westerners see the world as one, they see it as a threat." Ibid., 66.

18. Kedourie, "Feature Article: Islam Resurgent," *Encyclopaedia Britannia Book of the Year 1980: Events of 1979,* 1980, 63.

19. See Mohammed Abed Al-Jabri, "Clash of Civilizations: The Relations of the Future?" in Gema Martin Munoz, ed., *Islam, Modernism, and the West,* 1999, 65–70.

20. Huntington, *The Clash of Civilizations and the Remaking of the World Order,* 188.

21. For further discussion of the debate on Islam in the United States, see Pinto, "The Intellectual Backdrop: Approaches to Political Islam," in *Political Islam and the United States,* 1999, especially 174–178.

22. Miller, "The Challenge of Radical Islam," *Foreign Affairs* 72, no. 2, Spring 1993, 45.

23. Ibid., 54.

24. Ibid., 47.

25. Pinto, *Political Islam and the United States,* 184.

26. Booth, "Huntington's Homespun Grandeur," *Political Quarterly* 68, no. 4, 1997, 425–428; Chan, "Too Neat and Under-thought a World Order: Huntington and Civilizations," *Millennium: Journal of International Studies* 26, no. 1, 1997, 137–140; Halliday, *Islam and the Myth of Confrontation,* 1995; Jacinta O'Hagan, "Civilisational Conflict? Looking for Cultural Enemies," *Third World Quarterly* 16, no. 1, March 1995, 19–38; Tarock, "Civilisational Conflict? Fighting the Enemy Under a New Banner," *Third World Quarterly* 16, no. 1, March 1995, 5–18; Welch, "The Clash of Civilizations Thesis as an Argument and as a Phenomenon," *Security Studies* 6, no. 4, 1997, 197–216.

27. Jervis, Book Review of *Clash of Civilizations* by Samuel Huntington, *Political Science Quarterly* 112, no. 2, 1997, 307–308.

28. O'Hagan, "Civilisational Conflict? Looking for Cultural Enemies," 33.

29. Pfaff, "The Reality of Human Affairs," *World Policy Journal* 14, no. 2, 1997, 93.

30. Ajami, "The Summoning," *Foreign Affairs* 72, no. 4, September–October 1993, 4, 7.

31. Ibid., 9.

32. Huntington, *The Clash of Civilizations and the Remaking of the World Order*, 58.

33. Barber, *Jihad vs. McWorld*, 1996, 389, 4.

34. Ibid., 157.

35. Booth, "Huntington's Homespun Grandeur," 425.

36. Welch, "The Clash of Civilizations Thesis as an Argument and as a Phenomenon," 197.

37. Ibid., 212.

38. Hudson, "To Play the Hegemon: Fifty Years of U.S. Policy Towards the Middle East," *Middle East Journal* 50, no. 3, Summer 1996, 341.

39. Pinto, "U.S. Policy Towards Political Islam," in *Political Islam and the United States*, 206–207.

40. Halliday, *Islam and the Myth of Confrontation*, 12–13.

41. *Tehran Declaration on Dialogue Among Civilizations*, adopted by the Islamic Symposium on Dialogue among Civilizations, Tehran, 3–5 May 1999. Text reproduced on the homepage of the Permanent Delegation of the OIC to the UN Offices in Geneva and Vienna, http://www.oic-un.org/8/tehdec.stm.

42. See the United Nations website, http://www.org/dialogue.html.

43. "Arabs Demand Berlusconi Apology," BBC News Website, World: Middle East, Thursday, 27 September 2001, http://news.bbc.co.uk/hi/english/world/middle_east/newsid_1565000/1565664.stm; "Berlusconi Comments Dominate Italian Debate," BBC News Website, World: Middle East, Friday, 28 September 2001,http://mews.bbc.co.uk/hi/English/world/middle_east/newsid_1569000/1569039.stm.

44. Buzan and Little, "Beyond Westphalia? Capitalism After the 'Fall,'" *Review of International Studies* 25, Special Issue, December 1999, 101.

45. Buzan and Little, "Beyond Westphalia?" 102.

3

The Pax Americana
in the Middle East

The United States was the principal agent of the Western hegemony. At the end of the Cold War, the United States was the world's only global superpower, and although the international system could not be characterized as unipolar, the influence of the United States spanned the world. For all the questions about the future of the state in the age of globalization, the United States remained the most powerful actor in world affairs, with a clear sense of its own national interests and proactive strategies aimed at achieving them. U.S. power was projected by a breadth of preponderant capabilities and through its position in international organizations. To the extent that broader Western hegemony required security management services, it was the United States that provided them in most places. Britain and France had a role in regional security management in parts of the world, but the Muslim heartlands of the Middle East and South Asia were America's sphere.

Muslim peoples and states had little choice but to deal with America's moment. The United States was at the center of an alliance system that included the Muslim powers of Turkey, Egypt, Saudi Arabia, Pakistan, Indonesia, and Malaysia. Where Muslims were involved in conflicts, the United States assumed an even greater importance. Whether it was engaged in or distanced itself from regional conflicts had great bearing on the lives of millions of Muslims. In the war in Bosnia, the United States delayed its intervention but finally came to help beleaguered Muslims with decisive military aid. U.S. forces were sent in to back up the UN in Somalia, but after running into trouble, the Somalis were left to their anarchy and their starvation. In Christian East Timor, the United States was no longer prepared to acquiesce to the Indonesian occupation, and after considerable pressure, the Muslim

Indonesians left. The United States applied great military force to end the Serbian oppression of the Muslim population in Kosovo and to establish what amounted to a North Atlantic Treaty Organization (NATO) protectorate. When the United States resolved to bring down the Taliban movement's rule in Afghanistan following the 11 September 2001 attacks on it, it did so in two months with ruthless efficiency. In Kashmir, Chechnya, and Tajikistan, the United States took no decisive position, and the conflicts dragged on in the hands of their participants.

Above all, U.S. and Muslim interests met each other in the Middle East, a region at the junction of Europe, Africa, and Asia; the heartland of Islam and Judaism; and in possession of over two-thirds of the world's reserves of oil. The Middle East was of such strategic importance that it was difficult to imagine that U.S. leadership in the world could exist without a significant degree of control over the region. U.S. preeminence within the Western hegemony was based on relatively low and stable prices for energy. Without reasonably priced oil, the much more energy efficient Europeans and Japanese had a competitive advantage over Americans. It was no coincidence that the revival of U.S. power in the 1990s coincided with a sustained period of low oil prices; or that when oil prices rose in 2000–2001, the long U.S. boom faltered. Thus, nowhere else did Muslims feel the presence of U.S. power in quite the same way as they did in the Middle East.

For all the talk of a new era of international relations following the Cold War, realpolitik continued to be the name of the game in the Middle East. In this sense, the United States did regard the Middle East as a "zone of conflict," as distinct from a "zone of peace" requiring different methods. Israel remained the principal ally and obsession of U.S. policymakers, whereas those that defied the United States were to be locked in a zero-sum struggle with an implacably belligerent foe.

The United States had both friends and enemies in the region, but it was the deep political divisions that existed between Middle Eastern states that really gave U.S. power its entry points. Above all, the United States enthralled the Middle East with its role in two long-running regional crises: the Arab-Israeli conflict and the problem of Saddam Hussein's Iraq. In its position as hegemonic security manager, the United States had to deal with the endemic instability of the Middle Eastern state system, as well as a great body of Muslim opinion that was deeply hostile to it.

The New World Order System

In the aftermath of the Iraqi invasion of Kuwait, President George Bush addressed the U.S. Congress on 11 September 1990 and proclaimed that the world had an opportunity to now make a new world order. Echoing presidents since Woodrow Wilson, Bush talked of a new basis for peace and security in the international system. The new world order promised to foster liberal aspirations across the world, including greater justice, democracy, and prosperity, but in the midst of the Kuwait crisis, it was the rule of law that preoccupied Bush. From its very inception, then, the new world order was an idea closely associated with the furtherance of U.S. objectives in the international system; it would always be difficult, Chris Brown observed, to "distinguish between the New World Order and the New World giving orders."[1]

What emerged in the years after the Kuwait crisis was what could be called a new world order system. Dealing with Iraq set the tone from the start. For U.S. policymakers, international order was best managed through the multilateral organizations of the international community, which raised the legitimacy and cut the costs of policy interventions, but it was the United States that must have the definitive voice, especially in areas of its interest. The UN Security Council was the principal institution of the new world order, and although permanent members Russia, China, and France were not always at ease with U.S. preeminence, they rarely had the will or interest to contradict U.S. diplomacy. Where multilateral organizations could not be successfully utilized, the United States was prepared to bypass them. America's liberal ideals and its proclivity for unilateralism did not sit easily together.

For the Middle East, the new world order was to be practically synonymous with the terms of a pax Americana. Saddam Hussein–style adventures in nation building and economic development were not permitted on the U.S. watch. Middle Eastern states must follow the rules of the new world order, or they would face the penalty of the U.S. rule of law. In the case of the Iraqi occupation of Kuwait, the United States restored the "rule of law" with the organization of an unprecedented international coalition and UN sanctions regime, as well as an expeditionary force of over 500,000. The Iraqi army and Saddam Hussein's chanting supporters in such places as Morocco, Jordan, and Yemen were no match for the armies of the new world order. The Iraqis were blasted out of Kuwait, and Iraq was left desperately isolated. U.S. policymakers took note.

What resistance the new world order faced came largely from a group of disgruntled states and regional powers, notably Cuba, Serbia, Libya, Iran, Iraq, and North Korea. The dissenters were difficult and potentially dangerous, but the threat they represented was often overstated by the United States. The liberal order was inherently inclined to self-righteousness. The dissenters were condemned as "rogue states," "terrorist states," or "backlash states," sometimes with limited or fading evidence, and the validity of the grievances that produced their roguishness was denied. The superpower machinery of the United States was redirected into regional arenas in order to bring the rogues to heel. Thus, even though the language and practice of war were in general receding after the Cold War, where the dissident local power met U.S. regional hegemony, the threat of violence was growing. According to Waltrund Queiser Morales, the new U.S. willingness to clear up the "strategic slums" of the Third World was first marked by its intervention in Panama in 1989, and a "New World Order militarism" had quickly taken shape after that.[2] Doubtless, there were vested interests in the United States and in its giant security establishment that were happy to find new enemies.

For the "rogues," the disappearance of the Soviet Union had seriously weakened their positions and raised the chances of U.S. intervention against them. The United States took on the "rogues" in many ways but put most effort into preventing their military development, especially the proliferation of weapons of mass destruction to them. The U.S. effort was spurred by the "what if" thinking that followed the Kuwait crisis; how could Iraq have been handled if it had been armed with nuclear weapons? Strategic missile defensives were planned—and were to become the obsession of George W. Bush's administration beginning in 2001—but the more practical responses were political. In December 1993, the U.S. Department of Defense launched the Counter-Proliferation Initiative. The United States put much more time and money into a global intelligence and prevention campaign aimed at interfering with the flow of arms and equipment to the rogues.[3] NATO allies were conscripted. The task of nonproliferation was a difficult one—such was the spread of technology and the limitations of the Non-Proliferation Treaty (NPT)—but the Clinton administration was determined to make the point that containment and even rollback were possible and necessary.

Whether the United States could finish off the rogues was another matter. U.S. policy was limited by the international rule system that it had helped create and by the ambivalence of many Americans about the human and financial costs involved in policing the world. The United States found it difficult to close the gate on the rogues as long as they had something to offer, especially if they had oil and dollars. The states of the European Union and Japan preferred the strategy of "constructive engagement," and if a rogue avoided gross challenges to international order, it was possible to maneuver around U.S. sanctions. Only where the troublesome threatened the vital interests of the United States and outraged the liberal sensibilities of the Europeans were they liable to face the full force of the new world order.

Forging the Pax Americana in the Middle East After the Gulf War

The United States achieved a dominance of Middle Eastern affairs after the Gulf War not seen since that of the British Empire in the first half of the twentieth century. Soviet power had gone, and the United States was now at the center of an alliance system that linked Egypt and the Gulf states to Israel and Turkey. Two vital sets of interests had outlived the Cold War, and they now came to dominate U.S. policy in the region: first, the maintenance of a secure and prosperous Israel; and second, the security of reasonably priced oil supplies to the industrialized world. To achieve these goals, the United States needed to do a number of things: preempt strategic threats to Israel and its Gulf allies, encourage a resolution of divisions within its own alliance system, and make the region more accessible to its political and military presence.

The Gulf War put the United States in a vastly stronger position in the Gulf than before. The Gulf states were exposed as "military midgets dependent on U.S. might."[4] Before the Kuwait crisis, most of the Gulf monarchies had screened their countries from U.S. forces and security guarantees. When the United States had intervened in the Gulf during the Iran-Iraq War in 1987–1988, for instance, Kuwait and Saudi Arabia had refused to directly support U.S. operations on their behalf. Kuwait was now a de facto protectorate of the United States, with U.S. access formalized in a joint defense agreement reached in September 1991.[5] Saudi Arabia avoided a formal agreement, but U.S. forces were in the kingdom for the foreseeable future. The United States maintained a permanent Gulf establishment of over 20,000 men and women, with at least three fighter squadrons and a carrier battle group on station.[6] From this new base, President George Bush and Secretary of State James

Baker could move to construct a new regional order in which U.S. power was institutionalized in an Arab-Israeli peace process, an upgraded alliance system, and a much greater U.S. military presence.

The success of the United States in the Middle East to that point was all the more impressive because it had long fallen afoul of strong Arab and Muslim public opinion over its relationship with Israel. Doing something about resolving the Arab-Israel conflict was more difficult. U.S. policymakers were transfixed by Israel: they were often emotionally committed to the Jewish state themselves or beholden to the political influence of the Jewish lobby in the United States. The Jewish lobby could mobilize money, votes, and sympathies in the U.S. political system that few U.S. politicians could ignore.[7] Gaining a significant majority of the Jewish vote was vital to the Democratic Party's success in presidential and congressional elections, and denying them that vote was vital to the Republican Party. Israel was a sacred cow in U.S. politics.

Israel was the Middle East's only democracy, but it was a highly illiberal one. Israel ran its liberalism beside the quite contradictory Zionist ideology of nationalism and colonialism; the combination harbored fair elections and a free press alongside institutionalized racism, excessively violent policing, legally recognized torture, and government sanctioned extrajudicial assassinations, both inside and outside its jurisdiction. Israel aspired to be Western but could not be described as a liberal state, especially after the conquests of 1967. For all the profound flaws in Israeli democracy, though, there was really no serious questioning of the connection in the United States. Indeed, the U.S. commitment to Israel continued to be translated into high levels of political and material support that enabled it to transgress world opinion and international law in a way that no other state could.

The colonial settlement of Arab lands occupied in the Six Day War of 1967 was a brazen breach of international law, notably of that defined in Article 49 of the Fourth Geneva Convention. U.S. officials were aware of the issue, but not even the agreements reached during the peace process after 1993 reversed what was happening. In May 2001, the report of the Mitchell Commission, investigating the breakdown of the peace process, recognized that the settlements were illegal under international law and pointed out Palestinian concerns that since the Israel-Palestinian Declaration of Principles in 1993, Israel had constructed thirty new settlements and expanded others, and as a result the settler population in the West Bank had doubled to 200,000 and that in East Jerusalem had risen to 170,000.[8]

The Western hegemony paid a price for U.S. support to Zionist Israel. The different way in which Israeli violence and lawbreaking were treated undermined the very idea of the rule of law in the international system. Until Israel was held accountable, UN lawmaking could only be regarded as a system of biased hegemonic rules. For most Muslims, the story of violence, dispossession, and injustice that Israel continued to represent was synonymous with the self-interest and hypocrisy of the West. Israel got in the way of a more cooperative relationship between Muslims and Westerners in general. Supporting Israel meant such things as terrorism, nonproliferation, and missile defense were at the top of the Western agenda with regard to the Muslim world, not economic development and democratization. Violence haunted relations between Westerners and Muslims largely because of Israel. Because the Arab-Israeli conflict was apt to destabilize both the U.S. security system in the Middle East and the progress of the entire liberal international order, something needed to be done about the situation.

The Arab-Israeli Peace Process

During the Gulf War itself, the U.S.-Israeli link was the international coalition's most serious liability. Saddam Hussein had made the connection between Kuwait and the Arab territories occupied by Israel, and although the United States resisted the ploy, Bush indicated it would pursue an Arab-Israeli peace after the Kuwait crisis was over. Most Arabs were skeptical about the impartiality of the United States as an arbiter in any peace process, but the United States was the only option, because only it could bring Israel to the table.

Bush made good on his commitments, and with its enormous prestige just after the Gulf War, the United States was able to bring the conflicting parties to a peace conference in Madrid in October–November 1991. Israel sat down to talk peace with many Arab states for the first time, most notably with Syria. The Madrid conference itself was troubled, but the process it set off was an important development and inaugurated a whole series of bilateral and multilateral talks that made real progress in settling differences between Israel and Arab states.[9] The land-for-peace principle outlined in UN Security Council Resolution 242 and 338 formed the basis of the dialogue. Jordan went on to work out a full peace, Syrian entered into negotiations with Israel over the Golan Heights, and a number of other Arab states, including some of the Gulf states, began to have dealings with Israel. The United States provided aid or security to all those that made peace with Israel.

The negotiations represented an enormous step forward in securing Israel's acceptance in the region. Israel was soon attending conferences on regional economic development with Arab states. Even more unprecedented, when Israel fell victim to Islamic suicide bombers in 1996, Arab states agreed to gather in Sharm el-Shaikh, Egypt, to express support for Israeli premier Shimon Peres and to work out ways of improving the security situation. After fifty years of conflict, the prospect of Israel's peaceful absorption into the region finally seemed a possibility. A great achievement was just around the corner, and the potential benefits looked enormous. In 1995, William B. Quandt observed that

> one can imagine the emergence of a zone of peace in the Eastern Mediterranean in the coming decade that would allow for a flourishing of democratic politics and economic growth in Israel, Palestine, Jordan and Lebanon, with beneficial spill over in Syria and Egypt as well.[10]

However, a stable Arab-Israeli peace required an Israel-Palestinian peace. The dispossession of the Palestinians could not be pushed aside and was constantly emphasized by their civil uprising, the *intifadah,* in the Occupied Territories since late 1987. The Palestinian Liberation Organization (PLO) led by Yasser Arafat was not officially represented in Madrid, and the Likud bloc under Yitzhak Shamir refused to talk. It was the formation of the Labor government under a forward-looking Yitzhak Rabin in 1993 that allowed for the real jump forward. In September 1993, following secret negotiations in Oslo, the Israelis and the PLO signed the Declaration of Principles, establishing the terms and timetable for a resolution to the conflict. In exchange for peace and recognition for Israel, the Palestinians were to be allowed a form of rolling devolution in Gaza and parts of the West Bank. The deal may have been negotiated in Oslo, but it was given authority in Washington with a signing ceremony on the White House lawn. The Israel-Palestinian peace process was an extremely troubled one, but the deal was a breakthrough moment.

The prospective peace had real benefits for the United States. The end of the *intifadah* and the formation of the Palestinian National Authority (PNA) may not have pleased hard-line states, Islamic militants, and other rejectionists, but most Arabs were prepared to go along with the PLO. Certainly, the peace process did much to diffuse the constant pressure on Arab states to do something about Israel and made closer relations with the United States less difficult to explain. A weight had been lifted from U.S. foreign policy, although U.S. presidents and envoys would have to keep shoring up the peace process to maintain a degree of viability.

The peace process delivered significant benefits to both sides, but the terms of the process were only ever supposed to be interim, and the absence of a final settlement, projected for 1999–2000, undermined the entire enterprise. Neither Israel nor the PNA could easily come to terms over fundamental differences about territory, sovereignty, Jerusalem, and Jewish settlers. Meanwhile, violent extremists hovered in the wings. The Islamic bombers of Hamas and Islamic Jihad provided the sternest test of Israel's will to go on. The process appeared to hit a turning point in May 1996, when a series of bus bomb attacks in Jerusalem, Ashkelon, and Tel Aviv killed nearly sixty people. The subsequent arrival of the government of Benjamin Netanyahu set the peace process back years. The Likud-led government did not accept the land-for-peace principle and advocated further colonial settlement; this hard-line attitude made resolution of the conflict impossible. The growth of trust and goodwill between Israel and both Arab states and Palestinians was squandered.

The subsequent government of Ehud Barak raised new hopes again, but they were disappointed. Barak lacked the authority to get a deal without extracting something more from the Palestinians. A key moment of failure came in talks under U.S. auspices at Camp David in July and August 2000. President Bill Clinton was fully engaged, and the creation of a Palestinian state was on the table at Camp David. Barak offered more than any Israeli prime minister before him, but Arafat had few further compromises to give and could not bring himself to accept the delineation of territory or the limitations on Palestinian sovereignty that the deal still involved, especially in East Jerusalem. The issues of Israeli settlers and Palestinian refugees also got in the way of a successful negotiation. The ebbing trust between the two leadership teams— and between Israelis and Palestinian more generally—sealed the failure of negotiations. On the ground, the conditions for an upsurge in violence had already come into place. Most Palestinians in the West Bank and Gaza lived under the PNA, but most wanted more than the life of the ghetto allowed to them. Palestinians wanted an independent state, an end to Israeli settlement, a viable economy, and rights to East Jerusalem. Palestinians sought the end of Israeli domination. By the autumn of 2000, Palestinian frustrations were explosive. When the then

Likud opposition leader, Ariel Sharon, made an inflammatory visit to the Al-Aqsa mosque in Jerusalem on 28 September 2000, it was the spark for an upsurge in violence.

After September 2000, Palestinians embarked on a sustained period of protest with predictable results. Young stone-throwing protesters were shot down in the hundreds by the Israel Defense Forces (IDF), and the Palestinian police and armed members of Arafat's Fatah organization were inevitably drawn in. The cooperation between Israeli and Palestinian security forces totally broke down. The PNA had done much to contain the terrorism of Hamas and Islamic Jihad, but its will to go on doing so was strained past the breaking point. Israelis began again to suffer new shootings, mortar attacks, and suicide bombings. An upsurge of religiosity among young Palestinians fueled the threat of Islamic terrorism. Israelis dug in, too, and after elections in early February 2001, Ariel Sharon became prime minister.

The new Likud-led government remained committed to an undivided Jerusalem and to the further expropriation of the Occupied Territories. The peace process could no longer produce even a minimally acceptable final settlement—not that that was an issue because even talks were now coming to an end. Sharon's insistence on a moratorium on violence, including stone throwing, effectively prevented any dialogue on conflict prevention or resolution getting under way. The period of calm was eventually defined as only seven days, but even that could not be managed, even after the stunning impact of the 11 September attacks in the United States. The United States backed the Israeli position, and a plan introduced by Central Intelligence Agency (CIA) director George Tenet in June 2001 essentially offered the Palestinians the status quo in return for what amounted to an end to all protest and the arrest of Islamic militants. Arafat could not concede so much for so little. Most Palestinians believed that their resistance was legitimate under international law, especially with the breakdown of the Oslo agreement and the continuance of the occupation. According to Alan Dowty and Michelle Gawerc, Palestinian leaders did not accept the Israeli premise that they had to make a simple choice between peace and terror.[11] In any case, all Palestinian resistance could not be turned off at will by the PNA, even if it had an incentive to do so. The renewed conflict made Arafat much weaker vis-à-vis Palestinian radicals and reluctant to test his authority against the anti-Israeli belligerency of Islamic militants, his own security forces, and the mass of the Palestinian population. Between them, Islamic extremists and the IDF made sure that talks could not get going.

Whether Sharon actually had a grand design for proceeding with the Arab-Israeli conflict by this stage in his career was rather unclear, but hanging on to the occupation of something over 50 percent of the West Bank and Gaza by staying the course in a campaign of disproportionate attrition appears to have been the bottom line of his government's policy. The IDF ensured that far more Palestinians were killed in the conflict than Israelis. The long-established strategic doctrine of Israel to meet threats with preemption and disproportionate escalation was applied, and surely enough the conflict escalated. Sharon regarded the PNA areas as a setting to use Israel's big stick. Tanks, helicopter gunships, and even fixed-wing bombers were deployed in what was really a job for policing. Moreover, a military strategy required turning Palestinian officials and police into the enemy, whether they were or not. Killing Palestinian police and bombing their stations while urging that they do more to enforce order on their side looked nonsensical. Israeli blockades around most Palestinian towns also prevented the effective deployment of Palestinian police and undermined the practical capacity of PNA to control its jurisdiction. Increasingly, Arafat did not have the political or policing strength to meet Israeli demands that the Islamic groups be broken up and their members arrested. A return to cooperative policing between Israel and the PNA was increasingly difficult to imagine. The impasse that Sharon presided over took the entire Arab-Israeli peace process ever further down the road to failure.

The tempo of the conflict reached a new pitch in the summer of 2001. Amid purposefully provocative Israeli attacks, incursions, house demolitions, and assassinations, Islamic suicide bombers struck. A bomb at a Tel Aviv nightspot in June killed twenty-one Israelis, and another at a Jerusalem pizza restaurant in August killed fourteen. The bombing of the Jerusalem restaurant appeared to have been precipitated by the IDF's assassination of eight Hamas members and civilians in a helicopter attack in Nablus.[12] More was to follow. Israel also moved against the infrastructure of the PNA following the August attack, most notably by seizing the PNA's Jerusalem headquarters, Orient House. The seizure of Orient House was of great political significance, and the U.S. State Department publicly communicated its dismay at the move.[13] The United States drew a line at the reoccupation of Palestinian buildings and land. The cycle of killing, revenge, and escalation seemed without end. Even if a cease-fire could eventually be engineered, it was difficult to imagine that the necessary concessions for a final settlement would come into place.

The success of the Arab-Israeli peace process was central to U.S.

Middle East policy, but its inability to keep the process on track marked U.S. limitations as a regional arbiter. The Clinton White House was as closely attached to Israel as any U.S. administration of recent times, and this connection ultimately prevented it from applying sufficient pressure to impel the key concessions from the Israelis. The arrival of George W. Bush in early 2001 did not help matters, as it became clear that the administration sought to step back from its role as a third-party mediator. Bush did not want to become too involved in a failing process. U.S. policy became less about conflict resolution and more about the tactical concerns of restraining Israel's military responses and managing the anger of Arab states. Keeping the UN and Europeans out, as well as diffusing the spotlight of international law on Israel, were also objectives. Bush prioritized the avoidance of any wider Arab-Israeli conflict but was prepared to put up with a certain level of Israeli-Palestinian violence. Needless to say, most Arabs and many Europeans found the situation less tolerable, and U.S. policy embodied a tricky balancing act.

What was really required for an Israel-PLO settlement was quite clear. Israel had to withdraw its army and settlers from most of the West Bank and Gaza, allow a substantially independent Palestinian state, and come to some arrangement over sharing Jerusalem. The Palestinian authorities had to unreservedly recognize Israel existence, fully renounce and suppress any violence toward Israelis, and give up the rights of most Palestinian refugees to return to Israel. The problem was that there was far too much talking about the process and not enough about the final resolution. Commissioned by President Clinton in an effort to get the peace process back on track, the report of the Mitchell Commission presented in May 2001 was an enlightened document that pointed the way in detail to de-escalation, confidence building, new peace talks, and a final resolution, but it was very much a case of leading the horse to water but not being able to make it drink.[14] The key problem was that Israel had not yet made the decision to completely withdraw from the Occupied Territories. Changing the mind-set of enough Israelis and getting the withdrawal commitment was the fundamental task for the United States as a security manager. The rest was just process. However, it was far from clear that policymakers in either the Clinton or George W. Bush administrations understood the fundamental problem or were prepared to exert the kind of pressure that was required to persuade Israel to give up on its illiberal nationalism and colonialism.

In the meantime, the conflict was bound to drag on amid fundamentally different views as to where the process was going and what actually constituted "peace." For the Israelis—and in this regard they were essentially supported by the United States—peace really meant "pax": it was synonymous with maximizing security, establishing order, and ensuring the control of the Palestinian entity. For Rabin, Peres, Netanyahu, Barak, and Sharon alike, the Palestinians could not be allowed too much land or too much freedom because doing so would reduce Israel's ability to control them. Ultimately, the peace process was about making the continued occupation of the West Bank and Gaza easier and more effective.

For the Palestinians, peace involved a significant degree of national self-determination. Arafat had given up the historic claim to all of Palestine in an effort to secure a peace deal, and needed to get Gaza and the West Bank back and some control over East Jerusalem because that was the minimum that most Palestinians could accept. Until Israel could grind down Palestinian resistance to the point of capitulation, or, alternatively, until it accepted that it had to withdraw from the West Bank and Gaza, both sides would continue to talk about peace at cross-purposes. As the peace process floundered, the progress that had been made was lost, and the hard-won concessions were gradually withdrawn. A return to the all-out conflict of the past was a possibility. Israel might one day come to the conclusion that it cannot live with the existence of the PNA as constituted. Similarly, Palestinians and Arab states that had joined the peace process might also roll back their acceptance of Israel's right to exist.

The decay of the peace process raised real questions about the future of the pax Americana in the Middle East. The searing injustice felt by all Arabs and Muslims was bound to fuel continuing outbreaks of terrorism and put many Muslim allies of the United States under real political pressure. Jerusalem especially was a sleeping giant of instability in the Muslim world. Arab states were not ready to take on Israel directly, but the unending violence invited a confrontation with Arab states at some point in the future. The Israel-Syria-Lebanon border remained a conflict zone. The withdrawal of the Egyptian ambassador from Israel in November 2000 also tarnished one of the jewels in the crown of Arab-Israeli reconciliation. The Egyptians were reluctant to take this step, but the goodwill of the United States' Arab allies was beginning to wear very thin. The United States paid a price for its inability to sort out the Israel-Palestinian conflict; until it did, U.S. hegemony in the Middle East would be a very unstable structure.

Dual Containment: Taking on the Counterhegemons

The Gulf War was a spectacular demonstration of U.S. power, but it left major questions over the future of international security in the Middle East. The two biggest powers in the Gulf—Iran and Iraq—were completely opposed to any security system that included the United States and were among the most vocal opponents of any Arab-Israeli peace process. Iran and Iraq also represented a continuing threat to another principal U.S. interest in the region: the security of the Gulf states and their enormous reserves of oil. Iraqi troops still stood on the borders of Kuwait and Saudi Arabia.

The principal issue in controlling the threat from Iran and Iraq was their military development, especially their efforts to acquire ballistic missiles and weapons of mass destruction. The large numbers of ballistic missiles acquired by states like Iran, Iraq, Syria, and Libya could reach Israel and Europe and were very difficult to counter. By far the most important security headache, though, was the potential for the development of nuclear weapons in Iran or Iraq. The possibility was a security problem for the United States itself but also represented a fundamental threat to the existence of Israel. Israel had successfully bombed the Iraqi nuclear program in Baghdad in 1981, and the possibility that it might do something again was a regional crisis in waiting. Israel's incentive to preempt the nuclear threat was very high, and the means that it might use could be extraordinary. To forestall the prospect of a calamity, the complete de-nuclearization of Iran and Iraq was adopted as U.S. policy.

A completely new security system in the Gulf was needed. Notwithstanding the Damascus Declaration shortly after the Gulf War, the failure of the Gulf states to agree with Egypt and Syria about security arrangements meant that the United States had to do more itself. Although the Gulf states could not be relied upon to defend themselves in any full-scale conflict with Iran and Iraq, local forces could be developed to meet a range of security missions. The transfer of billions of dollars' worth of arms to Saudi Arabia after the Gulf War was quantitatively and qualitatively great by any standards: more M1 tanks, more F-15s, new Apache helicopter gunships, and new artillery rockets. However, the willingness and ability of the Gulf states to take up their own defense was limited, and the noticeable lack of progress toward defense coordination within the Gulf Cooperation Council (GCC) betrayed the caution among them.[15] The smaller states remained wary of Saudi influence, and most were concerned about overplaying what they could do on their own. For the foreseeable future, U.S. forces simply had to be the supreme guarantor of Gulf security, taking up a role of policing and supervision not seen since the British withdrew their forces and security guarantees in the 1970s.

As for Iran and Iraq, what emerged by the time the Clinton administration took office in 1993 was the policy of "dual containment." The idea was developed at the National Security Council under the direction of the assistant to the president for national security affairs, Anthony Lake, and the special assistant to the president on Near Eastern and South Asian affairs, Martin Indyk (later ambassador to Israel). Indyk unveiled dual containment in a speech to the Washington Institute for Near East Policy in May 1993, and the idea was further filled out by Lake in an article in *Foreign Affairs* in March–April 1994. In *Foreign Affairs,* Lake argued that as the sole superpower, the United States had a special responsibility to promote the rule of law and democratic values in the post–Cold War world, and doing so necessarily meant standing up to a number of "aggressive and defiant" countries he called the "backlash states." The United States needed to develop a "strategy to neutralize, contain, and, through selective pressure, perhaps eventually transform these backlash states into constructive members of the international community."[16] Of course, all this rhetoric implied that the United States claimed a superior right to define what counted as a good state and acceptable behavior, as well as to intervene when its new world order was challenged.

Turning to the Gulf, Lake perceived that previous U.S. attempts to play Iran and Iraq against each other had failed because neither was capable of acting responsibly, but the United States was now in a position to contain both states simultaneously.[17] Lake argued that dual containment did not mean duplicate containment. The Iraqi regime represented an "aggressive, modernist, secular avarice" that was irredeemably criminal, and the United States should seek its overthrow.[18] Iran was a different matter: "a theocratic regime with a sense of cultural and political destiny and an abiding antagonism toward the United States," but one that Lake thought the United States could deal with, if the regime was induced to change.

The Islamic legitimacy of the Iranian regime clearly gave it a different status from the Iraqi regime, with Lake making it clear that "the American quarrel with Iran should not be misconstrued as a "clash of civilizations" or opposition to Iran as a theocratic state. . . . It is extremism, whether religious or secular, that we oppose."[19] The objective was not to overthrow the Islamic Republic but to purge it of its extremism and thus domesticate it. Iran should be tested not according to its rhetoric but to its actions, for Lake believed that the United States could not trust the pragmatic language of Iranian moderates. In short, Iran was expected to give up its opposition to the Arab-Israeli peace process, stop its efforts to develop weapons of mass destruction, and cease to meddle in the affairs of its regional neighbors. Changes in Iranian rhetoric were insufficient.

The closeness of the Clinton administration to Israel gave dual containment its backbone. Clinton was also under constant pressure from the Republican-dominated Congress not to go soft on Iran or Iraq. With something of a mania for sanctions policies gripping U.S. policymakers in the 1990s, both Clinton and Congress agreed that the United States had to develop a portfolio of political, economic, and military instruments to exert sustained pressure on Iran and Iraq until they changed in the desired ways. Both regional powers were to be marginalized, and, if necessary, military force was to be used to directly contain their ambitions and capabilities. In the event, sanctions regimes—especially unilateral U.S. sanctions—were no panacea, but U.S. policymakers believed that they could change the world by such means.

Containing Iraq

For the United States and its hegemony in the Middle East, Saddam Hussein's Iraq was both the greatest threat and the greatest asset. Hussein's survival after the Gulf War was a headache for U.S. policymakers, dramatically highlighted in the humanitarian crisis in Iraqi Kurdistan that required the dispatch of Western protection forces. Bush sent forces to protect the Kurds in northern Iraq only reluctantly, although once committed, the "safe havens" turned into a de facto Kurdish state under NATO protection. Hussein continued to be defiant, threatening his Gulf and Kurdish neighbors, constantly battling the UN sanctions and control regimes, and refusing to come clean about hundreds of disappeared Kuwaitis.

Of course, in reality, in the cat-and-mouse game between Iraq and the United States, it was Hussein who was the mouse. The United States was quick to adapt to his survival and to turn the problem into a bulwark of its regional hegemony. Iraq was defiant and vengeful, and so some of Iraq's neighbors would require U.S. military services for the foreseeable future. The Gulf states especially were beholden to the United States, granting unprecedented basing rights as well as working more closely on a whole range of issues designed to bolster regional security, including the Arab-Israeli peace process. Indeed, by the late 1990s, it could reasonably be argued that the loss of the specter of Saddam Hussein would much reduce the leverage that the United States possessed in the region. A rehabilitated Iraq might also represent a greater challenge to the future of U.S. and Israeli interests in the region than did the run-down disaster area that was Saddam Hussein's realm.

U.S. containment of Iraq was founded on a series of UN Security Council resolutions passed during the Kuwait conflict of 1990–1991 and its aftermath. Once passed by the Security Council, these resolutions were practically set in stone, protected as they were by the U.S. veto. The most important of the control regime resolutions was UN Security Council Resolution 687 of 3 April 1991, which established an unprecedented arms control and disarmament regime. Iraq was banned from possessing chemical, biological, and nuclear weapons and became liable to highly intrusive supervision enforced by the UN Special Commission (UNSCOM) and the International Atomic Energy Agency (IAEA). Officials chosen by the UN would spend most of the 1990s roaming Iraq in search of its weapons and production capabilities.

A whole raft of further UN resolutions refined the sanctions regime, reinforced the UNSCOM mission, and added new powers. The creation of UN-authorized no-fly zones for Iraqi aircraft above the 36th parallel in the north and below the 32nd parallel (later 33rd) in the south was the most important supplement to the control regime. Originally designed to offer some protection to the Kurds in the north and the Shia population in the south, the no-fly zones gave the United States and Britain carte blanche to dominate Iraqi airspace and gather aerial intelligence for the indefinite future. Patrolling the no-fly zones also gave the allies real coercive leverage. U.S. and British air forces attacked Iraqi radars and air defense installations almost on a weekly basis, as well as other targets when the practice of coercive diplomacy required it. Iraqi attempts to evade UNSCOM oversight, to interfere in the Kurdish zone, or to challenge the no-fly zones were liable to be met with bombing. The boundaries of UN authorizations were pushed to the limit.

The control regime on Iraq was the most comprehensive ever authorized by the UN and was just about as successful as any control regime could ever be expected to be. Iraqi ambitions and capabilities were contained, and much that was missed by allied bombers during the Gulf War was found and destroyed. All manner of production facilities, masses of information about the Iraqi procurement networks, thousands of tons of chemical agents, and most of Iraq's ballistic missiles were accounted for under the inspection regime. The Iraqis spent much time evading the restrictions, but at various points, notably in autumn 1993 and August 1995, Hussein let many of Iraq's secrets go.[20] Moreover, following Iraqi military threats against Kuwait in October 1994—leading to a rapid deployment of U.S. military power—the Iraqi regime was reluctantly compelled to recognize Kuwait's borders under the terms of UN Security Council Resolution 833 of 1993, although Hussein's own acceptance of Kuwait's existence was still less than complete.[21]

The UN control regime on Iraq was presented by the United States and Britain as a lawfully constituted plan to get Saddam Hussein to live up to his commitments on disarmament. The façade initially worked brilliantly as a way of managing both domestic and international opinion. The routine bombing of Iraq was almost invisible on the world news agenda. Of course, what the allies were really doing was waging a prolonged limited war against Iraq, in which the United States and Britain intended quite literally to disarm their opponent and subject it to their will. UNSCOM was one of the weapons used in the long war, but a preparedness to use actual force was just as important. Indeed, the use of force was set to mount as the 1990s went on, as the Iraqis became exasperated by the unending sanctions, and as the Iraqi regime began to perceive and respond to the security threat that the control regime represented to it. Iraqi attitudes toward UNSCOM significantly hardened after 1995, and relations worsened still further after Australian diplomat Richard Butler became its head in 1997. The Iraqis were now aware that the Central Intelligence Agency and others had taken up residence in the UNSCOM mission and were gathering all manner of intelligence, including information that put Saddam Hussein's life directly at risk. Iraq stonewalled UNSCOM and soon expelled U.S. and British members of the inspection teams. The Iraqis also decided to lock UNSCOM out of a significant number of sites that Hussein designated as "presidential palaces."

The deadlock over the extent of UNSCOM access in 1997–1998 came to a head in December 1998, when the United States and Britain launched Operation Desert Fox, a major nationwide bombing campaign. The allies targeted Iraqi military production facilities—although how many good targets were left must be debatable—but also extended their attack to the Iraqi regime and army. The attacks on the regime took UN authorization past its limits. The bombing of Republican Guards barracks had nothing to do with weapons of mass destruction, and the killing of sleeping Iraqi soldiers was of very dubious legality.

After the bombings, the Iraqis saw no point in further cooperation. UNSCOM was not allowed back. The U.S. attitude hardened, and Iraqi suspicions about U.S. intentions were soon further confirmed. The Clinton administration announced in January 1999 that it was making $97 million available to Iraqi opposition groups under the terms of the Iraq Liberation Act of 1998.[22] A special coordinator, Frank Ricciardone, was appointed by President Clinton to oversee the overthrow of Saddam Hussein under the terms of the act, and this included liaising with forces of the Iraqi opposition.[23] The forgotten air war in the no-fly zones also continued, with the Iraqi regime claiming that over 300 civilians were killed by U.S. and British bombing in the two years up to January 2001.[24]

The control regime achieved much for U.S. policy, but keeping it together proved increasingly difficult as the 1990s went on. The endless debilitation of Iraq and its people was the cause of great anger among most Arabs and Muslims and deepening worry on the part of their governments. Few in the Gulf states were sympathetic to Saddam Hussein's regime, but what was happening to the Iraqi people looked bad. The United Arab Emirates (UAE), Oman, and Qatar were all reported to be talking about how Iraq could be brought into general Arab reconciliation.[25] The willingness of all the Gulf states to go on supporting bombing was in particularly sharp decline. Saudi Arabia moved to limit U.S. military operations against Iraq from the kingdom. Later, in the aftermath of U.S. and British bombing in February 2001, Saudi Arabia took the noticeable step of signing a joint statement with Syria condemning the attacks.[26] More generally, Gulf Arabs were reportedly tiring of constant U.S. efforts to extract money from them to pay for the military presence as well as political backing for the Arab-Israeli peace process.[27] In an article in 1997, Abdullah Al-Shayeji reported that the strong public sympathy for the United States in the Gulf states after the Gulf War had largely subsided; the conflict with Iraq had gone on too long, and most were suspicious of U.S. intentions.[28]

By the late 1990s, the control regime was beginning to look ragged. The policy of sanctions was a blunt instrument, and the costs involved for people of the Middle East were enormous. Sanctions were a huge drag on the regional economy but, more important, impoverished ordinary Iraqis and further weakened them vis-à-vis the regime by virtue of its power over rationing. Meanwhile, Saddam Hussein and his associates seemed as well entrenched in power as ever and, after the expulsion of UNSCOM, got on with their weapons programs relatively untroubled. The biggest management problem in keeping the control regime together, though, was the fact that it killed thousands of ordinary people. UN Security Council Resolution 706 of August 1991 allowed the sale of $1.6 billion worth of oil over six-month periods, to be used by the UN to fund food and medical supplies, but it did not work. Hussein refused to allow the UN such control over Iraq's oil until after 1995, and thus many Iraqis went hungry, and many of the sick went untreated. In November 1994, the Iraqi Health Ministry claimed that by March 1994, some 385,000 deaths were attributable to sanctions.[29] The lack of reliable statistics on Iraq made assessments difficult, but international observers agreed that there was enormous suffering among the young and old, especially from malnutrition, disease, and lack of medical care. Infant mortality rates were at least double prewar levels in parts of Iraq. A survey carried out in Iraq for the UN Children's Fund (UNICEF) in 1999 reviewed the differences between prewar and postwar child mortality rates and came to the alarming conclusion that there would have been half a million fewer deaths of children under the age of five for the period 1991–1998 if child mortality rates in Iraq had remained at the prewar levels; this was a siege on a dreadfully huge scale.[30]

To ease some of the concerns about the human disaster that was taking place in Iraq, the United States was prepared to see sanctions relaxed, although Hussein himself moved slowly in the hope of forcing a fuller lifting of sanctions. UN Security Council Resolution 986 allowed oil sales worth $2 billion every six months to pay for food and humanitarian aid. In early 1996, Iraq accepted the deal. The program was further extended, with the United States and Britain accepting a suggestion from UN Secretary-General Kofi Annan that oil sales be expanded to $5.25 billion every six months.[31] In fact, in the subsequent years, Iraq was able to sell about as much oil as it could pump. Thus, the United States and Britain blamed Saddam Hussein for the human disaster, but they could not escape the misgivings of a mounting body of international opinion, let alone that of the Muslim world, where a dangerous legacy of hatred was in the making. The human disaster continued because the United States and Britain were locked into the policy by the moral and political investment made by the occupants of the White House and Downing Street. To even discuss whether the policy was wrong was to admit something quite dreadful. Parliamentarians and foreign ministry officials might call for a review, but Iraqi policy had become a sacred cow of the U.S. president and British prime minister.

The control regime also continued because even if Hussein had wanted to—which he did not—Iraq would find it impossible to "verify" that it had done all the things that the United States was demanding.

The United States was not really seeking verifications that would have allowed Iraq to get off the control regime hook anyway. Indeed, after the senior UNSCOM inspector, Scot Ritter (a former U.S. Marine Corps captain), resigned in late August 1998, he went on to testify to the U.S. Senate's Armed Services and Foreign Relations Committees that the Clinton administration had "undermined UNSCOM's efforts through interference and manipulation" and had pressured it to cancel and delay inspection visits. Ritter had thought his job was to get on with Iraq's disarmament. U.S. secretary of state Madeline Albright had already perceived that Ritter "didn't have a clue what the overall plan had been."[32]

How long UN sanctions could be maintained was unclear. Support for sanctions in the UN Security Council faded as time passed, with France, Russia, and China looking for an end point. After allied bombing in December 1998, France argued that further investigations into Iraq's past were no longer practical and that what was needed was a new system that controlled Iraq's future without causing unacceptable suffering for ordinary Iraqis.[33] Controls should be made sharper and confined to the arms and oil sectors. The United States was inclined to agree, and what eventually emerged was British-sponsored UN Security Council Resolution 1284 of December 1999: some sanctions could be "suspended" if Iraq fully cooperated with newly constituted inspection teams of the UN Monitoring, Verification, and Inspection Mission (UNMOVIC) and the IAEA.[34] Consciences were eased in the Security Council, but the Iraqis still had too few incentives to cooperate. Hussein held out for a full lifting of sanctions.

Beyond the Security Council, where none of the permanent members really thought it worth taking on the United States for Saddam Hussein's sake, the control regime was being challenged by a number of small but significant steps being made by regional states; these steps were speeded by the outbreak of the new Palestinian *intifadah* in late September 2000. Sanctions could be decreed from on high, but they could not be enforced without the cooperation of Iraq's regional neighbors. Sanctions on Iraq permanently stifled the development of the regional economy; this significant cost—mostly overlooked in the West—was largely carried by Iraq's neighbors. Egypt, Turkey, Jordan, Syria, and Iran wanted to do business with Iraq again. Flights to Iraq, especially from France, Russia, Egypt, and Jordan, carried aid and businesspeople. Iraq also restored diplomatic ties with a number of Arab states, notably Egypt. In November 2000, Iraq and Egypt upgraded their relations, and then in January 2001, Iraqi vice president Taha Yassin Ramadan became the most senior Iraqi official to visit Egypt since 1990, where he signed a free trade agreement.[35]

Iraq was also about to begin generating a source of oil income that was separate from UN supervision. Talks between Iraq and Syria about restoring the oil pipeline link from northern Iraq to the Mediterranean, a route barred since 1982, were a major step in the direction of bypassing the UN. To the annoyance of U.S. officials, Syria was also reported to be importing between 100,000 and 150,000 barrels of oil a day from Iraq.[36] With Iraqi oil going to Jordan, Syria, and Turkey, the Iraqi regime was beginning to generate a significant income beyond the supervision of the control regime.

By February 2001, the control regime seemed to have reached an important moment. U.S. and British air forces attacked an Iraqi air defense and communications system near Baghdad in response to determined Iraqi efforts to shoot down an allied aircraft. The bombing was initiated partly because Iraq appeared to have updated its air defense system, possibly with Chinese help, but future allied operations would have to be less frequent and more measured to avoid the political nightmare of losing an aircraft crew over Iraq. Allied bombing also faced real political resistance. The round of criticism after the February bombings was universal, with France, Russia, and China speaking out strongly. French officials were candid: the attacks had no basis in international law and were illegal. After February 2001, the dispatch of allied air patrols was much more cautious and less proactive.

By February 2001, the sanctions regime was also beginning to hit the buffers. The February bombings had coincided with the visit of Egypt's economy and finance minister, Youssef Boutros Ghali, to Iraq, where enhanced ties and increased trade were again on the agenda. Flights between Cairo and Baghdad were about to become regular events. Ultimately, the United States might try to tighten up the sanctions regime by pressuring regional states, but with three of the permanent members of the Security Council supportive of relaxed sanctions and all Arab states certain to resist new pressures, taking the coercive route risked failure. Indeed, in a meeting in late March 2001, the Arab League states made it clear that sanctions should be lifted.

In response to the growing difficulties, the United States and Britain talked of "smart sanctions." In UN Security Council discussions in May and June 2001, it was clear that smart sanctions meant the lifting of restrictions on civilian goods but the tightening of controls on arms-related equipment and on oil smuggling.[37] The theory of the control regime was moving from blanket controls to specific prohibitions, although since ordinary Iraqis could not afford imported consumer goods, it made little real difference to them. What the proposals really sought to do was make UN oil-for-food supervision more efficient, end the Iraqi regime's alternative sources of income, and again refocus the blame for civilian suffering on Saddam Hussein. Not surprisingly, Hussein held out for the full lifting of sanctions but was now backed by Russia and other Arab states. The repackaging of sanctions failed to pass through the UN Security Council in summer 2001. Russia stopped it. The gradual decay of sanctions and progressive U.S. compromises seemed the only realistic outcome. The standoff continued without a clear end in sight, but the U.S. policy of containment and rollback against Iraq had about reached its limits by mid-2001. Iraq was smashed but remained defiant.

Containing Iran

Much had passed between the United States and Iran since the Islamic revolution in 1978–1979: a favored client overthrown, a bitter ideological conflict, diplomats and journalists taken hostage and murdered, over 240 U.S. Marines killed in Lebanon, U.S. airliners hijacked, plots to overthrow the governments of Arab Gulf states, and an Iranian airliner with nearly 300 civilians on board shot down. Relations were severed in 1980, and Iran was placed on the State Department's list of terrorist states in 1984. Indeed, the Islamic Republic gloried in its struggle against the "Great Satan," and Iranians were responsible for a significant increase in the level of international terrorism in the 1980s.

U.S. hostility toward the Islamic Republic was, above all, fed by its unremitting hostility toward Israel. Iran did not recognize Israel as a legitimate state and provided real support to the militants who wished to destroy it. Hizballah, the Shia militant organization in Lebanon, was the most serious threat to Israel's security in the 1990s. Iranian opposition to the Arab-Israeli peace process was keenly felt, not only because the United States was concerned that Iranian-backed terrorism might successfully sabotage it, but also because the United States feared that Iran might rally a wider body of anti–peace process forces. Iran and Syria were regarded as the potential coordinators of a united front that might include the Islamic groups Hamas and Islamic Jihad as well as secular rejectionists.

Within Iran, the Islamic regime continued to draw its legitimacy from the struggle with the United States. Most of the political establishment—including reformers—had vested themselves in the language of the Great Satan. Wherever Muslims were suffering, many Iranians saw the malign hand of the United States. Reform may have been on the agenda in the 1990s, but among the key political personalities, there was little real sign of a mellowing toward the United States. Few Iranians could conceive of even talking to the United States, and the regime refused to allow any contacts. The spiritual leader, Ayatollah Ali Khameini, made it one of his principal missions in life to remind Iranians of U.S. evils: Muslims must know their enemy and must prevent them from "sending over their junk."[38] The American ringleaders of global arrogance, Khameini argued in a speech in November 1994,

> only like meek and feeble nations. . . . When a nation appears in the arena with such a spirit of independence and with such strength, and when a government does not look up to them [the United States] and refuses to consider them a superpower, then they cannot stand it any longer. . . . As long as Quranic, Islamic and divine aspirations rule over us and over the system, hatred against and confrontation with the ringleaders of the global arrogance, headed by the United States, will remain in force.[39]

For Khameini, it was the Islamic Republic's religious duty and destiny to counter U.S. hegemony.

President Hashemi Rafsanjani (1989–1997), too, was consistent in his hostility to the United States and Israel, and this inclination appears to have increased after he left the presidency in 1997. In January 1998, Rafsanjani even ventured into the realm of Holocaust denial, citing French author Roger Garaudy to claim that a careful study indicated that no more than 200,000 Jews were killed by the Nazis: since then, Israel's crimes against the Palestinians had been "far greater" than those of Adolf Hitler.[40] Rafsanjani remained an important political figure, chairing the key Council for the Determination of Exigencies. The obsession of Iranian leaders with the United States knew little discretion. In September 1994, Chief Justice Ayatollah Mohammad Yazdi felt that he had no choice but to respond to a reported comment by a White House official about the killing of some annoying pigeons in Qom: all lies, Yazdi said; pigeons were safe from the Islamic state, for "Islam had recommended its followers to be kind to pigeons."[41] Such is the nature of hegemony and its discontents.

Nevertheless, the Islamic Republic was changing in the 1990s. The original vision of the Revolution—which aimed to establish God's government on Earth through the *velayat-e faqih* (the guardianship of the jurisconsult), to actively support the oppressed peoples of the world and fight their oppressors, and to spread the word of Islam across international borders—had faded over the years. The Revolution of 1999 was not the Revolution of 1989, much less that of 1979. Iran was becoming a conventional state, increasingly restrained by the norms of international law. The Rafsanjani government reined in the Iranian Revolution's most radical supporters. Burgeoning foreign debts, high inflation, high unemployment, and rapid population growth created an economic crisis that left little time for grandiose dreams of world revolution. Iran wanted to be recognized as a great Muslim power, but its use of subversion and terrorism was on the wane. In most of the Middle East and Central Asia, the Islamic Republic did not push for Islamic rebellion but for stable borders and trade. Beyond the Middle East, Iran looked for economic exchange, especially with Europe and Japan.

The election of Mohammad Khatami in May 1997 was a reaffirmation of the changes. Khatami struggled to prevail against domestic conservatives, but the official foreign policy of Iran was bound to be further moderated. In a major interview with Cable News Network's Christiane Amanpour in January 1998, Khatami set out a foreign policy agenda. He made it clear that the rule of law and political moderation was his preferred course, and he emphasized his wish for a positive "dialogue among the civilizations." Iranians had done things as a result of their revolutionary fervor, but that was no longer required, and the Islamic Republic would now "fully adhere to all norms of conduct that should regulate relations between nations and governments."[42]

In the interview, Khatami made a particular effort to take a measured approach toward Americans, noting that "American civilization is worthy of respect" and that Iranians could learn from it; this kind of comment was certainly a considerable step forward from President Rafsanjani's earlier thoughts that Iranians had had a great civilization when Americans were "savages and eating fruit from trees in the jungle."[43] Khatami pointed out that Iranian slogans—"Death to America" and the like—had to be taken in the proper context and that they were not directed at U.S. citizens as such but at the policies of the U.S. government.[44] Khatami's comments on the Arab-Israeli peace process were also relatively measured. Iran opposed the process, but the Palestinians had the right to self-determination, and the Iranian government did not intend to stand in their way.[45] All that said, Khatami's reformism was tempered with an underlying skepticism about the possibility of relations with the United States, and he still had some scathing things to say in his interview about the U.S. role in the world since World War II. The Iranian president cautioned the United States that

> we feel no need for ties with America, especially as the modern world is so manifold and diverse that we can reach our objectives without American assistance. We especially feel that many progressive countries, including the Europeans, are far more advanced in their foreign policies than the Americans. We can carry out our own activities and have no need for political ties with America.[46]

Neither Rafsanjani nor Khatami could ever be seen currying U.S. favor, although some kind of dialogue did seem possible by the 1990s. It was paradoxical, then, that at a time when the Islamic Republic was reforming, the United States chose to intensify its campaign to isolate and impoverish Iran. Unlike Iraq, the United States did not seriously entertain the overthrow of the regime—that was beyond U.S. powers— but throughout the 1990s, the United States showed no inclination to reach any kind of accommodation.

A number of clear U.S. demands were communicated to Iran. First of all, the United States continued to regard Iran as one of the principal sources of international terrorism. The Iranian regime must stop all official and unofficial support for terrorists and stop the alleged flow of Iranian advice and money to such places as Lebanon, Israel and the Palestinian Authority, Algeria, Bahrain, Saudi Arabia, Bosnia, and Tajikistan. Whether Iran could ever satisfy the United States on this matter was another question, partly because the way each defined "terrorism" was so different. What the U.S. government regarded as terrorism, most Iranians regarded as national liberation. Moreover, Iran had influence in Lebanon, Sudan, and northern Afghanistan, but elsewhere its foreign activities had tailed off and were largely directed at controlling the regime's Iranian opponents.

The other major issue in U.S.-Iranian relations was Iran's military development. Iran was reportedly spending some $2 billion a year acquiring some significant new equipment, notably from the former Soviet bloc, including MiG-29 and SU-24 fighters, T-72 tanks, and Kilo class submarines.[47] Bearing in mind the vastly greater scale of U.S. transfers to the Gulf states, U.S. protestations about an Iranian conventional buildup lacked credibility. The idea of containing an Iranian nuclear program attracted more interest in the international community. After Iraq had been smashed, if any Muslim Middle Eastern state was going to build a nuclear weapon, it was Iran. Israel regarded the possibility of an Iranian bomb as a fundamental threat, and the Clinton administration agreed. The intensification of political and economic pressures on Iran was the preferred course for the United States and Israel, but military options were also on the table.

During the days of Grand Ayatollah Ruhollah Khomeini in the 1980s, there were moral and material restrictions on both the nuclear and chemical programs. Iran was also a member of the NPT, the Chemical Weapons Convention, and the Biological Weapons Convention. As Iran drifted away from its revolutionary priorities and toward those of a more typical regional power, the Rafsanjani government probably initiated a more coherent look at strategic weapons. The government moved to finish the Bushehr nuclear plant—one of the shah's dreams that had been left unfinished by German contractors— initially with German help but subsequently with Russian assistance. Iran made efforts to order further Russian and Chinese equipment and fittings, although much of this equipment was safeguarded against proliferation. Following President Rafsanjani's visit to Beijing in September 1992, China agreed to supply two 300-megawatt power plants.[48] North Korea and Pakistan may also have been cooperating with Iran on nuclear research. To deliver any strategic weapons, Iran had its own ballistic missile program and with North Korean assistance was gradually extending its reach. Iran's Shahab-3 missile reportedly had a range of 1,500 kilometers, long enough to reach Israel. North Korea's development of the Taepo-Dong missile pointed to the possibility that southern Europe might come within Iran's range.

Exactly what the Iranian regime intended with regard to nuclear weapons was far from clear, and it seems unlikely that it was entirely sure itself. The denials of Iranian leaders were open and straightforward, and Iran was in compliance with its NPT commitments. The IAEA made regular forays into Iran, including "special visits," but could find nothing overtly suspicious.[49] Bearing in mind the way that Israel was allowed to blatantly maneuver around the NPT, though, Iranian leaders regarded the treaty as unfair and incomplete. To highlight the issue of Israel's unregulated nuclear weapons, Iran promoted the idea of a nuclear weapons free zone in the Middle East—an idea supported by other Muslim states at the Non-Proliferation Review Conference in Vienna in April 1995—but with no success. The injustice implicit in the NPT certainly provided some scope for a later reformulation of Iran's commitment to it: as Foreign Minister Ali Akbar Velayati noted prior to the Non-Proliferation Review Conference, Iran would sign up again, but it regarded the existing NPT as temporary and its future contingent on existing nuclear powers beginning to negotiate the destruction of their weapons.[50]

Iran had no urgent requirement for nuclear weapons, but there was a certain logic to acquiring them. Israel and Iraq were potential nuclear threats. Nuclear-armed U.S. naval vessels plied the Indian Ocean and the Gulf. Going nuclear would also reflect Iran's status as a major regional power and one of the leading Muslim states. In an article in *Survival* regarding Iran's nuclear program, Shahram Chubin thought that

> Iran will seek nuclear weapons both for general political reasons and as a response to specific threats: that Iran's "decision" to acquire them is not firm and could be reversed; and that acquiring nuclear weapons would not make a significant difference to Iran's international behaviour, except possibly to moderate it.[51]

For the United States and Israel, a policy of better safe than sorry seemed sensible. The Iranians had to be convinced that nuclear weapons were not worth the trouble, and to this end the United States stepped up its nonproliferation efforts in 1995, with a diplomatic campaign aimed at curtailing Iran's access to critical materials and dual-use technology. The United States pursued its campaign with some success within the Group of Seven (G7, later the G8) and NATO, and among a wider group of suppliers. It was reported to have interrupted deals between Iran and India, the Czech Republic, Argentina, and Brazil. Even Russia acquiesced to U.S. pressure on nuclear assistance and conventional arms supplies to Iran. Russia ceased supplying all weapons to Iran in 1995, although these ties were reestablished in late 2000 after the arrival of the more confident Putin government.[52] Iran's ability to acquire weapons and equipment related to manufacturing weapons was undoubtedly limited.

The U.S. effort against Iran also expanded into a broader economic campaign. In the early 1990s, U.S. trade to Iran was growing, with the United States reportedly exporting some $748 million a year to it by 1992 and with indirect exports adding another $500 million to $1 billion.[53] U.S. oil companies were moving in. The prospect of improved ties was opposed in the U.S. Congress and by the Clinton administration.[54] In fact, U.S. politics saw a bidding war between the Democratic president and Republican-dominated Congress to appear tough on Iran.

The hostility toward Iran manifested itself in the early part of 1995, when the U.S. oil company Conoco reached a breakthrough deal to develop an offshore oilfield near Sirri Island. If the Iranians had been seeking to send a positive message, it was quickly shot down. Senator Alfonse D'Amato introduced tough sanctions legislation. In May, spurred into action by Congress, Clinton announced his intention to impose a comprehensive regime of sanctions on Iran at a speech to the World Jewish Congress. U.S. companies and their subsidiaries would no longer be able to do business with Iran.[55] All imports from Iran were banned, as was the export of all engineering and oil equipment. The Conoco deal was terminated.

Clinton went further in 1996 when he signed the Iran and Libya Sanctions Act, with provisions to punish foreign companies that did anything more than a small amount of trade with Iran. The 1996 act, though, risked seriously overplaying the U.S. hand; quite simply, extraterritorial law was not widely accepted in the international system. Without UN debate and authorization, unilateral U.S. lawmaking lacked authority and was bound to meet resistance from friends and foes alike. The "D'Amato law" was widely scorned in the Muslim world. The final communiqué of the Organization of the Islamic Conference (OIC) meeting in Tehran in December 1997 pronounced that its more than fifty members should reject "any arbitrary extra-territorial and unilateral measures" and consider the new law "null and void."[56]

The Western allies were also less than impressed. Coordinating sanctions with Europe and Japan proved nigh impossible, and unilaterally punishing their companies threatened to isolate the United States. The United States had failed to make a sufficiently convincing case to the Europeans in particular, and most continued to advocate a "critical dialogue" and "constructive engagement" with the Islamic Republic. Iran was a future trading opportunity on a scale that Europeans were reluctant to pass up. The French oil company Total had quickly moved in on Conoco's banned development project. U.S. relations with Russia, China, Turkey, and others were also liable to be complicated by the extraterritorial legislation. In fact, the Clinton administration quickly became aware that the United States was overreaching, and it sought to adopt a light touch. In May 1998, Secretary of State Madeline Albright waived U.S. sanctions against French, Russian, and Malaysian companies involved in Iranian oil and gas development.[57] A consortium led by Total was also given U.S. approval to explore and develop the South Pars gas field.[58] The world's oil companies were lining up to go into

Iran, as well as to use the country as a transit route for the Caspian Sea and Central Asian oilfields, although for the time being, U.S. companies had to sit out the opportunities. As long as Iran had oil and dollars, it would do business in the world without U.S. approval.

Khatami's election in 1997 weakened the U.S. argument still further. After some thought, U.S. policymakers came to the conclusion that he represented a public relations problem rather than a significant change. U.S. allies disagreed. Japan had done more than most to back the U.S. sanctions policy, but the Japanese urge to trade was reengaged during Khatami's visit to Japan in October 2000. He did much to publicly reassure the Japanese about security issues. The Japanese government cleared the way for enhanced cooperation in the oil and gas sector and for trade financing.[59] Oil exploration and production deals were to follow.

Political relations between Europe and Iran also further improved after the election of Khatami. The European Union's ban on high-level contracts—initiated after a German court found in April 1997 that very senior Iranian officials were implicated in the murder of Iranian-Kurdish dissidents in Berlin in 1992—was soon lifted, and the new Iranian president made landmark visits to Rome, Paris, and Berlin. European banks and official credit agencies took a more relaxed attitude toward Iran. France and Germany were well-established trade partners, although the improvement of ties was not without interruptions. German-Iranian relations were particularly accident-prone, often damaged by Iranian activities against dissidents in Germany. The arrest and death sentence given to German businessman Helmut Hofer in 1998 for having an affair with a Muslim woman was also a stark reminder of what kind of place Iran really was: Hofer's conversion to Islam allowed the Iranian Supreme Court to revoke the death sentence, although he was heavily fined for "insulting the law enforcement forces."[60] Later, Iranian-German relations were again set back by the long sentences given to seven Iranians who attended a conference in Berlin that was critical of the Iranian leadership. Despite everything, members of the European Union were resolved to engage with Iran.

When the Islamic Republic began to have increasingly friendly contacts with the United States' closest European ally, Britain, it was clear that U.S. policy was failing. Referring to a meeting with Iranian foreign minister Kamal Kharrazi at the UN in September 1998, British foreign secretary Robin Cook perceived that Anglo-Iranian relations had had a "fresh start."[61] The atmosphere took a further positive turn in early 2000, when Kharrazi made an official visit to Britain, with both

sides referring to the importance of the "dialogue amongst civilizations" and to respecting cultural identities. The Voice of the Islamic
Republic noted that Iranian-British ties seemed to have entered a "new
phase," although this change did not prevent ritual denouncements of
Britain in Iran.[62] Britain's role in the Gulf War and subsequent conflicts
with Iraq had become part of Iranian consciousness. Anglo-Iranian relations were further reconnected amid the high-level diplomacy that followed the 11 September 2001 terrorist attacks on the United States.
When the British foreign secretary, Jack Straw, visited Iran on 24–25
September, he did not act as a proxy for the United States. Indeed,
improving Anglo-Iranian relations may not have been welcome in some
quarters in the U.S. administration and Congress. Whether 11
September would eventually lead to a change in the U.S. approach to
Iran remained to be seen.

In the Gulf itself, the political atmosphere was also improving. The
antipathies across the Gulf ran deep, but the election of Khatami occasioned a wave of optimism. Kuwait regarded Iran as a long-term counter to Iraq. Oman and the UAE talked of the need to establish a regional
security system that included Iran. Saudi-Iranian relations noticeably
improved, especially after the OIC summit in Tehran in December
1997, a meeting attended by Crown Prince Abdullah. The two-week
visit of Rafsanjani to Saudi Arabia in February 1998 and President
Khatami's visit in May 1999 confirmed the thaw. By January 2001,
there was even talk of an Iranian-Saudi security pact to fight crime, terrorism, and drug trafficking.[63] The Gulf states remained wary of Iran,
and the issue of the Tri-Islands dispute (Abu Musa and the Greater and
Lesser Tunb Islands) between Iran and the UAE continued to poison the
atmosphere, but the kind of cold war that existed in the 1980s was a
thing of the past. Iran and the Gulf states could now do some serious
business. Indeed, the Saudi-Iranian reconciliation was a significant factor enabling producer restraint within OPEC by mid-2000, and it led to
marked increases in the price of oil in 2000–2001. In this respect especially, better Saudi-Iranian relations were not entirely in U.S. interests.

U.S. scare-mongering about Iran was a declining currency by the
late 1990s, and U.S. policy was in danger of being counterproductive.
Iran could live with unilateral U.S. sanctions. Aggressive U.S. posturing
also benefited the conservatives in Iran by reinforcing the idea that the
United States was a real security threat and that it was the Islamic
Republic's historical mission to stand up to such intimidation. No
Iranian politician could be seen bowing to overt U.S. pressure, no mat-
ter what the cost. Thus, the United States had little real leverage over

Iran. Clinton and Albright made occasional concessions to the atmospherics, notably from the early part of 1998, but did little to change the Iran policy. The "road map" to better relations that Madeline Albright mentioned in a speech in June 1998 never emerged.[64] Lifting U.S. sanctions on Iranian carpets, pistachio nuts, and caviar in March 2000 was about as far as it went, and the Iranians showed little sign of reciprocating.[65] Ultimately, Clinton needed to go beyond platitudes about civilizational dialogue and Iran's rich cultural heritage and on into the specifics of unfreezing seized Iranian assets and repealing the Iran and Libya Sanctions Act.

The way dual containment was working did not go unquestioned among the Middle East policy and academic community in the United States, though, and there was an awareness of the inefficacy of U.S. policy. In an article in *Foreign Affairs*, Gregory Gause III argued that U.S. policy was clear but misconceived and unstable and that

> dual containment offers no guidelines for dealing with change in the Gulf, and it ties American policy to an inherently unstable regional status quo. Worse yet, it assigns to the US a unilateral role in managing gulf security issues at a time when the American capacity to influence events in Iran and Iraq is at best limited. The policy could end up encouraging the very results—regional conflict and increased Iranian power—that the United States seeks to prevent.[66]

At a conference of Middle Eastern experts in Washington, William Rugh also thought dual containment a simplistic catchphrase that reduced U.S. flexibility and increased the inertia of a failing policy.[67] The United States did not have the necessary international support to make the policy work. Geoffrey Kemp also advised in an article that

> U.S. leaders must present a more compelling and coherent strategic rationale for an open-ended Gulf commitment that is credible and accepted by key allies. It is no longer sufficient to repeat mantras about "rogue states" and threats of radicalism if few others agree with this diagnosis.[68]

The Clinton administration was aware of the problems, but making effective foreign policy on Iran was not really possible in the Clinton years. The Iran policy was driven by Clinton's own commitment to Israel and by the enthusiasm of Congress for talking tough. Even if Clinton had been inclined to change track, any easing on Iran was bound to cause a fight with Congress and the Jewish lobby, and he was just not about to expend political capital on Iran. To the extent that the

Clinton administration did seek more policy flexibility, it did so rather late and by rather indirect means. In mid-2000, the administration officially dropped the term *rogue state* for the more politically correct "states of concern." The rogue concept, Meghan O'Sullivan observed, had not only conveyed the impression of imperial arrogance to Europeans and Asians but had also institutionalized the idea that some countries were beyond rehabilitation and could only be subject to policies of punishment.[69]

The hostility toward Iran was entrenched in U.S. politics, and any change in approach was bound to take some time to develop. For the foreseeable future, the Iran policy would not change. George W. Bush's administration was less tied up with Israel than Clinton, and Bush had U.S. oil interests on his mind, but both the Republican president and Congress would continue to have an investment in the idea of a rogue Iran. Indeed, Bush's missile defense scheme was absolutely contingent on the existence of significant rogues. No one was much inclined to move with any speed to significantly alter the tenor of the Iran policy. Indeed, when a chance to meaningfully alter the Iran policy came up on the occasion of the automatic review of the Iran and Libya Sanctions Act in August 2001, U.S. policymakers did not take it. Any suggestions that the term of renewal be amended or reduced were brushed aside as the full five-year renewal went through Congress without serious opposition and Bush signed it. European Union external relations commissioner Chris Patten criticized the move and indicated that the European Union would take measures against the United States through the World Trade Organization if actions were directed against European companies trading with Iran.[70]

In the meantime, the Iranians could live without the United States. Indeed, many Iranians continued to draw their self-worth from U.S. hostility toward their country. The Iranian leadership was not troubled: as Ayatollah Khameini put it to a gathering of Revolutionary Guards in February 1998, "America cannot do a damn thing against the Islamic system. The enemy, with all its extensive cultural support, economic sanctions, political intimidation and various conspiracies will not be able to create the least bit of instability in this high and divine establishment."[71]

The United States and Islamic Militants

The United States had long had to face the hostile inclinations of many Arabs and Muslims toward it, but in the aftermath of the Gulf War, the level of tension rose markedly. The sight of Western forces demolishing Iraq, the suffering of ordinary Iraqis under UN sanctions, and the continued presence of U.S. forces in the Gulf inflamed Muslim opinion. Muslims from all backgrounds were hostile to the United States, but a new breed of Islamic activists turned this hostility into the greatest security threat facing the United States and the pax Americana in the Middle East. U.S. regional allies, especially Saudi Arabia and Egypt, bore the brunt of this Islamist hostility, but the United States too would directly experience the dreadful ruthlessness of the new militants.

During the Gulf War itself, political Islam was divided, partly because of the ambivalence of many Islamists toward Saddam Hussein, but also because of Saudi Arabia's influence across the world's Muslim networks. The kingdom had spent decades supporting Muslim organizations, publishing houses, and education centers, including the Muslim Brotherhoods and other, more militant groups.[72] The Saudis also had contacts with the Jamaat-i-Islami movement in Pakistan and, through it and the Pakistani government—specifically, Pakistan's Inter-Service Intelligence (ISI)—could pull strings in the Islamic milieu of the mujahidin in Peshawar and Afghanistan. However, Saudi Arabia, Pakistan, and the United States had created a monster in supporting the anti-Soviet jihad in Afghanistan in the 1980s. After the war, highly indoctrinated Arab veterans of the Afghan war returned home to Algeria, Egypt, Jordan, the Occupied Territories, Pakistan, the Philippines, and elsewhere to lead their own struggles for militant Islam. A loosely connected network of violent young men spread out across the world.

Muslim anger proved manageable during the Gulf War itself, but a crisis was building. The Gulf War led to a rift between much Islamist opinion and the Saudis; a moderating influence was removed. In Algeria, Saudi money did not prevent the Front Islamique du Salut (Islamic Salvation Front, FIS) from siding with Iraq during the Gulf War and did nothing to stop the outbreak of the Algerian civil war. In Egypt, too, the Mubarak regime came under renewed attack from Islamists. Both the Saudis and the United States sought to stave off the instability in Egypt with aid, debt write-offs, and technical support. The United States contributed billions of dollars, regardless of the real questions about the Mubarak regime's effectiveness and its human rights record.

The Gulf War sparked particularly significant trouble, especially in Saudi Arabia. Prior to the invasion of Kuwait, the Saudis had always declined requests to base U.S. forces in the kingdom, and the reasons quickly became evident. Islamic militants regarded the presence of infidel forces protecting the land of the two holy mosques of Mecca and Medina as an outrage against Islamic doctrine. In Saudi Arabia itself, the minority Shia community had long harbored dissidents to the Saudi regime. However, it was the emergence of a new cadre of urban and educated Sunni fundamentalists that was the really significant development.[73] The new Islamists agitated against the Saudi state in a political form, notably with a number of petitions to the king in 1992–1993, but a violent undercurrent quickly became evident.

The seriousness of the emerging security threat in Saudi Arabia became clear in November 1995 when a bomb attack on the National Guard headquarters in Riyadh left five U.S. advisers dead. Worse was to follow. In June 1996, a massive explosion at the Khobar Towers residential facility in Dhahran killed nineteen U.S. citizens. Following a long investigation by the U.S. Federal Bureau of Investigation (FBI), fourteen Shia Muslims—thirteen Saudis and a Lebanese—were indicted in the United States in June 2001.[74] The indictment suggested that Iranian-supported Saudi extremists were trained in Lebanon before the Khobar attack. None of those indicted were in U.S. custody. A number were being held in Saudi jails, but the Saudi government was unlikely to hand them over. The involvement of the Iranian government in the attack was debatable, although the United States was poised to pursue the connection further. The allegations remain to be proven.

U.S. forces in Saudi Arabia were principal targets for Islamic militants, but bombings in the kingdom proved to be a rather rare event; such was the coercive clout of the Saudi state. The war that was to be fought between the United States and Islamic militants would be waged far beyond the borders of Saudi Arabia. Islamic terrorism was an emerging global phenomenon. The militants lived, studied, worked, and raised funds in dozens of countries, including in Europe and North America. To the extent that they were coordinated, it was as a rather diffuse nongovernmental network. Militants from different countries—many of whom knew each other from meeting places in Afghanistan, Pakistan, Sudan, and Europe—often drifted toward each other under the roof of a local mosque, in an Islamic organization, or simply through a committed individual. The militants at these meetings sometimes plotted acts of violent struggle before moving on. The diffuse and personalized organization of the "Islamic international" made it very difficult to penetrate and control.

One of the few figureheads of the Islamic international was the doyen of Saudi militants, Usama Bin Laden. Bin Laden came from a wealthy family, but his passion for jihad had taken him to Afghanistan in the 1980s. His subsequent activities against the Saudi regime had prompted the revocation of his Saudi citizenship, and he was forced to make his home in the Islamist havens of Sudan, Pakistan, and, finally, Afghanistan. Bin Laden and his al-Qaeda (the base) organization became unusually significant for a number of reasons. The resources available to Bin Laden pump-primed a fund-raising and recruitment network that eventually spanned the world and acted as a pole of attraction to other significant Islamist personalities and aspiring young activists. Bin Laden forged personal and even family relationships with the Sudanese Islamic leader Hasan al-Turabi and the famous blind Egyptian cleric, Omar Abdel Rahman. Most important, though, was Bin Laden's alliance with the exiled Egyptian militants of al-Jihad, especially with al-Jihad leader Ayman al-Zawahiri and Mohammad Atef.[75]

Al-Qaeda was greatly aided by the developing situation in Afghanistan in the 1990s and the relatively secure haven that it helped to create there. The Afghan sanctuary was founded on a personal relationship between Bin Laden and Mullah Mohammad Omar, the leader of the Afghan Taliban movement. Al-Qaeda's money and men helped the Taliban emerge from microsovereignties in Pashtun tribal areas and refugee camps in southern Afghanistan and Pakistan to become a national phenomenon. From almost nowhere, the Taliban swept away the fractious and corrupt sectarian politics of mujahidin rule between 1994 and 1996 to establish a strict traditionalist Islamic order across most of Afghanistan.

From Afghanistan, Bin Laden and the al-Qaeda organization offered inspiration, intellectual guidance, training, and financial sponsorship for local groups of militants across the world willing to wage a military jihad against the United States, its citizens, and its allies. In Somalia, Yemen, Chechnya, Pakistan, Kashmir, the southern Philippines, and a host of other places, local Islamic militants and al-Qaeda developed mutually supportive relationships. Local militants headed to Afghanistan for training and to act as the foot soldiers of the new Taliban regime. Al-Qaeda networks were also active in planning attacks directly on U.S. interests and citizens. Many facts remain unclear, but al-Qaeda appears to have played a direct or indirect role in most of the major terrorist incidents of the 1990s.

The first real hint of where the new Islamic terrorism was going came in February 1993, when a truck bomb exploded in the basement parking lot of the World Trade Center in New York. The bomb killed six, but if the terrorists' plan had been successful, one tower would have collapsed into the other, and the loss of life could well have numbered in the tens of thousands. The bombing was organized by a group of émigré militants based in the El Salaam mosque in New Jersey. The group was clustered around another of the Islamic international's few figureheads, Omar Abdel Rahman. Rahman was wanted in Egypt for terrorist crimes but had found refuge in the United States from May 1990 with the help of interested U.S. intelligence agencies.[76] Doing business with the new militants was clearly problematic; U.S. agencies might try to cultivate and co-opt them in various ways, but they felt no loyalty to or respect for any non-Islamic authority. Rahman and a number of his followers were indicted and convicted of the World Trade Center bombing.

The ruthless modus operandi of the new militants was again seen on 7 August 1998, when two bombs blew up outside the U.S. embassies in Nairobi, Kenya, and Dar es Salaam, Tanzania. The blasts were indiscriminate, killing 224 people, mostly innocent Africans, but also twelve Americans. A group calling itself the Islamic Army for the Liberation of the Holy Places claimed responsibility, and al-Qaeda associates were thoroughly implicated by subsequent U.S. investigations. Some of the militants who were eventually apprehended were an international group: Tanzanian, Lebanese, Saudi, and Jordanian.[77] Quite a few others remain on the FBI's most-wanted list. On 20 August 1998, the United States responded to the East African bombings by launching cruise missiles at al-Qaeda training camps in Afghanistan and a medical factory in Sudan said to be linked to Bin Laden. Little of real consequence was hit. Getting at the militants in their Afghanistan sanctuary would require a lot more than a few limited strikes. Later, a suicide attack that nearly sank the U.S.S. *Cole* in Aden harbor in October 2000, killing seventeen sailors, may also have been linked to al-Qaeda. The use of a rubber speedboat packed with explosives to blow a gaping hole in the side of the vessel suggested a significant level of planning and support, and a number of militants arrested and accused in Yemen were former Afghan veterans.[78]

Of course, it was all just a prelude to the catastrophic events of 11 September 2001 in the United States. After hijacking four U.S. airliners, Islamic militants armed only with knives perpetrated the worst act of terrorism in modern history. By crashing an airliner into each of the World Trade Center's towers, thereby demolishing both, and another into the Pentagon in Washington, they struck at the heart of U.S. economic and military power in a way that no terrorist had seemed capable of. Apart from the colossal loss of life, the sense of peace and security that Westerners had enjoyed since the end of the Cold War was shattered. On 11 September 2001, the new Islamic terrorism had clearly become the principal threat to the peace and security of the Western world. The impact of the attacks and its aftermath were bound to resonate in the relations between Westerners and Muslims for years to come. At the time of this writing, it was still too early to assess the success and direction of the global campaign against terrorism launched by the George W. Bush administration.

The scale and determination of the U.S. and world response to 11 September left al-Qaeda and the Taliban leadership with a grim future. The events of 11 September stunned the world, and the breadth of sympathy and solidarity with the United States was unprecedented. A powerful antiterrorist coalition that included European states, Russia, China, and India was forged, and it undoubtedly has had many successes in reducing the ability of international terrorists to operate. Among Muslim states, only the Iraqi regime initially refused to condemn the attacks or sympathize with the American people. A global campaign to arrest al-Qaeda activists and destroy their financial support networks got under way. The enhanced policing of the militants' networks in their European refuges was among the most important accomplishments of the war on terrorism. Policing was not enough for the United States, and predictably the U.S. response was quickly militarized. The military regime of General Parvez Musharraf in Pakistan was quickly cowed into cooperation. Pakistan cut off its Taliban client and assisted in the initiation of an air war in Afghanistan on 7 October 2001.

Afghanistan was so large, rugged, underdeveloped, and already ravaged by war that the task of destroying the Taliban and al-Qaeda seemed likely to be a prolonged one, but the United States found its leverage in supporting the opposition forces of the Northern Alliance in the north and Pashtun tribal leaders in the south. Resources were pumped into the new clients, and U.S. special forces coordinated U.S. airpower and the forces of local allies. The massive power of U.S. intelligence and airpower worked more quickly and effectively than many anticipated. In the second week of November, Taliban control of northern Afghanistan collapsed as its forces began to withdraw south or defect to the opposition. On 13 November, the Northern Alliance swept into Kabul. Clearly, the Islamic ideology that was at the heart of the Taliban movement was not enough to prevent the reassertion of the traditional Afghan practices of selling loyalty to the winner or the highest bidder. The Afghan way under military pressure was to merge back into the landscape, and without the support of Pakistan and Pashtun tribal leaders, the Taliban leadership could not stop many of its members from switching sides or returning to their microsovereignties in villages, local fiefdoms, drug gangs, and refugee camps. Pockets of resistance led by foreign and al-Qaeda forces, notably in Kunduz and Masar-e-Sharif, were soon blasted away. The final stronghold of Kandahar in southern Afghanistan was ceded to Pashtun tribal leaders on 7 December after negotiations. At the time of this writing, the Taliban was on the verge of dissolving, but Bin Laden and his key al-Qaeda associates were yet to be fully accounted for.

Whatever the final outcome of the war in Afghanistan, though, the security problem represented by the Afghanistan-Pakistan-Kashmir Islamic milieu was likely to remain. The Islamic infrastructure in Pakistan and Kashmir remained. In Afghanistan, picking up the pieces was bound to be difficult. Exhaustive talks between the various factions in Bonn, Germany, under the auspices of the UN led to the signing of a deal on an interim government on 5 December 2001 and gave some hope that a new peace and order in Afghanistan could be constructed. The UN plan established an interim coalition government for six months under Pashtun tribal leader Hamid Karzai, with the aim of a later meeting to elect a transitional government until a fuller constitution could be drawn up and elections held in about two years hence. The new order was constructed rapidly, and it begged many questions. It was very easy to imagine the various Pashtun, Tajik, Uzbek, and Hazara factions falling out with each other at some point in the future. The end of the Taliban had fractured the country into a myriad of fiefdoms, and whether a national rule of law could be reestablished remained to be seen. Without substantial and sustained Western aid to build up a new central authority, the end of the Taliban threatened to take Afghanistan back in time to an era of fractured sectarian politics and lawlessness. Under the conditions of sectarian division, it was not impossible that something like the Taliban and al-Qaeda might one day reemerge from the microsovereignties of the Pashtun ethnic areas.

With the endgame in Afghanistan in sight, the next phase of the war on terrorism was being considered in Washington. A number of Muslim countries—Iraq, Yemen, Sudan, Somalia, Syria, and Iran—were often mentioned as problem cases. The military campaign in Afghanistan had gone well for the United States, but whether military solutions could successfully be applied elsewhere remained to be seen. The United States would undoubtedly face more serious political opposition from Muslim countries and in the broader international community if it pressed the "war on terrorism" in too many places or used it to pursue others objectives that it had so far failed to accomplish. In the aftermath of 11 September, fear of what the United States might do in the Middle East produced a conspicuous outbreak of reconciliation between the key regional powers. The senior foreign ministry officials of Egypt, Syria, Saudi Arabia, and Iran did much traveling to each other's countries, with an Egyptian-Iranian rapprochement a particularly significant development. If the United States launched another war in the Muslim world or turned its war on terrorism toward the Arab-Israeli conflict, it would find little support among either its friends or foes in the Middle East. Many people in the Muslim world were acutely sensitive to the idea that the United States might pick off another major Muslim state and thus further retard the progress of the Muslim world. Iraq was enough.

The U.S. conflict with Islamic militants stemmed from its dominant role in managing international relations in the Middle East, and it was at that level of politics that the threat really needed to be met. The 11 September attacks were unexpected, but they could not be seen as bolts from the blue. The disaster originated in a crisis that had been in the making for over a decade, and it was one that had gone critical in the year 2000. The attacks had a lot to do with the failure of the pax Americana in the Middle East. U.S. policymakers had had their chance to create a sustainable security system in the region after the Cold War and Gulf War but had not come up with the ideas or policies to turn the opportunities into something more lasting. The real problem was that the pax Americana did not bring peace and order to the region, but presided over—indeed sustained—a number of endemic conflicts that had gradually slipped beyond the ability of even the United States to manage and contain them. Creating a deeper peace and reducing the causes of the pervasive anti-Americanism in the Muslim world required a final Arab-Israeli settlement as well as some kind of security system in the Gulf that did not encourage the belligerency of Iran and Iraq or necessitate the permanent stationing of sizable U.S. forces in Saudi Arabia. Moreover, with Palestinian and Iraqi Muslims dying in such large numbers, it was really very easy for Islamic militants to justify desperate acts of resistance to themselves, no matter how murderous. The pax Americana did not work very well, and it elicited violent responses.

Whether the George W. Bush administration could come up with the ideas and policy initiatives to improve the architecture of the Middle East's peace and order remained to be seen, although the 11 September attacks put the entire regional situation into a state of flux. At the time of this writing, it was not obvious that U.S. policymakers had come up with a new way of relating to Iran and Iraq. Indeed, Iraq seemed likely to face a new round of coercive pressure from the United States. At the very least, the heightened state of cooperation between the United States and Russia following 11 September opened the possibility that a new regime of "smart sanctions" that targeted Saddam Hussein's regime more effectively might be put through the UN Security Council.

The need to restart the Arab-Israeli peace process was also clear, with a number of European leaders pressing for something significant to be done. President Bush's comment to the media, following a meeting with members of Congress, that "the idea of a Palestinian state has always been part of a vision, so long as the right of Israel to exist is respected," was a significant moment.[79] The U.S. administration went on to send former general Anthony Zinni to the region as a peace envoy, but a breakthrough seemed as far away as ever. The series of suicide bomb attacks in Jerusalem and Haifa on 1–2 December 2001 that killed twenty-five Israelis during Zinni's first visit represented acts of business as usual in a long conflict of attrition to which both sides were committed. Israel's response was predictably tough, and the suggestion that it might remove Yasser Arafat threatened a future that was even more uncertain, chaotic, and violent. Arafat's political authority was further damaged. What was left of the peace process was being broken on the back of Sharon's insistence on a period of seven days of complete calm before talks could even begin. The conflict was stuck in the process. The influence of Israel in the U.S. political system was profound, and a number of the Bush administration's key members were biased toward it, so it was unclear whether the administration had the will or capacity to push Israel toward the key peace concessions.

Getting regional security architecture right, though, was not the end of dealing with the causes of Middle Eastern terrorism. The other basic cause of political instability lay in the nature of politics in the region, including those states allied to the United States. U.S. policymakers knew that the lack of democracy, economic development, and social justice had much to do with Islamic resistance. The problem here was that the United States had few sensible alternatives to the likes of Hosni Mubarak, King Fahd, and King Abdullah, not least because the Islamic opposition was as undemocratic as and much more anti-American and anti-Israeli than the status quo. Promoting democratic reform was likely to promote the forces that threatened U.S. interests, especially its oil and Israeli interests.

In addition, Arab allies of the United States were often quick to react angrily if the United States either made contact with the Islamic opposition or criticized the abuses of democracy and human rights taking place. U.S. officials and members of Congress sometimes commented on the need for improved governance in Mubarak's Egypt, for instance, but the United States was loath to deviate too far from the imperative of keeping Mubarak afloat. Mubarak was not looking to do business with anyone from the Islamic opposition and refused to countenance U.S. advice on such matters. U.S. policymakers chose not to rock Mubarak's boat, although this meant that a more sophisticated initiative to counter the causes of Islamic violence could not be developed. Mubarak got by, but Egypt remained chronically unstable.

In the last analysis, the Arab allies of the United States were just too important to risk destabilizing in the short term by trying to force changes. U.S. officials could do little more than establish intelligence-related contacts with Islamists, even the relatively moderate ones. Islamic reformers in Morocco, Tunisia, Algeria, Egypt, Jordan, and Saudi Arabia were essentially on their own.[80] The result was a vicious circle: the United States acquiesced to poorly performing regimes who perpetuated violent opposition, which in turn perpetuated their misrule. Thus, the pax Americana in the Middle East had very little to do with democracy and human rights, at least not among its allies. Order, oil, and Israel came first, and U.S. policymakers simply lived with the double standards involved. What all this meant was that U.S. policy was limited to policing the rage of the Muslim crisis rather than seeking ways to resolve its causes.

The United States had not done a very good job as the principal security manager for Western hegemony in the Middle East in the 1990s. The security architecture of the region was unstable, and until a more positive peace was engineered, the West could not win the war on terrorism; it could only suppress it. Most Muslims were shocked and saddened by the enormous loss of life on 11 September, but Bin Laden struck a chord that resonated wider than most Western and Muslim governments were prepared to admit. Bin Laden's methods were extreme, but many of his stated objectives—the withdrawal of U.S. forces from Saudi Arabia, a jihad against Israeli occupation, the restoration of Jerusalem to Islamic rule, and political reform in Muslim countries— were almost indistinguishable from much mainstream opinion. Over a long period of time, so many Muslims had become so enraged with the world that they wanted to see someone fight back. A few Islamists were committed to a violent option to the point of killing themselves—it was part of their statement of resistance—and for the foreseeable future it would be very difficult to stop some of them from doing just that.

Securing the world's air travel, much less every burger bar and pizza parlor in the world, was impossible. Moreover, even if the United States was able to hunt down the few figureheads of the "Islamic international," as it seemed likely to do with Bin Laden and his closest associates, no matter how many Bin Ladens were killed or cruise missiles fired, new militants were likely to take their place because the grievances were so very deep. A low-level war between the United States and the Islamic militants seemed likely to rumble on for years.

The Future of U.S. Preeminence in the Middle East

The United States was always going to have clout in the Middle East after the end of the Cold War, but the Gulf conflict in 1990–1991 opened the way for a presence that was unimaginable even a year before. The United States was able to station forces permanently in the Gulf; develop an Arab-Israeli peace process; subject the deviants—Iran, Iraq, and Libya—to tough regimes of containment; encourage a de facto alliance among Israel, Turkey, Egypt, Saudi Arabia, and Syria; and pursue Islamic terrorists to the margins of the Muslim world. In the absence of a global-level counterbalance or a Muslim body capable of articulating a unified voice, the United States had made itself the undisputed arbiter of the Middle Eastern state system. After the Gulf War, it was impossible to imagine, in Michael Hudson's words, that any Middle Eastern state had the "will and capability to explode the region."[81]

The United States was preeminent in the Middle East, but the pax Americana did not look very stable. A system that left the Palestinians as guardians only of besieged ghettos and purposefully estranged the two biggest powers in the Gulf—Iran and Iraq—was dysfunctional. U.S. influence stemmed from its position as the principal arbiter of the Arab-Israeli and Gulf conflicts, but this role could not be sustained indefinitely. By the end of the 1990s, Middle Easterners were tiring of the endless dragging out of the control regimes on Iran and Iraq and the all-too-obvious failure of the Arab-Israeli peace process. The awful violence of Islamic militants highlighted the costs of the U.S. approach. Destroying the lives of thousands of innocent people cannot be justified under any circumstances, but the 11 September attacks on the United States stemmed from a flawed and unstable security system that the United States presided over in the Middle East. To go on failing to make a better future for the region—or rather, failing to provide the hegemonic services that Arabs and Muslims expected of the United States after the Gulf War and Madrid conference—was to invite a further loss of authority.

By 2000–2001, it was beginning to look as though the post–Gulf War pax Americana in the Middle East had already seen its best days. The George W. Bush administration that took office in early 2001 did little to address the decay in the U.S. security system that had set in during the Clinton years. Bush was reluctant to become too deeply involved in foreign entanglements in general but also stood back from an Israeli-Palestinian peace process that seemed very unlikely to satisfy either side. Without the power and authority of the United States, however, the Middle East risked drifting beyond anyone's management, and the final implications of an escalating Arab-Israeli conflict were very difficult to predict. The 11 September attacks on the United States and the subsequent declaration of the war on terrorism put the entire security situation in the Middle East into a state of flux. At the time of this writing, it was too early to say whether the Bush administration would be able to use the war on terrorism to create something more positive and lasting in the region. The United States would undoubtedly try to use the situation to revive the pax Americana, but yet more coercive solutions would be just as likely to further destabilize and damage its security system as to recover it.

In the longer run, U.S. preeminence in the Middle East is also likely to face greater challenges stemming from the interests and concerns of other major outside powers. The importance of energy security is bound to go up the international agenda as the twenty-first century goes on, with the price and stability of the Middle East's oil supplies a concern for everyone. Indeed, U.S. policy in the Middle East itself was partly designed to put off the fateful day when the energy-hungry United States will experience a profound energy crisis that seems likely to sap its powers. In the Middle East, the United States will more than likely have to deal with the squeeze of the emergent superpower interests of China on the one side and Europe on the other. China's growing interest in Gulf oil was significant, and Chinese weapons were already flowing to Iran and Iraq. Reports in the aftermath of the U.S. and British bombing of Iraq in February 2001 that China was helping Iraq to enhance its air defense and communications capabilities might well portend things to come. A future of proxy wars in the Gulf was far away, but China was likely to be a force to be reckoned with.

The other emergent superpower that might cast a much larger shadow across the Middle East is the alternative leader of the Western hegemony, the European Union. U.S. supremacy at the end of the twentieth century consisted of its dominance of military security and the Arab-Israeli conflict, but the Europeans were quietly moving into a number of issue areas. European political and military integration was likely to proceed in the twenty-first century, but even if it did not, the Middle East and North Africa were in Europe's economic, intellectual, and cultural shadow much more than in that of the United States. It was to a version of Europe and its regulated capitalism that most Middle Eastern elites aspired. Far more Middle Easterners traveled to London, Paris, Rome, Madrid, and Berlin than to Washington, New York, and Boston. Furthermore, Europeans were not myopically devoted to Israel, and they were more willing to develop ties with states that the United States regarded as rogues. European constructive engagement was building bridges to Iran and Iraq, while the United States clung to containment and rollback strategies that were bound to retard its ability to do business in the Middle East for years to come. The United States had proved itself an adaptable hegemon; it would need to be so in the future if it was to retain its preeminence.

Notes

1. Brown, "History Ends, Worlds Collide," *Review of International Studies* 25, Special Issue, December 1999, 47.

2. Morales, "U.S. Intervention and the New World Order: Lessons from Cold War and Post–Cold War Cases," *Third World Quarterly* 15, no. 1, 1994, 78.

3. Krause, "Proliferation Risks and Their Strategic Relevance: What Role for NATO?" *Survival* 37, no. 2, 135–148; Joseph, "Proliferation, Counter-Proliferation and NATO," *Survival* 38, no. 1, Spring 1996, 111–130.

4. Hadar, "America's Moment in the Middle East," *Current History* 95, no. 597, January 1996, 2.

5. Anthony, "The US-GCC Relationship: A Glass Half Empty or Half Full?" *Middle East Policy* 5, no. 2, May 1997, 23–24.

6. Khalizad and Ochmanek, "Rethinking US Defence Planning," *Survival* 39, no. 1, Spring 1997, 53–54.

7. See Pinto, "US Middle East Policy Making," in *Political Islam and the United States,* 1999, 31–42.

8. The Mitchell Commission was a group of experts chaired by former U.S. senator George Mitchell. The group was formed following commitments made by U.S. President Bill Clinton to a peace conference in Sharm el-Shaikh in October 2000. It was tasked with investigating the breakdown of the peace process and recommending ways of restoring it. See "The Mitchell Report," BBC News Website, In Depth: Key Documents, Thursday, 29 November 2001,

http://news.bbc.co.uk/hi/english/in_depth/middle_east/Israel_and_the_ Palestinians/key_document/newsid_1632000/1632064.stm.

9. The Madrid process, as Michael Hudson observed, "envisaged not only loosely parallel bilateral negotiations between Israel and its several Arab antagonists, but also a multilateral, functional dimension involving states throughout the Middle East and the industrialized world. The broader regional focus appealed to the Israelis, and drew in countries like Saudi Arabia that could influence the Arab parties to the bilateral talks. The Madrid process, in short, was designed for bandwagoning, or developing a centrifugal momentum to create a new Middle East, with Israel playing a central role in it." Hudson, "To Play the Hegemon: Fifty Years of U.S. Policy Towards the Middle East," *Middle East Journal* 50, no. 3, Summer 1996, 336.

10. Quandt, "The Middle East on the Brink: Prospects for Change in the 21st Century," *Middle East Journal* 50, no. 1, Winter 1996, 17.

11. Dowty and Gawerc, "The Intifada: Revealing the Chasm," *Middle East Review of International Affairs* 5, no. 3, September 1991 (MEIRA online journal).

12. "Israeli Helicopters Attack Gaza Police," BBC News Online, Monday, 30 July 2001, http://news.bbc.co.uk/hi/english/world/middle_east/newsid_ 1465000/1465081.stm; "West Bank Tensions Escalate," BBC News Online, Wednesday, 1 August 2001, http://news.bbc.co.uk/hi/english/world/middle _east/newsid_1467000/1467869.stm.

13. "U.S. Condemns Israeli Takeover," BBC News Online, Friday, 10 August 2001, http://news.bbc.co.uk/hi/english/world/middle_east/newsid_ 1485000/1485151.stm.

14. See "The Mitchell Report," BBC News Website, In Depth: Key Documents, Thursday, 29 November 2001, http://news.bbc.co.uk/hi/english/in_ depth/middle_east/Israel_and_the_Palestinians/key_document/newsid_163200 0/1632064.stm.

15. Anthony, "The US-GCC Relationship," 22–41.

16. Lake, "Confronting the Backlash States," *Foreign Affairs* 73, no. 2, March–April 1994, 45–55.

17. Ibid., 48.

18. Ibid., 49.

19. Ibid., 52.

20. Hashim, "Iraq: Fin de Regime?" *Current History* 95, no. 597, January 1996, 11.

21. The Iraqi Revolutionary Command Council issued a decree accepting Kuwait's sovereignty under the terms of UNSCR 833 on 10 November 1994. Reported by the Iraqi News Agency, Baghdad, in Arabic, 1310gmt, 10 November 1994. Reproduced in the BBC's *Summary of World Broadcasts (SWB)*, ME/2150, 11 November 1994, MED/1.

22. Toby Ash, "In Search of a New Consensus on Iraq," *Middle East Economic Digest (MEED)* 43, no. 4, 29 January 1999, 3.

23. Gause, "Getting It Backward on Iraq," *Foreign Affairs* 78, no. 3, May–June 1999, 54.

24. "No Change in Iraq Policy, UK Insists," *MEED* 45, no. 3, 19 January 2001, 2.

25. Al-Shayeji, "Dangerous Perceptions: Gulf Views of the U.S. Role in the Region," *Middle East Policy* 5, no. 3, September 1997, 3–4.

26. Brian Whitaker, "U.S. Urges Syria to Be Tougher on Iraq," *The Guardian*, 27 February 2001, 18.

27. Rugh, "Time to Modify Our Gulf Policy," *Middle East Policy* 5, no. 1, January 1997, 50.

28. Al-Shayeji, "Dangerous Perceptions," 1.

29. Reported by the Iraqi News Agency, Baghdad, in Arabic, 1035gmt, 21 November 1994. Reproduced in *SWB*, ME/2160, 23 November 1994, [27], MED/15.

30. Report based on a survey carried out in Iraq between February and May 1999 by UNICEF and the World Health Organization. Report released by UNICEF on 12 August 1999. Hoskins, "The Impact of Sanctions: A Study of UNICEF's Perspective," http://www.unicef.org/newsline/99pr29. htm.

31. Toby Ash, "Saddam Takes the U.S. to the Brink," *MEED* 42, no. 8, 20 February 1998, 2.

32. Statement made by Scott Ritter on 3 September 1998 to the U.S. Senate's Joint Legislative Hearing of the Committees on Armed Services and Foreign Affairs. In the archive (105th Congress) of the Senate Armed Forces Committee, http://www.senate.gov/~armed_services/statemnt/980903sr.htm.

33. Ash, "In Search of a New Consensus on Iraq," 3–4.

34. David Butter, "Dancing on the Sanctions' Grave," *MEED* 44, no. 49, 8 December 2000, 7.

35. "Iraq Makes Egyptian Breakthrough," *MEED* 45, no. 4, 26 January 2001, 2.

36. Whitaker, "U.S. Urges Syria to Be Tougher on Iraq," 18.

37. Barbara Plett, "Analysis: Will 'Smart' Sanctions Work?" BBC News Online, Saturday, 2 June 2001, http://news.bbc.co.uk/hi/english/world/middle_ east/newsid_1366000/1366201.stm.

38. From comments made by Ayatollah Ali Khameini in a live broadcast for Iranian radio and television, 0620gmt, 27 October 1994. Reproduced in *SWB* 28/10/94, MED/2138, 28 October 1994, [19], MED/8-9, MED/9.

39. Broadcast by the Voice of the Islamic Republic of Iran, Tehran, in Persian, 1104gmt, 2 November 1994. Reproduced in *SWB*, MED/2144, 4 November 1994, [1], MED/1-3, MED/1-2.

40. Comments made by Rafsanjani at Friday prayers in Tehran, 23 January 1998. Broadcast by the Voice of the Islamic Republic of Iran, in Persian, 1230gmt, 23 January 1998. Reproduced in *SWB*, ME/3134, 26 January 1998, [31], MED/11-14.

41. Reported by the Islamic Republic News Agency, Tehran, 27 September 1994. Reproduced in SWB, ME/2114, 30 September 1994, [32], MED/11.

42. The full CNN interview was broadcast by the Vision of the Islamic Republic of Iran, in Persian, 0430gmt, 8 January 1998. Reproduced in *SWB*, ME/3120, 9 January 1998, [1], MED/1-9.

43. Comments made by Rafsanjani at a Friday sermon on 4 November 1994. Broadcast on Voice of the Islamic Republic, in Persian, 1130gmt, 4

November 1994. Reproduced in *SWB, ME/2146,* 7 November 1994, [5], MED/2-5, MED/4.

44. Khatami, CNN interview, *SWB,* 9 January 1998, MED/4.

45. Ibid., MED/6.

46. Ibid., MED/4.

47. Khalilzad, "The United States and the Persian Gulf," *Survival* 37, no. 2, Summer 1995, 99–104.

48. Chubin, "Does Iran Want Nuclear Weapons?" *Survival* 37, no. 1, Spring 1995, 86–104.

49. Spector, "Neo-Nonproliferation," *Survival* 37, no. 1, Spring 1995, 75.

50. From comments made by Foreign Minister Ali Akbar Velayati to a two-day national seminar on the NPT in Tehran on 19 December 1994. Reported by the Islamic Republic News Agency, in English, 2059gmt, 19 December 1994. Reproduced in *SWB,* ME/2184, 21 December 1994, [1], MED/1.

51. Chubin, "Does Iran Want Nuclear Weapons?" 86.

52. "Russia Resuming Weapons Supplies to Iran," *MEED* 45, no. 2, 12 January 2001, 2.

53. Vahe Petrossian, "U.S. Has a Serious Problem with Iran," *MEED* 39, no. 18, 5 May 1995, 2.

54. See Pinto, "The Intellectual Backdrop: Approaches to Political Islam," in *Political Islam and the United States,* especially 184–197.

55. Rugh, "Time to Modify Our Gulf Policy," 47–49.

56. "Solidarity with Iran and Libya Concerning D'Amato Law" (Point 64), Final Communiqué of the 8th OIC Summit in Tehran, 9–11 December 1997. Text reproduced on Homepage of the Permanent Delegation of the OIC to the UN Offices in Geneva and Vienna, http://www.oic-un.org/8/fincom8.htm.

57. "United States: Meanwhile, There's Iran," *The Economist,* 27 June 1998, 58.

58. Vahe Petrossian, "Investors Lap up Iranian Oil Field Offers," *MEED* 42, no. 29, 17 July 1998, 4.

59. "Khatami Visit Brings Japan and Iran Closer," *MEED* 44, no. 26, 30 June 2000, 5.

60. Reported by the Islamic Republic News Agency, in English, 0818gmt, 20 January 2000. Reproduced in *SWB,* ME/3743, 21 January 2000, [7], MED/3.

61. Comments made by Foreign Secretary Robin Cook at the Ismaili center in London on 8 October 1998. Reproduced in "A New Dialogue with Islam," UK Foreign and Commonwealth Office, http://www.fco.gov.uk/news/speechtext.asp?1578.

62. Reported by Voice of the Islamic Republic of Iran, in Persian, 0430gmt, 13 January 2000. Reproduced in *SWB,* ME/3737, 14 January 2000, [1], MED/1.

63. "Iran, Saudi Arabia Plan Security Pact," *MEED* 45, no. 3, 19 January 2001, 3.

64. Kemp, "The Persian Gulf Remains the Strategic Prize," *Survival* 40, no. 4, Winter 1998–1999, 146.

65. Kemp, "Iran: Can the United States Do a Deal?" *Washington Quarterly* 24, no. 1, Winter 2001, 122.

66. Gause, "The Illogic of Dual Containment," *Foreign Affairs* 73, no. 2, March–April 1994, 57.

67. Rugh, "Time to Modify Our Gulf Policy," 55.

68. Kemp, "The Persian Gulf Remains the Strategic Prize," 147.

69. O'Sullivan, "The Politics of Dismantling Containment," *The Washington Quarterly* 24, no. 1, Winter 2001, 70.

70. "Libya and Iran Hit by New Sanctions," BBC News Website, World: Americas, Saturday, 4 August 2001, http://news.bbc.co.uk/hi/english/world/americas/newsid_1473000/1473176.stm.

71. Comments made by Ayatollah Khameini to a large gathering of Islamic Revolutionary Guards in Khuzestan Province. Broadcast on the Vision of the Islamic Republic Network 1, in Persian, 1530gmt, 19 February 1998. Reproduced in *SWB*, ME/3157, 21 February 1998, [34], MED10-11, MED11.

72. Roy, "The Geostrategy of Islamism: States and Networks," in *The Failure of Political Islam,* 1994.

73. See Dekmejian, "The Rise of Political Islamism in Saudi Arabia," *Middle East Journal* 48, no. 4, Autumn 1994, 627–643.

74. "U.S. Brings Saudi Bombing Charges," BBC News Website, World: Americas, Friday, 22 June 2001, http://news.bbc.co.uk/hi/english/world/americas/nedsid_1401000/1401266.stm; details of some of those wanted for the Khobar Towers bombing can be found on the "Most Wanted List" of foreign terrorists at the Federal Bureau of Investigation (FBI) website, http://www.fbi.gov/mostwant/terrorists/fugitives.htm.

75. Details of leading members of al-Qaeda can be found on the FBI's website: http://www.fbi.gov/mostwant/terrorists/fugitives.htm.

76. Friedman, *The World Trade Center Bombing and the CIA,* October 1993, 1.

77. "Four in U.S. Embassy Bombings Trial," BBC News Website, World: Americas, Monday, 5 February 2001, http://news.bbc.co.uk/hi/english/world/americas/newsid_1153000/1153812.stm.

78. "Cole Suspects Arrested," BBC News Website, World: Middle East, 19 February 2001, 0021gmt, http://news.bbc.co.uk/hi/english/world/middle_east/newsid-1177000/1177865.stm.

79. "Bush 'Endorses' Palestinian State," BBC News Online, 2 October 2001, http://news.bbc.co.uk/hi/english/world/middle_east/newsid_1575000/1575090.stm.

80. See Pinto, "U.S. Policy Towards Political Islam," in *Political Islam and the United States.*

81. Hudson, "The Middle East Under Pax Americana: How New, How Orderly?" *Third World Quarterly* 13, no. 2, 1992, 315.

4

The Impact of the Global
Economy in Muslim Countries

The global economy was at the heart of Western hegemony. Far more than U.S. fighter wings and aircraft carriers, it was the global dominance of a model of liberal market capitalism that shaped the world that most people lived in. The values and practices of liberal capitalism and the goods that its adherents produced were ubiquitous. Liberal capitalism drove what became familiarly termed *globalization,* as well as the growing sense that the fortunes of almost all humans were interdependent. The new expansion of globalized liberal capitalism was speeded by a simultaneous technological revolution in communications and transportation that vastly reduced effective distances and gave an unknown immediacy to the idea of a single global economy.

The new globalization was sometimes presented as a natural and inevitable phenomenon, but it really involved purposeful practice that was driven by an alliance of Western states and multinational corporations (MNCs) that formed a global hegemonic grouping. Markets did have an ideology, and they were governed. In fact, the world economy had never before labored under a system in which the rules of participation were so clear and transgressions of them so transparent. Markets were supervised by states—above all, by the collusion of Western states—as well as by a number of multilateral institutions, the foremost being the International Monetary Fund (IMF), the World Bank, and the World Trade Organization (WTO). At the center of the world economy was the so-called Triad: an intense trading and investment community linking the United States, Europe, and Japan. The corporations, markets, and governments of the Triad were highly interdependent, with the Group of Seven (the United States, Japan, Germany, United Kingdom,

France, Italy, and Canada) acting as the premier forum for multilateral consultation and coordination.

The relationship between global markets and Western states was not entirely straightforward, but if global markets were working for anyone, it was for states, societies, and corporations of the Triad countries. Indeed, market capitalism was making the world much more unequal, with those properly engaging with new technology and global markets forging ahead and those left behind becoming even more marginal. In 1997, the top 20 percent of the world's population earned 86 percent of the world's gross domestic product (GDP), the middle 60 percent only 13 percent of GDP, and bottom 20 percent just 1 percent.[1]

The expansion of globalized liberal capitalism in the late twentieth century challenged all societies with enormous change. Freer markets had profound implications for familiar patterns of social identity, authority, and loyalty everywhere. The implications of the new markets were as profound in the less developed world as in the West itself. In the 1980s, the idea of a Third World had ceased to be meaningful as interests fragmented and as some states and elites became more fully integrated into the global economy while others did not.

The experience of Muslim countries in the 1980s and 1990s was diverse. Malaysia embraced capitalism and freer markets and was an economic success story. The Gulf states continued to benefit from oil-based development, but depressed oil prices from the mid-1980s slowed their progress. The Islamic Republic of Iran sought to exclude foreign influences but paid a crippling price for its autarky. Most Muslim countries struggled, especially in the Middle East. Low oil prices were partly responsible for low rates of growth, but economic failure was also rooted in a lack of dynamism and the overblown character of most Muslim states. Inefficient public sectors continued to crowd out private economic activity. Nevertheless, economic reform was in the air. State-led development practices had run into the ground by the 1970s and 1980s, and most Muslim states were aware that economic reform was by necessity on its way.

Embracing liberalization and the new globalization presented Muslim states and societies with two major challenges. First, reform was liable to destabilize local economies as markets were liberalized, industries were privatized, state spending was cut, and currencies floated. Second, economic reform was designed to engage with foreign capital and global markets; apart from the direct impact on economic life, liberalization opened societies to the culture of the market as well as the individualism and consumerism that went with it. Global culture tended to homogenize societies along the lines of a Western model that did not always sit easily with local cultures.

The imperatives of economic viability tended to offset local concerns about the downsides. Muslim countries feared the consequences of Westernization, but they also feared falling further behind, and so risks were to be borne. Whether Muslims could catch up with Westerners and Asians within the foreseeable future, though, was far from clear. Certainly, Muslim politics and Islamic culture sometimes represented serious compatibility barriers to freer markets and to effective engagement with the world global economy. Yet reforms were put in place, and the new globalization began to make its mark. Almost all Muslim societies faced change in very significant ways.

The Long Experience of Globalization in the Muslim World

Globalization is not new. The origins of the contemporary global system can be traced back at least to the sixteenth century. European technology, organization, and entrepreneurship created a widening gap between Europe and the rest of the world. With their ships, guns, railways, and telegraphs, European soldiers and entrepreneurs went out into the world to trade and to conquer. Europeans established global trading systems that were essentially extractive and exploitative. The lives of the subject peoples of European empires were bound up with forces that lay many miles over their horizon.

The capacity of Europeans and Westerners to absorb others into their global systems has been the principal issue facing Muslim societies since the eighteenth century. As Europeans forged ahead, Muslims were absorbed into European empires. The Dutch took the East Indies. The Muslim states of India were picked off by Britain. Czarist Russia absorbed the Caucasus and Central Asia. Napoleon's expedition to Egypt in 1798 was also a fateful moment. Britain and France had arrived in the Middle East, heralding over a century of retreat for the principal Muslim authority, the Ottoman Empire. France established its empire in North Africa, and the British forced entry into Egypt and the Arabian Peninsula. Egypt was contained by debt and military threat, and its cotton and the Suez Canal (constructed 1859–1869) eventually led to its full subjugation by a British invasion in 1882. The final collapse of the Ottoman Empire at the end of World War I finished the process of penetration and absorption. Britain created a new state system, and dominated Iraq, Transjordan, and Palestine, while France took on Syria and Lebanon. Almost all Muslims had been pressed into the global trading systems of the European empires.

The Europeans brought the two revolutions of modernity to the Muslim world: the industrial revolution and the revolution of political and social ideas. European technology opened Muslim areas to new kinds of economic activity. Modern ideologies also took hold, with Arab, Iranian, and Turkish nationalisms superseding Islam as the dominant political philosophy. In Turkey, Mustafa Kemal (Atatürk) argued that Islam was *the* cause of Muslim backwardness and decline. To compete, Muslims had to be more like the Europeans. In Turkey and Iran, the secular state moved to break the power of Islam and to make Muslims more European. Turkish law enforced a European calendar and European forms of script and dress. The Arabs never went as far in rejecting Islam as did the states in Turkey and Iran, but in such places as Algeria, Egypt, Iraq, and Syria, the model adopted was secular, socialist, and nationalist. Arab modernizers remained Muslim, but they ceased to be Islamic in any meaningful sense. When real political independence was achieved after World War II, "progressive" Arab regimes sought economic independence from European domination by means of state planning, public ownership, and import substitution. Local markets were protected from foreign control and competition.

The nationalist and socialist states of the Middle East were never really successful, but for a time it seemed that a new independence was being forged. It was all a false dawn. State planning failed almost as soon as it was implemented. Gamal Abdul Nasser's regime in Egypt led the way into state planning, as well as toward the consequences of its failure. Tunisia, Iraq, Syria, Libya, Yemen, and Algeria followed. Middle Eastern economies were characterized by overly rigid bureaucracies, poor planning, inefficiency, and corruption. Sheltered behind protected borders, local economies were unproductive, and the demand for goods, employment, and welfare quickly outstripped the resources available. In Egypt, state control had been extended over the economy in the early 1960s, but even by the end of that decade, it was clear that the policy was unsustainable.

Reform came onto the agenda in Egypt. With Nasser's death in 1970 and the consolidation of Anwar Sadat's regime, reform was embraced. The state remained the principal force in the economy, but Sadat introduced the *infitah* (opening) in 1974. Regulations were eased, private and foreign capital was encouraged, more foreign trade was allowed, and public spending was cut. The *infitah* also embodied a new alliance between the bureaucracy and private sector, although as Nazih Ayubi argued, this cooperation really represented a readjustment of state capitalism rather than the abandonment of a socialism that never existed.[2] The entrenched power of the bureaucracy in the form of the Arab Socialist Union (ASU) was curtailed, and a number of chambers of commerce and business clubs were promoted as new nodes of political consultation and patronage.[3]

Egypt had readopted the market idea, then, some years before the rest of the world followed. By the 1980s, the *infitah* model had spread to most other states in the Arab world, with liberalization planned or implemented in Morocco, Algeria, Tunisia, Iraq, and Syria. No matter their origin—secular socialist or conservative Islamic—a capitalist-bureaucratic alliance that ran a mixed economy came to dominate almost all Arab countries.

Late-Twentieth-Century Globalization

Globalization was not new, then, but an entirely new phase began to take shape after World War II, reaching a culmination in the 1980s and 1990s. The new globalization had its origin in the Western economic system that was the backbone of the Western alliance during the Cold War. A number of multilateral institutions were created to supervise the gradual opening of Western markets, although the Western alliance incorporated what is often called "embedded liberalism": a compromise between U.S.-style free markets and European and Japanese concerns for social stability. The system tolerated a significant degree of state ownership and protectionism, as well as fixed exchange rates. European social democracy was embodied in the widely used Keynesian model of macroeconomic management that prioritized state planning and social welfare. In Europe and Japan, citizens were protected from the full implications of markets, which created the stable conditions for their postwar redevelopment.

The Western system was global, but it was not *the* global system; however, this was to change with the coincidence of a number of developments in the 1980s. New technologies that brought cheap and instantaneous communications facilitated an unknown quantity and quality of human interactions across the globe, but the full implications of the technology could not have been realized without two great political changes that unfolded in the 1980s.[4]

The first great change, stemming from the "neoliberalism" of

Margaret Thatcher and Ronald Reagan in the 1980s, was the "capitalist revival" in the West. Market reforms cut public spending, privatized state-run industries, lifted trade controls, freed financial services, and deregulated foreign exchange markets. The revolution in economic practice that all this represented changed the conditions for economic competitiveness and success. As a result, most value was created not in fixed manufacturing production but in the more ephemeral financing and marketing of goods and services. The influence of MNCs and of global financial networks centered on New York, London, and Tokyo increased noticeably. In liberalizing and supervising the new open global markets, the multilateral institutions of the Western economic system also significantly upgraded their power.

The second major political change was the end of the Cold War. The dissolution of the Soviet threat to the West lifted the remaining internal and external restraints on Western market reforms. Socio-economic stability in the West, or anywhere else for that matter, was no longer as vital as it had been, and so the ethos of the Keynesian social consensus further gave way to the impulses of liberal capitalism. Elsewhere, the collapse of the Soviet model left large parts of the world politically and economically bankrupt. New frontiers for Western global markets lay out there for the taking. The new technologies provided the means by which these new opportunities could quickly be exploited.

The combination of new technology, the capitalist revival, and the end of the Cold War produced a new era of globalization. All states and societies had little choice but to respond to the incredible force of what had happened. The future role of the territorial state came under particular question, with supranational authorities seemingly challenging it from above and MNCs and nongovernmental organizations (NGOs) chipping away from below. New understandings about sovereignty were indeed required. States remained powerful, as well as the essential facilitators of the new globalization, but the myth of their absolute supremacy was no longer sustainable. For all but the largest states, the traditional mechanisms of macroeconomic management were now less useful. The chairman of the U.S. Federal Reserve still had the capacity to move the markets, but few other state-bound managers did. The state's ability to manage its economy and society was now less a matter of traditional legal jurisdiction and more one of the quality of its understanding and the extent of its economic capabilities.

The new liberal capitalism provided a particular challenge to many states in the way that it made capital into a highly mobile commodity, one increasingly indifferent to the claims of the nation or state. Capitalists sought out low-cost and high-efficiency locations and could slip port when the logic of the market pointed elsewhere. MNCs were sometimes particularly difficult to pin down. Although almost all MNCs remained tied to headquarters, markets, and regulators in the United States, Europe, or Japan, all states had to work harder to create the setting for domestic and foreign investors. Above all, state managers were expected by private and foreign capitalists to provide the right macroeconomic conditions for investment: law and order, low taxes, clear regulatory codes, secure property rights, a sound financial sector, reasonably free markets, a regime of tariffs, stable and properly valued currencies, and an educated labor force.[5]

The state and the market could go hand in hand, but only if the state knew what to do. The way states responded to the needs of the market constituted, as Deanne Julius observed, part of the "strategic assets (or liabilities) that create a firm's competitive edge": all governments had to upgrade their technical expertise in the ways of the market.[6] The problems facing less developed countries were particularly acute. Almost all less developed states had a mountain of reform to contemplate because they had been so committed to state-led industrialization and import-substitution strategies that were no longer viable. To develop, borders had to be opened, and less developed states had to find some way of managing the tidal wave of information and commercial exchange that inevitably followed. Parts of the world that had structural weaknesses, were not geared to global markets, or could not easily assimilate foreign business operations were unlikely to attract economic activity. Countries that raised too much tax in order to support systems of welfare and subsidies were also at a real disadvantage.

The Expansion of Western Hegemony
Through the Institutions of Global Governance

The big Western states had the knowledge, capabilities, collective organization, and credibility to shape the emerging economic context and to be players in the networks of the new globalization. Western states adapted successfully, partly by ceding further powers to the Western-created multilateral institutions that were capable of reaching across global markets. The world economy was supervised through the IMF, WTO, Group of Seven, North American Free Trade Association (NAFTA), and the European Union (EU), which were not neutral vessels of international bargaining but were tilted in favor of the powerful.

Multilateral governance made rules and practices in the world economy more transparent than they had ever been before. Global institutions monitored behavior against rules directly but, just as important, created systemwide moods and inclinations that quietly shaped understandings about economic principles and practices in the world economy.

Less developed states had great problems in understanding and responding to the new globalization. A number of organizations were established in the less developed world, such as the Group of 15 and the Group of 77, but the Organization of Petroleum Exporting Countries (OPEC) remained the only really significant body of coordination for the non-Western world.[7] In fact, less developed states were largely the subjects of Western-created multilateral institutions.

Growing indebtedness was one of the principal forces driving global integration under Western terms. The prospect of defaulting on foreign debts put developing countries in the hands of the IMF and World Bank. The IMF's ability to organize loans to countries where options were drying up was a powerful tool. In the 1980s, the IMF and World Bank embraced a certain mission creep, as they turned their hand to designing packages of structural reforms aimed at rescuing the struggling, and consulting with others about how best to engage with the global economy.[8] The IMF and World Bank became missionaries and took the liberal orthodoxy into places where Western states could not go.

The structural adjustment programs (SAPs) of the IMF in the 1980s took their lead from the neoliberal example of the Thatcher-Reagan revolution. The neoliberal orthodoxy meant getting government budgets into balance by cutting spending and improving tax collection, followed by implementing monetary and foreign exchange policies designed to bring down inflation. States were encouraged to deregulate markets, reduce external trade barriers, and encourage private investment as a prelude to exporting their way out of trouble. The vulgar advocacy of market forces by the IMF and the World Bank was tempered in the 1990s, and states were often given a bit more leeway in adjusting, but adjust they must. States were expected to converge on the liberal model, and the errant would simply be left behind in a zone of failure, indebtedness, and marginalization. The overly authoritarian, arbitrary, taxing, and introverted need not apply.

The further liberalization of international trade was another key manifestation of the new globalization. The General Agreement on Tariffs and Trade (GATT) was the intergovernmental forum through which the rules of trade had been liberalized since 1947. The trade regime had very gradually lowered tariffs, eased trade quotas and other restrictive practices, and reduced the levels of unfair state subsidies. The West's move to widen and deepen global trade put GATT center stage. The Uruguay Round (1986–1994) of GATT negotiations came to its final act in December 1993, with agreement to formalize GATT in a new multilateral body, the WTO.[9] It came into existence on 1 January 1995, with a structure of functional committees, a permanent staff of economists and technicians, and a charter that gave it the power to monitor world trade, settle disputes, and enforce the rules. WTO surveillance was to identify any back-peddling toward protectionism and was authorized to redress or penalize improper practices.

The kind of import-substitution strategies that could be found all over the less developed world were ruled out by the WTO. The philosophy was clear: hiding industries behind barriers merely made them inefficient, and although the blast of foreign competition might be painful, it was the only way of making real progress. Important new areas were also covered by WTO monitoring, including agriculture, trade-related property rights (TRIPS), and trade-related investment measures (TRIMS).[10] The move into intellectual property and finance was particularly significant because they were the levers of control in the new globalization. Developed countries were clearly determined to protect their inventions and trademarks everywhere while breaking open the financial systems of other countries. Within a decade, all signatories were to have fully implemented WTO rules.

The WTO represented something new: it moved trade, agriculture, services, investment, and intellectual property rights from the realm of international mediation into that of global governance. The agreement was to be policed. The WTO was also involved in monitoring nonsignatory states and in inclining them to sign up on preexisting terms. Notwithstanding claims to the contrary, the WTO implied a ceding of sovereignty for all states involved. For the most powerful, the exchange of sovereignty for economic benefits was planned. For the less developed, the benefits of membership were often less clear.

The WTO was set to accelerate the new globalization by making the global rules on trade intrusive, transparent, and enforceable. The organization had another hegemonic function in that when states signed up, they were signifying their positive consent to the terms of the global economic order and, by implication, were rejecting the alternatives. States might haggle about the specifics of trade, but once they had become WTO members, they were tied to the principle of an open trading system. The carrot for this consent was full membership in a club that was widely believed to be a prerequisite for a prosperous future. Benefits from increased trade and greater foreign direct investment (FDI) were thought to be associated with WTO membership. With a few exceptions, to be outside the WTO was to be marginalized in both in global economic practice and in the global economic debates.

The internalization of structural adjustment as inevitable fact and vital imperative was an achievement of some importance for those forging the new globalization, not least because it was something of a self-fulfilling prophecy. For the forces of globalism, Linda Weiss argued, it was important to show that

> the political geography of nation-states, and with it the territorial principle, is being outflanked by the economic geography of capital flows, that national forms of governance are thus swiftly becoming outdated and redundant, and that the task of intellectual analysis is to prepare the ground for political and policy transformation to better adapt to the new geo-economic reality.[11]

Whether the less developed had no option but to join the WTO was debatable. Only the most liberal and competitive countries could really get the most out of the organization. Nevertheless, by the 1990s, most political and economic elites around the world were convinced that being a part of the new globalization was absolutely vital. Indeed, non-Western states were lining up to jump into the institutions of global governance, sometimes without a clear understanding of what they were really doing and why. Muslim states were among those that joined the line. Morocco, Kuwait, Bahrain, and Pakistan were signatories of the WTO. Tunisia, Egypt, Turkey, Qatar, and the United Arab Emirates (UAE) had been members of GATT and were on a fast track to WTO membership.[12] Oman joined in autumn 2000. Saudi Arabia wanted to join. Iran had expressed an interest in joining from the mid-1990s, but the United States vetoed its application in May 2001, even though Iran had been supported by a number of other developing countries, including Egypt.[13]

For the vast majority of developing countries, bringing their economies into line with WTO rules was bound to involve a difficult and prolonged reform process, and achieving full membership was likely to take many years. Developing countries were supposed to have ten years to come into compliance. Even though most Muslim states had reservations, few felt that they could be left out of the club. Amid the stampede to join, though, there were real compatibility issues, and it was unclear whether open markets were an optimal course for some Muslim countries.

The loss of control in the home market that WTO membership implied was only really worth contemplating if it could be offset by increased performance in export markets. Compared to its emerging-country competitors in Asia, especially India and China, the business and labor of the Muslim world did not look particularly competitive, although in Morocco, Egypt, Turkey, Iran, Pakistan, and Indonesia, the potential was clearly there. The blast of competition could mean company failures, job losses, inflows of foreign goods, and more foreign ownership. In fact, neither Western countries nor Asian tigers had developed under free market conditions, but rather under public-private partnerships and protected markets. The new liberal market model was, as George Joffé noted, "completely experimental."[14]

The Inherent Instability of Globalizing Capitalism

The tide of liberal capitalism was bound to lead to all sorts of problems for less developed states, but two categories of trouble stood out. First, liberalization threatened political and economic destabilization wherever it was introduced. Easing controls on foreign trade, foreign exchange, pricing, and the private sector almost universally led to a burst of consumption and inflation, followed by worsening balances of trade and indebtedness, then a real or de facto devaluation in the value of the local currency, and finally a further stoking of inflationary pressures. Along with the cuts in public spending required by structural adjustment, the debt-devaluation-inflation cycle put people out of work and undermined standards of living. Economic instability was bound to have political side effects. Second, embracing the market also meant opening cultural borders. The cultural implications of global engagement were many, but they included more contact with foreigners through business and tourism, more pressure to adopt secular ideas and market principles in society, and greater immersion in the products and images of global capitalism, many of which were explicitly of Western origin.

The common problems faced by developing countries in the globalizing economy were brought into sharp focus by the Asian economic crisis in 1997–1998. Speculative business activity, poor regulation, and high indebtedness had seriously undermined business confidence and led to a collapse of local currencies. In South Korea, the Philippines, Thailand, Malaysia, Indonesia, and other countries, there was a major contraction in economic activity and serious falls in the standard of living. The Asian crisis had come in the wake of pressure from the United States and multilateral institutions for Asian states to reform the crony capitalism that they hosted and open local financial markets. Relaxing controls on banking, the flow of capital, and exchange rates proved particularly destabilizing. The Asian economic crisis subsequently spread to Russia and Latin America and had negative effects around the world, including in the Middle East. Global institutions were powerless to prevent the global economic crisis.

The Asian crisis was initially regarded as a vindication of and victory for those promoting the Anglo-American neoliberal model of capitalism, as against the more corporatist-oligarchic Asian model; the crisis might be a "blessing in disguise" if it led to further economic reform. However, as Richard Higgot and Nicola Phillips have argued, the Asian crisis may ultimately have represented a setback for the liberal orthodoxy, as new "sites of resistance" at a local and regional level questioned the nature and pace of global markets.[15] Liberalization was far from the only culprit for what had happened in Asia and beyond—bad local practices were a major factor—but many of the locals chose to blame liberal orthodoxy, and to take another look at the alternatives. Asians states reaffirmed the role of the state and resumed controls that had been eased, especially over capital movements and foreign exchange trading.

A new mood also seemed apparent in the more flexible approach adopted by the IMF and World Bank after 1997. The neoliberal orthodoxy remained the basic pattern, but the implementation of SAPs was sensitized to local conditions and desires. One thing seemed clear: the purveyors of global capitalism ignored political and social stability at their peril. Both Western and local leaders realized that liberal capitalism was best "embedded" with a social consensus that included a degree of economic planning, concern for the welfare of the population, and poverty alleviation—as it had been in the West. The so-called Washington consensus of the neoliberal orthodoxy was supplemented by the thinking of a "post–Washington consensus," which sought to incorporate the issues of justice, equity, welfare, development, and culture.[16]

The Anglo-American neoliberalism shaping the global economy seemed a bit less triumphant after the Asian crisis. A new discourse that referred to social and democratic issues got firmly under way. Certainly, any convergence on the Anglo-American model was put back in 1997–1998, although for how long remained to be seen. The West wanted open markets, and it would continue to directly and indirectly influence the ongoing contributions being made by local capitalisms to the global whole. Living on the same planet as Anglo-American capitalism tended to put a competitive imperative in place. Crony capitalisms could not compete. Notwithstanding the post–Washington consensus discourse, most of the world's capitalisms needed to make their states more efficient and introduce some degree of market liberalization. For the time being, though, it was clear that the world would continue to harbor a number of different models of capitalism.

To the extent that local preferences could take a distinctive path in the global economy, much depended on the abilities of local states and peoples. The locals needed an alternative system with a viable degree of efficiency, but they also had to be clear about what they actually wanted to run alongside capitalism. Muslim countries were some way behind in the liberalization game, but Muslims had long asked themselves how far they could go in engaging with the West and its economics. The big question for Muslims was whether Islamic values provided the basis for an alternative capitalism that could successfully meet the imperatives of the new globalization. Across the Muslim world, Islamic thinkers were pondering the problem, but an authoritative Islamic economic model was yet to emerge. In fact, the way most Muslims met the new globalization was in ad hoc increments of experience and policymaking. The experience was varied, and the results were not entirely satisfactory.

Economic Reform and
Instability in Muslim Countries

The problems that the Muslim world faced in engaging with the global economy looked particularly stark. In the 1980s, an economic crisis precipitated by falling oil prices pushed most Middle East and North African states toward economic reform. The non-oil economy was dependent on the oil sector for growth. In the first instance, states unloaded public obligations in order to conserve scarce resources. In Egypt, Jordan, Morocco, Iraq, Syria, and Tunisia, there were privatization programs. A fundamental break with the state's economic domination was not made, though, and the principal result of reform was to promote a kind of illiberal public-private crony capitalism. The economics of crony capitalism were often based on political and social criteria rather than market principles; business ties were often cemented with marriage alliances, and who made profits was determined by the decisions of state regulators. Asia had had a similar model of capitalism, although much more successful. Fundamental economic reform could only really stem from fundamental political and social reforms.

Egypt

A significant moment for economic reform came in 1991, when Egypt was forced to turn to the IMF for assistance with its budget deficit and spiraling external debts amounting to over 90 percent of GDP. The Mubarak government took on a full-blown SAP: fiscal balancing in the form of a sales tax and income tax reform; cuts in public spending; reduction of subsidies on energy and food; the pegging of the Egyptian pound to the U.S. dollar; and further privatization and market deregulation.[17] In fact, IMF-inspired reforms in Egypt must be counted as one of the IMF's successes. The budget deficit fell to less than 1 percent of GDP, and inflation fell to only around 4–5 percent per annum.[18]

The Egyptian government pressed on, and scores of state companies were partly or wholly sold into the private sector. The financial sector was reformed, too, although capital controls remained much firmer than had been the case in Asia. The Egyptian stock market was revived in 1996 as public companies were put up for sale to private investors. Plans were eventually put in place to privatize four public sector commercial banks. As elsewhere in the Middle East, public-private partnerships were a favored method of upgrading the public power and telecommunications infrastructure, and there were successful ventures in these advanced sectors that included the involvement of major foreign companies.[19] The Egyptian economy was growing, and the state was able to begin paying its bills.

Keeping the reforms on track was always going to be a struggle in Egypt. Debts and deficits constantly stalked Egyptian policymakers. Heavy public investment and a significant downturn in the economy from early 1999 saw sharply rising deficits, with the budget deficit rising fourfold to over 4 percent of GDP in 1998–1999, and the balance of payment deficit going up to $3.5 billion.[20] Increasing indebtedness and a devaluation of the Egyptian pound—pegging to the dollar could not be sustained—soon followed, leading to uncertainty about Egypt's exchange rate policy and a loss of business confidence. Reforms were no panacea because the task of development was so huge and Egypt was particularly vulnerable to outside economic shocks. The Asian economic crisis of 1997 and the fall in oil prices in 1998–1999 set back the progress made.

A psychological jump was made in Egypt, but acceptance of the market was, as Ray Hinnebusch observed, as much one of pragmatism as of conviction.[21] Senior cabinet ministers disagreed about the need for reforms and their pace, although Mubarak's resolve to press on was seemingly reaffirmed by a significant cabinet reshuffle in 1998. It made Privatization Minister Atef Obeid the prime minister, left Youssef Boutros Ghali as economy and foreign trade minister, and removed a number of long-serving ministers thought to be less than enthusiastic about the whole reform process.[22] For the bureaucrats and managers of public companies, too, a more competitive environment was threatening. The bureaucratic opposition did not have to look far to find a constituency. Reform put industrial and agricultural workers under pressure, as well as threatening what living the urban poor were able to eke out. Cuts in subsidies for basic goods and services were a potential catalyst for trouble, and the regime was mindful of past experiences with rioting. Fears about bureaucratic resistance and social protest slowed the momentum for reform. The Egyptian government shied away from rigid IMF timetables, and Mubarak was often given to openly castigating the organization.

Algeria

The problem of structural adjustment bringing with it austerity and political instability was repeated across the Middle East, sometimes with even more dramatic consequences. Civil disorder was sparked in a number of places, often by cuts in subsidies, notably in Morocco in 1984, Tunisia in 1984, and Jordan in 1989 and 1996. The worst breakdown of reform came in Algeria. Following serious urban rioting in October 1988, President Chadli Benjedid initiated radical reforms. Benjedid recognized the need for concurrent political changes to support economic restructuring, but this loosening allowed the outbreak of explosive social frustrations that were seized upon by militant Islamists. Before the regime could do anything about turning the economy around, Algeria was spiraling off toward civil war. The reform process continued after the start of the civil war in 1992, with IMF assistance after 1994, but it could come to nothing as long as there was such civil disorder.

Iraq

Events in the Gulf were also instructive of the potential for trouble following structural adjustment in highly authoritarian systems. In Iraq, the failure of economic reform following the end of the Iran-Iraq War in 1988 was one of the principal reasons Saddam Hussein took the road to the invasion of Kuwait in August 1990. The lifting of trading restrictions and price controls had quickly led to the vicious cycle of debt-devaluation-inflation. A few Iraqis got rich, but most got poorer as the buying power of the average Iraqi plummeted. Neither blatant threats against businesspeople nor the reintroduction of price controls in April 1989 could bring the problems of inflation and capital outflow under control. The subsequent falls in oil prices left the regime feeling the pressure even more keenly. Saddam was not prepared to wait and see whether conventional techniques could rescue the Iraqi economy and moved to pursue economic policy by other means. Of course, Saddam's violent economics was a spectacular failure, and Iraq was to be completely knocked out of both the global and regional economies.

Iran

In Iran, a command economy had emerged from the Islamic revolution of 1978–1979. Oil, banking, and foreign trade came under state control. The payment of interest was made illegal. Foreign companies were banished. A raft of business-unfriendly laws were passed. Great numbers of companies were nationalized or absorbed by quasi-state Islamic foundations known as *bonyads*. The *bonyads,* as Anoushiravan Ehteshami observed, made the clerical establishment more than just another political group; it also made them a powerful socioeconomic class, which entrenched their power more deeply in society.[23] Patron-client reciprocities were the basis of what market relations existed in Iran. Thus, when economic reform was initiated at the end of the 1980s, it was bound to run into the socioeconomic position of the religious bureaucracy and their dependent associates in the private sector.

The election of Hashemi Rafsanjani as president in 1989 marked a move toward private sector capitalism, although Rafsanjani was far from a free marketer. Not all ran smoothly. A modest relaxation of trading restrictions led to a burst of consumer imports that left Iran carrying significant foreign debts for the first time. Rafsanjani also initiated a five-year plan that looked forward to easing regulations, privatizing public concerns, cutting subsidies, and even attracting foreign capital, notably to a number of free trade zones in the Gulf. Doing something about the multitiered exchange rate by devaluing the Iranian riyal (IR) was also a priority, although it raised the prices of imported goods and created other problems. Speculative foreign exchange trading became rife. With privileged access to foreign exchange, the *bonyad*s were also reluctant to see a unified rate that reduced their scope for trading between tiers. The tiers remained, but most Iranians had to put up with a massive devaluation of the riyal, from an official fixed rate of 72 riyals to the dollar in the 1980s to a floating rate of 9,400 riyals to the dollar by mid-1999.[24] Devaluation meant shortages of foreign goods, an inflation rate of over 50 percent, and an ingrained problem with black market trading.

The reform process in Iran was underlined by the election of Mohammad Khatami as president in May 1997, amid great hope for further reform and economic improvement. Khatami did not have the kind of personal links to patron-client capitalism that Rafsanjani had, and so the reforms he could envisage were potentially more radical. The problem was that no one really knew how to go about transforming the flagging economy. Further tax reforms, subsidy cuts, privatization, and trade deregulation—with a view toward an application to the WTO— were on Khatami's agenda in principle, but the policy specifics were slow to emerge.

Entrenched interests blocked the way to further reforms. Serious levels of resistance to privatization and deregulation could be found in the cabinet, parliament, judiciary, and bureaucracy. Offsetting his desire to initiate reform were Khatami's sensitivity to rising unemployment and mindfulness of his commitment to social justice. Most Iranians would take years to benefit from any prosperity that a revived private sector could produce. Rafsanjani's efforts to reduce subsidies in the mid-1990s had led to widespread rioting across Iran's major cities in the spring of 1996, and Khatami was reluctant to follow this lead.

Even if the politics had been easier for Khatami, the task facing him was enormous. With over 70 percent of the economy under state control and many state concerns reportedly working at less than 50 percent of capacity, the implications of structural adjustment were alarming. The entire Iranian economy was a massive loss-making concern, with state industries absorbing up to two-thirds of Iranian government spending. To initiate real privatization reform was bound to create serious unemployment in the midst of a desperate situation in which the unemployment rate was already over 20 percent. Iran needed to create 800,000 new jobs each year just to employ the young people entering the job market. Privatization also ran into legislation passed by the Majlis (the

Iranian parliament) in 1994 that gave "deprived groups," such as families of the war dead and injured veterans, special rights to hold shares in public companies that were privatized.

With privatization seemingly dead in the water, it was left to the existing private sector to provide growth, but here too there were real political restraints. The Islamic revolution was basically hostile to large private capitalists and foreign interests as inherently corrupting. The very pursuit of profit by an independent private sector was regarded as "profiteering" and "corruption" in parts of the revolutionary establishment, and there were frequent clampdowns, with long terms of imprisonment and even threats of the death sentence, for those considered "profiteers" or "parasites." The private and foreign sectors were hampered by many restrictions, including high import tariffs, inflexible labor laws, limits on the movement of capital, and an uncertain legal framework. Moreover, the state's monopoly on banking was enshrined in the constitution, and the concession enabling private banks to operate in the offshore free trade zones fell short of what was needed. Foreign investors could now own businesses in Iran but were barred from repatriating profits unless they were earned by exports. Other than in the oil sector, there was really very little point in investing in Iran.

The IMF itself was advising the Iranian government, and IMF-style reforms were on Khatami's agenda, but actually turning ideas into practice was seemingly beyond the grasp of his government. In the first Khatami government, there was too much opposition, and the will to take on the really big issues was lacking. As with other oil exporters, it seemed more likely that rising oil prices would rescue the economy from the doldrums than any proactive reform process. With oil revenues rising significantly in 1999–2000 to account for $11.4 billion of Iran's $14 billion of export revenues, there seemed little chance that non-oil exports could pay the bills any time soon. Oil encouraged the government to believe that the most disruptive reforms might be avoided because one day there would be light at the end of the tunnel. Until that day arrived, Iran would have to scrape along as a chronic underachiever.

The Gulf States

On the other side of the Gulf, the oil-rich Gulf monarchies were insulated from many of the pressures to get on with economic reform, although a drop in oil receipts following the mid-1980s had led to a slowdown. GDP dropped sharply, and debts and deficits appeared.

Nevertheless, the impetus for reform in the Gulf States was less IMF- and World Bank–driven and more WTO-related.[25] Indigenous self-sufficiency in capital meant that the Gulf states did not have to pander to international organizations and foreign investors in the way that most of the developing world did. Crucially, too, all had hard currencies pegged to the U.S. dollar.

Capital gave the Gulf states a great advantage in engaging in global markets. Global companies in arms, oil, construction, power, telecommunications, and financial sectors beat a track to the Gulf because there was money to be made. Gulf banks and investors were also active in Western capital markets and were a significant force in other Muslim countries. Riyadh, Jidda, Kuwait City, Abu Dhabi, and Dubai were conduits of the global economy in a way that no other Middle Eastern cities could match, and that perhaps only Kuala Lumpur could parallel in the Muslim world. It was sometimes said that the likes of Kuwait and the UAE were no more than an oil well with a flag, but in truth they had an existence in the networks and cyberspace of global capitalism as great as any state in the Muslim world.

The Gulf states could play in some global markets, but they did not have anything like open economies. The Gulf states had always been loath, Roger Owen observed, to allow foreigners positions of control, nor did they want to subject themselves to international standards of transparency and accountability.[26] The state remained the principal force in all the Gulf economies, and markets were organized on the basis of public-private patron-client relations. An extensive system of state subsidies and welfare supported the activities of Gulf businesspeople. Foreign participation was tightly controlled by means of restrictive laws, licensing rules, and import/export controls and tariffs. Equity partnerships with foreign interests in the oil, power, and communications sectors were not allowed. The ownership of land was confined to Gulf citizens. Many foreigners worked in the Gulf, but casual travel and tourism were difficult. Access to foreign media and the Internet was controlled. International copyrights and patents were not fully enforced. In short, the Gulf markets were difficult to penetrate, and there were real limitations on what could be traded successfully. Compared to Asian competitors, the Gulf states attracted relatively little foreign direct investment, and most of that was confined to the petrochemical sector.

A reasonable degree of solvency kept the Gulf states out of the way of the IMF and World Bank, but they were being nudged by Western states to do something about reforming their markets. In an address to the American Businessmen of Jidda and the Jidda Chamber of Commerce in March 1997, the counselor to the U.S. Department of Commerce, Jan Kalicki, argued that the Gulf states should

> undertake the economic reforms necessary to free the private sector, to attract private foreign investment and technology, and to diversify and expand the economies of this region. Waiting to make necessary reforms will only make them more painful in the future. The Gulf countries should open their economies further to private investment. Let the investors decide for themselves how to negotiate and structure their businesses. Give them the freedom to expand and develop transportation, infrastructure, telecommunications, energy resources and other industries. Provide greater protection to intellectual property rights and thereby attract the technologies that create more and higher paying jobs. Further liberalize your commercial laws to allow your industry and consumers greater access to diverse products and services. . . . Governments in other parts of the world have realized this and have changed or are changing their business environment to attract foreign investment and technology. Frankly, this region is behind at the moment. Only three percent of the world's investment reaches the countries of the Middle East and North Africa. But the countries of the region do not have to remain behind—and cannot remain behind—if they are to be stable and prosperous.[27]

Most Gulf rulers accepted the idea that there might be benefits to making their economies more dynamic. Oil money alone was unlikely to be enough to meet the future demands of fast-growing populations: Saudi Arabia, for instance, reportedly needed to create over 100,000 new jobs a year just to employ the Saudi males entering the labor force.[28] The rulers of the Gulf also wanted their countries to operate at the higher-level positions of the global economy and be strong in advanced industrial, financial, and technological sectors. The Gulf states signaled their aspirations in their membership in or their applications to the WTO. Membership required privatizing state entities, reforming the tax structure, opening local financial markets, redrafting business regulations, increasing official and legal transparency, and tightening up rules on the enforcement of patents and copyrights. WTO membership also meant that the Gulf states could not go on discriminating against foreigners in almost every aspect of ownership and business operations.

A number of the Gulf states, notably Oman, went further than others in opening their economies. Even in Saudi Arabia, proposals granting foreigners the right to own property and to control certain local joint ventures in the kingdom came onto the legislative agenda.[29] Many sectors of the Saudi economy, though, would remain beyond the bounds of full foreign ownership; as of 2001, the "negative list" included oil exploration, drilling and production, insurance, real estate, investment in Mecca and Medina, telecommunications, fishing, education, sea and air transportation, television, radio, electricity distribution, health, defense-related industries, and publishing.[30] The Saudi state would only start giving up some of these sectors when the pressure from foreign states and companies, the requirements of the WTO, and, most important, local interests inclined them to do so.

Economic reforms were slow in coming in the Gulf states, but significant changes had been initiated or were under consideration by the end of the 1990s. Subsidies for water, electricity, and oil were trimmed or frozen across the Gulf. Privatizations were relatively few, but falling oil prices in 1998–1999 and the prospect of more debt—the Saudi budget deficit rose to some 10 percent of GDP—acted as a particular stimulus to get going. Across the Gulf, there were moves to privatize or to prepare markets and companies for it, especially in the power generation, transportation, and telecom sectors.[31] The UAE and Qatar led the way to markets and fiscal reforms, but the others gradually followed. In Saudi Arabia, following King Fahd's illness since 1996, the increasing influence of Crown Prince Abdullah appeared to have brought a new desire to modernize the terms of doing private business in the kingdom and make it a friendlier place for both Saudi and foreign investors. The benefits of reform could be great; an enormous quantity of Saudi wealth alone, reportedly up to $400 billion, was invested abroad.[32]

The Gulf states were potentially dynamic economies that might one day operate at the higher levels of the global economy, but much was still to be done if the possibilities were to be realized. Structural adjustment could only really be successful if it was introduced in association with advances in human, technological, and managerial capabilities. The non-oil private sector was the key to real progress, but the sector needed to be more innovative and competitive in the Gulf and beyond. Liberalization might work to gear up the local private sector, but the states and companies of the Gulf were apt to be reluctant reformers and were often better at talking about reform than actually delivering it. Real change would certainly require a cultural transformation, but the Gulf States were inherently defensive places, and almost everyone was wary about foreign influences. Whether the Gulf States had the will to go on with economic reform past the upturn in oil prices in 2000–2001 remained to be seen.

Islam and the Culture of the Market

The tension between local cultures and Western modernity has been the principal cultural dynamic across the world at least since the eighteenth century. In the age of twentieth-century modernization, Muslim political elites sometimes turned their backs on Islam and embraced the nation-state in association with ethnic nationalism and socialism. As in Europe, religion was de-politicized and privatized.

Modernity imposed itself on the lives of ordinary Muslims, as older and simpler landscapes—of the desert, the mud brick house, the palm, and the camel—faded everywhere.[33] Muslim cultures absorbed the effects of modern bureaucracy, military organization, and education, as well as foreign travel, railways, factories, wage labor, the clock, major road networks and motor vehicles, imported consumer goods, telephones, television, high-rise urban dwellings, and the nuclear family. Migration and urbanization often reduced the influence of the extended families, tribes, and village neighborhoods, and in a few places women emerged from behind their veils into public life. For individuals, breaking out of traditional structures was now possible, although doing so often only meant more formal and impersonal forms of subjugation. The traditional totalitarianism of village life was replaced by the likes of the Baath Party. Only a few enclaves of the premodern world survived in the more remote regions of the Muslim world.

By the last quarter of the twentieth century, then, almost all Muslim societies had already experienced enormous social and cultural changes. In many ways, late-twentieth-century globalization merely deepened and broadened things that had already arrived in the age of modernization. Modernization and the new globalization ran into each other, and it was sometimes difficult to distinguish between the two, but the new globalization did bring two major new developments.

First, there was heightened pressure to absorb idealized market economics. The West itself had never had free markets, but that did not stop it from privileging market principles through the global marketplace, multilateral institutions, and SAPs. The move to privatization and market reforms by many Muslim states also implied a greater submission to market principles. Marketization was bound to change the way Muslim societies were run, not least because it was liable to contradict basic Islamic understandings about the preeminence of the community in economics. Bringing market theory and Islamic principles together was not straightforward, and the halfway house often evident in the Muslim world was not an entirely satisfactory outcome. Second, the cultural implications of engaging with global markets were also immense, although the impact of cosmopolitan consumer culture on local identities is often difficult to pin down. Late-twentieth-century globalization threatened a level of everyday cultural penetration that had not really been faced by Muslim societies during modernization until that time.

Believing in the values and practices of markets is a profound business. The ideology of market economics postulated the idea, John Brohman reflected, of *Homo economicus:* of a rational economic person who behaved according to the natural logic of the market, based on competition and self-interest in a world of scarce resources and unlimited desires.[34] The practice of the market would eventually realize *Homo economicus* through the mechanism of profit and loss. Economic science reduced all other motives to a secondary status. Brohman noted that

> *homo economicus* becomes a creature solely of the marketplace, devoid of history, culture, and social and political relations. Moreover, markets are assumed to react similarly everywhere—as if non-market mechanisms had no bearing on market outcomes. The sphere of market exchange is abstracted from the realm of production and relations of power. In the end, an ideological conception of the market is offered as a substitute for particular, historically constituted markets in different countries.[35]

Homo economicus did not care about *Homo Islamicus* or any other sociocultural being, other than to point out that they were a distortion of the rational order. In a system of market economics, *Homo economicus* must be freed from restrictive or irrelevant social practices in order to get on with the business of generating "utility." Within liberal societies, Mary Ann Tétreault observed, the counting of utility was done in profits and votes rather than in the currency of duty, community, or godliness.[36]

In market theory, market relations were based on reciprocal self-interest and did not embody the kind of hierarchical patron-client rights and obligations that could be found in many nonmarket systems of exchange. The relative absence of restraints from the state and from social hierarchies was also needed for efficient market relations. Although no Western society had ever quite lived up to the full implications of its economic science, the Thatcher-Reagan capitalist revival had made *Homo economicus* a hero again. Materialism and individualism were at the heart of Western civilization, Akbar S. Ahmed argued, and even though the "sheer drive" for the material produced dynamic societies, it also meant a moral bankruptcy that Muslims must avoid.[37] For Ahmed, the market in the West ran into places that should be reserved for moral philosophy. *Homo economicus* was secular, materialistic, and ultimately on his or her own.

Muslims had long had markets, but Islam had never theorized economics as a value-free science. From the standpoint of Western economics, "Islamic economics" was hardly economics at all. Islamic economics was not an alternative to Western theory, Rodney Wilson argued; it had more to do with moral justification than economic explanation.[38] Islam had something to say about ownership, production, and distribution in markets, but economics alone was not enough for Islamic thinkers. Markets might describe a number of natural conditions facing humanity—self-interest and the laws of supply and demand—but they did not help Muslims live according to God's will. Muslim thinking and practice reflected the Islamic concerns for social justice *(adalah),* as well as for living up to a number of specific quranic injunctions on such things as *zakat* (a tax levied for the poor) and the prohibition on unearned wealth *(riba),* preventing the practices of interest payments and insurance.

For Islamic thinkers, humanity had to be very circumspect about the pure pursuit of wealth because God owned everything and merely devolved the stewardship of the earth's resources to humans; thus, human motives were more important than economic outcomes. Economics was not an end in itself, but the means to live a more virtuous life as outlined by Islam. Furthermore, God wanted everyone's needs to be met, and so unused accumulations of capital and "hoarded" goods were moral wrongs. Private ownership and markets were only legitimate as long as they served God's will and the interests of the whole Islamic community.

The capitalist's accumulation of capital had historically been regarded with suspicion in the Muslim world, and accumulations of capital were always vulnerable to punitive taxation. Islamic theory tended to have an inherent preference for small and medium-sized businesses rather than the larger corporation. The implications of these Islamic preferences were sometimes manifested in the contemporary world in quite striking ways. Time and time again, especially when times were tough, Muslim governments were inclined to accuse businesspeople of criminal corruption or of plotting economic sabotage. In some places, notably Iran and Pakistan, long terms of imprisonment and even the death penalty hung over those judged to be exceeding the bounds of "fair" prices and profits. Even in the most developed of Muslim countries, Malaysia, Prime Minister Mahathir Muhammad could not help threatening to throw businesspeople and foreign exchange traders into jail when things got tough during the Asian financial crisis of 1997.

The great problem with sustaining an economic system embodying Islamic preferences and morality is competitiveness. Strangely, since Islam stresses the importance of hard work and risk taking, Muslim theorists and practitioners have neglected to do much thinking about competitiveness. Muslim markets have always been characterized by significant levels of state control and patron-client social arrangements. The built-in opposition to the private MNC has clear implications for competitiveness at the global level of operations. Moreover, even today, most business decisions made by Muslims on behalf of states or private concerns are not arrived at on the basis of market principles but are made according to political and social relationships. In short, Muslims have a normative barrier to cross if they are to compete in fair and open markets.

To the extent that Muslims absorbed foreign economics in most of the twentieth century, it was socialism that they absorbed. The progressive Arab states of the 1950s and 1960s were socialist or state capitalist. In the conservative Gulf states, the private sector played a part, but it was the state that controlled the commanding heights of the economy and ensured that oil, minerals, and water resources were publicly owned and distributed. The Iranian Revolution had also produced a state-led economics. The Islamic Republic of Iran spent much of its early years nationalizing and regulating its economy according to the demands of social justice. The levels of state intervention went well beyond the enforcement of such things as *zakat* and *riba*. Islam was used to rationalize the overarching power of the Islamic state to run major industries, restrict accumulations of private wealth, support ordinary people with welfare, promote self-sufficiency, and prevent foreign influences in the community. The economic reforms of the 1990s represented a questioning of the Islamic model that the revolution had proposed.

Islamic economics has struggled to give Muslims a clear philosophy for dealing with the economic pressures on them in the era of globalization. The tradition of making economic decisions according to noneconomic criteria is well established, but the economic preeminence of states and patron-client networks is clearly under challenge from global-level competitors as well as the intersubjective power of the Western hegemony. Meshing Islam with the market remains rather difficult for Muslims to accomplish because an authoritative body of work on Islamic macroeconomics has not really emerged, and until it does, there is little to mesh. Muslims sometimes claimed that Islamic economics was a middle way between capitalism and communism, but whether it represented anything more than a shade of Third Worldist state capitalism was debatable. Of course, it was these kinds of local state capitalisms that the Western hegemony was consigning to the past.

In the meantime, Islamic economics was largely confined to a microeconomic realm that focused on the quranic injunctions about unearned income and how banks and companies can function without providing interest-bearing returns. The preference for profit sharing and cooperative investment solutions is distinctively Islamic, and Islamic banks have carved out a significant role for themselves in the Muslim world and beyond.[39]

The absence of a definitive Islamic economics has had significant consequences. Most Muslim economies were based on a mixture of Islamic and non-Islamic principles. Balancing on two stools was not always satisfactory, if that meant Islamic principles were not fully enforced and free markets were improperly established. Muslim states hosted many private sector activities that were at odds with Islamic ideals. The Gulf states are particularly associated with rentierism.[40] The Muslim world has a number of stock markets that are just as guilty of speculative gambling as those of the Nasdaq, techMARK, and Nouveau Marche. Although some Islamic states like Iran, Saudi Arabia, Sudan, and Pakistan have outlawed interest payments in the domestic economy, many more allow the operation of Western-style banking and use interest rates as a tool of economic policy. All Muslim states have found that they cannot live in the world economy without straining Islamic injunctions. To deposit money in a Western bank is to receive interest.

Most Muslims realized that they needed a compromise between Islam and modern markets, but few knew how a "moral competitiveness" in globalized markets could be forged. Until the solution was found, Muslim states were constantly in danger of falling short of their own Islamic values and were also often uncertain about how best to proceed in practice. In these respects, Iran was something of a paradigm. The Islamic Republic had been resolved to uplift the deprived *(mostazafin)* against the oppressors *(mostakbarin),* but when it came down to specifics, policy was paralyzed by constant disputes between the government, Majlis, and conservative Council of Guardians (a constitutional vetting body of clerics) about the powers of the state and the economic rights of the citizen. The system failed to formulate a balance between the public and private interests. For Grand Ayatollah Ruhollah Khomeini, "economics was for donkeys," and so the authoritative rulings did not come. The establishment of a new supreme body of arbitration, the Council for the Determination of Exigencies *(shura-i mashlahat-i nezam)*, was a way of breaking the institutional deadlock on occasion, but it was very slow in creating a body of consensus. To this day, Iranian political elites have failed to decide how the interests of the Islamic state and its concerns with social justice can be reconciled with the rights of the individual and the realities of existing in a competitive world.

The idea of an Islamic economy, Olivier Roy argued, was largely rhetorical, and the

> failure of the Iranian revolution to transform society chips away at the dream of a purely Islamic economy. . . . The idea of building a modern economy that would function only through the virtue of the economic actors is an illusion. . . . And, in economics as in politics, when virtue doesn't function, its opposite emerges; the abuse of power, speculation and corruption, the banes of Islamized economic systems.[41]

For Roy, Islamism could only really offer public morality, not a superior economic system.

A mixture of uncertainty and pragmatism has characterized the slow move of Muslim countries toward economic liberalization. To the extent that Muslim leaders proposed a reform model, it was to Asia that many looked. The Asian model of state-led capitalism, corporatized markets, and social consensus had certainly worked for Japan, South Korea, Taiwan, Singapore, and Malaysia in the past, although whether it would continue to do so in the future was the subject of some debate. Whether Muslim countries could emulate the Asian takeoff was altogether another question. What seemed clear was that the state would continue to dominate Muslim economics, and it was always reluctant to expose Muslims to the blast of the market. Mixing markets with too many social and moral purposes was liable to put Muslims at a serious competitive disadvantage against the more amoral. All Muslim countries were less competitive than Western ones.

Islam and the Culture of Cosmopolitan Consumerism

The other major development that the new globalization brought to the Muslim world was the sheer ubiquity of Western-style consumer culture. States and societies cannot engage in the world economy without accepting the globalized cosmopolitan consumer culture to some degree or other; it is an absolute prerequisite for doing business in the world in a way that accepting liberal politics is not.

Although it is a mistake to overequate Westernization simply with Western-style consumerism—real Westernization is better viewed as the penetration of liberal politics and economics—forms of consumption and lifestyle cannot be dismissed as mere ephemera. The culture of material satisfaction is what the vast number of people in the less developed world actually perceived Westernization to be. Western goods, trademarks, tastes, and entertainments have a great capacity to crowd out the local alternatives to the point of marginalization. The desire to consume also creates powerful lifestyle aspirations that can really disrupt the social fabric. The trivia of Western-styled consumerism is a cultural battleground.

Globalized consumer culture threatened to reach deep into the Muslim mind amid a myriad of day-to-day aspirations, practices, and experiences. Trade, travel, tourism, television, the Internet, and e-mail linked millions of Muslims to the global society. The big question for Muslims was how far aping Western patterns of consumption and entertainment would lead to the unconscious reproduction of the West in deeper political and social ways. The emergence of global cultural homogeneity was unlikely, but greater cultural synthesis seemed inevitable. Whether global culture threatened to change the essential character of Muslim culture—whether it altered the key totems and practices of cultural identity—was something that Muslims would probably find out only later.

The new technologies played their part in taking globalized modernity into the most isolated regions of the world. The media of globalization—the fax, multichanneled satellite television, and the Internet—conveyed information and entertainment with an unknown immediacy and depth of penetration. The big global news gatherers, producers, and distributors—Cable News Network, National Broadcasting Company, Fox, British Broadcasting Corporation, Reuters, and Agence France-Presse—were Western, and so were their news agendas. Entertainment was also patented in the West and, even if mediated by non-Western broadcasters, conveyed images, values, and dreams associated with the West. Bollywood films, Brazilian soap operas, and game shows and professional sports everywhere promoted the ideals of individualism, consumerism, romantic love and sex, images of youth and female liberation, and sanitized violence.

Technology and its software was a particularly prominent issue in the Islamic Middle East. Bans on satellite dishes might slow access to the global, but the capacity of Middle Easterners to rig dishes was very impressive. In Iran, for instance, a reported 250,000 satellite dishes serving some 2 million Iranians prompted a ban on the import, manufacture, and installation of dishes in late 1994. Iranian leaders recognized that the ban was problematic, though, not only because it was difficult to enforce but also because it denied Iranians advanced communications technology. The Islamic state was not against satellite technology as such, but only against its corrupting content—equated to the "cultural onslaught of colonialists and the arrogant"—although how the goodness of the technology and content could be brought into harmony was far from clear.[42] Satellite television was a case in which Western technology brought Western consumer culture into Muslim homes.

The Internet was also a window into types of information and entertainment that were forbidden in Muslim societies. The Internet and e-mail spread rapidly around the Muslim world. In Egypt, for instance, there were reportedly thirty Internet service providers in 1998, with another ninety waiting for licenses.[43] Islamic governments especially were uneasy about the corrupting possibilities of the Internet, but they simply could not hold back the tide or allow their peoples to be left behind in the information and economic slow lane. The way forward in some places was the difficult task of trying to censor cyberspace. Saudi Arabia, for instance, took a long time coming to the Internet, and the go-ahead was only given in principle in 1997. The kingdom planned to make all local Internet providers go through a supernode that could sift the material. Things would inevitably get past the word searches and the sampling of censors, but few Saudis were likely to want to chance it. In the meantime, thousands of Saudis were reported to be tapping into Internet service providers in freer neighboring states like Bahrain.

The guardians of Muslim society were right to be concerned about the cultural threat of global software, because it was powerful. The bureaucrats of parochial society might try to think up alternative distractions, but they were unlikely to be as entertaining as global providers. In his study of the global-local relationship, *Jihad vs. McWorld*, Benjamin Barber described globalized consumer culture as the product of utterly ubiquitous global companies like Coca-Cola, McDonald's, Levis, Nike, Philip Morris, Disney, AOL-Time Warner, Microsoft, Dreamworks, Mercedes, and Sony.[44] Much of this global company culture was American in origin and aspiration. American culture was often denounced as insubstantial, including by other Western-ers, but it was clearly attractive to people across the world, and its power could be measured in many billions of dollars of annual sales. Western consumerism had also changed the landscapes in which most people lived. Across the world, the shopping mall, sports stadium, cine-ma/entertainment complex, and branded fast-food restaurant had imposed themselves on familiar local settings.

The cultural pressure that McWorld brought with it was rarely planned or purposeful, but, as Barber observed, "the seemingly innocu-ous quest for fun, creativity and profits puts whole cultures in harm's way and undermines autonomy in individuals and nations alike."[45] Global capitalism may have had a friendly face—perhaps that of Ronald McDonald or the Little Mermaid—but it concealed a kind of cultural cannibalism. The cultural synthesis that McWorld forged was sometimes presented as mutually agreed and limited, but as Barber later remarked, "this is a peculiar reciprocity—the reciprocity of the python who swallows the hare: after a week or two of active digestion, the hare is gone and only the python remains."[46] Barber had no doubt that McWorld had, perhaps inadvertently, embarked on a conquest of local cultures, and in the end, it would probably succeed. The goods, tastes, styles, and stories of locals were being absorbed and appropriated by globalized capitalism, and adapted Americanized versions sold every-where as the definitive model.

A globalized culture of consumerism also threatened to disrupt lifestyles and social relations on a deeper level. Global modernity was materialist and secular, and as Bhikhu Parekh observed,

> modern social and political life inevitably encourages a quasi-utilitari-an attitude to morality. When the main concern is to get on in life, to pursue pleasure and promote self-interest, the rigours of moral life are found to be burdens, leading to a tendency to cut moral corners, bend moral principles to the requirements of personal conveniences and legitimise these acts with sophistry.[47]

The kind of social relations underwritten by notions of kinship, place, duty, and God were now vulnerable to the challenge of consumerist individualism and prudential morality. More complex identities were bound to emerge in the global milieu. Elites were the most enthusiastic participants at the global level, but other people were also aware of and interested in it. Most important, consumerism appealed to the aspira-tions of women and youth, or rather to their desire and ability to earn wages and make consumption decisions. The male head of a family might approve of his wife or daughter's pay packet, but he was accepting a benefit that was also transforming his family. The increased ability of women and young people to choose where to work and what to consume challenged existing power relations in all patriarchal societies.

The Battle for Relevance

The Muslim world met global culture with a combination of three responses: imitation, resistance, and synthesis. The combination fostered uncertainty within Muslim societies about the future of culture. Akbar S. Ahmed warned that the myriad of images and experiences that postmodern culture offered were vital and seductive, but they threatened to bewilder Muslims and pick off the religious and social values that made Islam and Muslims what they were.[48] In his book *Orientalism, Postmodernism and Globalism,* Bryan Turner agreed with Ahmed, describing the real threat to Islam:

> At the level of everyday life, the relativization of belief via commodities, travel, tourism and the impact of global TV shakes the bases of faith in the general population. . . . It is social being that determines consciousness and not consciousness that determines social being. In order to understand how a dominant ideology functions, one needs to examine how ideological beliefs and perspectives operate at the everyday level of consumption, production and distribution of beliefs. . . . The erosion of faith through the postmodernization of culture has to be understood in terms of how the diversity of commodities and their global character transform in covert and indirect fashion the everyday beliefs of the mass of the population. It is for this reason that . . . the presence of Western forms of consumerism and hedonism have a far more significant impact on the nature of traditional religious belief, at the level of the village for example, than the intellectual beliefs of religious leaders and other intellectual elites within the church or the Academy.[49]

The real danger that Islam faced was not that Muslims would stand up to oppose their faith but simply that they would lose interest in it for something more congenial.

The tension between global and local culture manifested itself in a battle for relevance amid a myriad of day-to-day experiences in Muslim societies. This battle was one that local cultures had struggled to win everywhere, in the face of McWorld's seductiveness and the power of the political and economic interests behind it. For those Muslims seeking to fend off the global, it was important to show that their cultural totems—the relatively authentic tastes, images, stories, and social practices that they related to themselves—were still relevant to the lives of most people in the community.

The urge to consume global products is as great in the Muslim world as anywhere, but many Muslims are conscious of the dangers. The drift from Islam is yet to come partly because enough Muslims are purposefully telling themselves that Islamic culture is better than global culture. Moreover, Islam and its social institutions continue to have intersubjective power from the top to the bottom of many Muslim societies. Islam dominates civil society with powerful codes of morality and social practice and a strong sense of community centered on prayer and local mosques that do indeed make it relevant to most Muslims. Islam defines what is normal and acceptable behavior across swaths of the Muslim social setting.

Islam's social relevance is often reinforced by Muslim economic systems. Islamic banking is a multibillion-dollar industry. Other Islamic organizations also run health, education, social welfare, and business schemes. Benevolent organizations are often privately run and are supported by Muslim civil society networks. In the more Islamic states, Islam and material interests are often clearly linked. In Iran, with its state subsidies and *bonyad* foundations, the religious establishment remains extremely relevant to the lives of most ordinary Iranians. Where Muslims continue to generate economic relevance, it is much easier to sustain the idea that Islam still has valid things to say. In a world where most Muslims live in a permanent state of economic insecurity, Islam's doctrinal connection to social justice is a powerful rallying point. From a base of social and economic relevance, Islamists continue to viably construct their vision of society.

The other noticeable thing about Islam's relevance is that it is still enforced by more than just persuasive argument and economic incentives. Islamic intersubjectivity sometimes involves fostering the meeting of minds by cracking heads together. For Islamists, Islam could not be allowed to decline into a mere brand or entertainment, competing for a market share of Muslim attention. Islam's grand narrative must be supreme—a monopoly—and many Islamists are willing to use force to control the competition and compel obedience to the faith.

In Islamic states, Islam is enforced by religious police and by groups of men organized around local mosques and Islamic committees. In most Muslim countries, the relevance of Islam is ensured by a kind of archaic totalitarianism, rooted in the patriarchal structures of society at family and community levels and an intolerance of alternative lifestyles among very large numbers of ordinary people. The pious unashamedly remain their brothers' keepers and the guardians of a communitarian ideal that resists the pluralism and individualism of the global culture. In many Muslim neighborhoods, the young woman who prefers not to wear the *hijab* or who breaks the conventions on marriage runs real risks of retribution from her family and neighbors. The student who seeks a more open debate about society, much less one about the Truth, may not only face the coercive state but also the personalized hostility of friends and family. Islam has deep roots in Muslim societies, and McWorld has much to do before it captures the souls of ordinary Muslims.

The social and cultural revolution heralded by the new globalization, then, was tempered in the Muslim world by conscious religious resistance. Yet, for all the resistance, Muslim cultures were undoing cultural synthesis. The patterns of "globalization" were rather complex, with Muslims taking steps forward and steps back in absorbing the global culture. For Mehran Kamrava, most non-Western societies faced a kind of "variable speed" Westernization, with partial reconstructions of identity incrementally moving communities and individuals through change. Kamrava observed that the

> fragmentation of attitudes allows the individual to hold and to practise different values without the debilitating moral and psychological dilemmas of having inconsistent beliefs. Once this fragmentation is accented and the contrast between values grows sharper, there is a tendency to change values completely and to acquire an entirely new frame of reference. Thus the partial change of attitudes gives way to a more complete attitudinal change. The individual is no longer confronted with conflicting values, his or her many beliefs and actions now being underwritten by principles that are consistent and uncontradictory.[50]

The outcome of global synthesis varied from place to place in the Muslim world. Whether Muslims remained "essentially" Islamic was something that only time would tell. Muslims faced stark choices, and finding a viable path for Islam in the global setting would substantially define their future.

The Economic Future of the Muslim World

Global capitalism is devoid of the spiritual and invites the Muslim world to integrate itself with the amoral and the infidel. Muslims have little choice but to come to terms with the market and with the culture of consumerism. In the university departments and Islamic banks of Egypt, Saudi Arabia, and Pakistan, Islamic thinkers have been trying to bring Islam and market capitalism together, but an effective and widely understood means of doing this has yet to be agreed.[51] Muslims will undoubtedly find ways of mixing Islamic culture and market principles, but whether they will be left with a genuinely Islamic economics at the end of the day is a good question. In the end, Fred Halliday perceived, Islamic economics is a deluded idea, presenting yet another Third World populism that will go the same way as its secular antecedents, Nasserism, Peronism, and the Indian Congress Party.[52] There is an alternative to engaging with global capitalism and that is isolation and backwardness. Only time will tell whether such pessimism is warranted.

The actual performance of Muslim economies reflected the problems that they had in modernizing their economic policies. Dependency on oil in the Middle East and North Africa (MENA) remained high, and economic performance was very poor after the sharp downturn in oil prices in 1985. In the decade after 1985, the MENA region was only underperformed by Africa. Other than Malaysia, no Muslim country had really moved toward the levels of economic and technical sophistication necessary to prosper in the global marketplace, although even its high short-term borrowing and exchange rate problems helped precipitate the Asian financial crisis of 1997.

The Arab Gulf states looked modern, but their development was very uneven and their prosperity completely tied to the price of oil. The potential for true global engagement existed in the gateway cities of the Gulf, but real cultural barriers stood in the way of an advanced economy. When information, goods, and services are restricted by authoritarian states, when women cannot fully participate in economic and social life, when temporary foreign workers do the bulk of the work, and when the state remains in control of economic growth, the more advanced stages of economic development cannot take place. The cultural setting in the Gulf states was changing—and in the case of Dubai, the arrival of "Russian capitalists" was bringing in some of the most startling and unpleasant aspects of globalization—but for the most part, cultural adaptation was very restricted. The peoples of the Gulf had yet to decide that they really wanted or needed to be advanced. Higher world oil prices might once again propel the Gulf states into the realm of the superrich, but their development would remain unbalanced.

Elsewhere in the Muslim world, underdevelopment and poverty were pervasive. For those with some oil income, like Algeria and Iran, the state had some capacity, although a diminishing one, to insulate their society from the most disruptive aspects of economic reform. For those without sizable oil reserves, including big states like Egypt, Morocco, and Pakistan, building an economy that was merely capable of keeping up with population growth looked to be a distant prospect. Rising oil prices after 2000 slightly brightened the outlook, but the trickle-down effect of oil wealth was simply not enough to turn economies around, much less get them into the game of global markets on anything like reasonable terms. Furthermore, even as producers of industrial and manufactured goods, Muslim countries struggled to compete with Asia and South America, and their exports of non-oil merchandise were very small elements in their GDP.

The political barriers to economic progress could be found everywhere in the Muslim world. Capitalism can work without democracy, but whether it can work very well in the longer term without a freeing up of society is another matter. Successful capitalism may well require political development in the contemporary world. Asian and South American states had liberalized their politics in the 1980s and 1990s, but Middle Eastern countries remained largely under authoritarian rule, which had inhibited the genesis of complex capitalism: too much capital was employed in public consumption and coercive capabilities, entrepreneurs were overregulated, domestic markets were rigged by entrenched crony capitalists, and labor lacked education, skills, and flexibility. All over the Muslim world, too many entrenched interests remained tied into the rent-seeking practices of monopoly, protectionism, subsidy, fixed exchange rates, and high state spending. The restricted position of women also denied Muslim countries the full benefit of a group of workers and consumers that were vital to economic success elsewhere. In the last analysis, Muslim societies suffer from the intrinsic competitive disadvantage of authoritarian systems: far too few people are genuinely productive, and they have to support far too many who are not.

Making the transition to an open and successful capitalism was going to be difficult. The basic infrastructures of economic development—health, education, transportation, and corporations—were poorly developed. Population growth of up to 3 percent per annum gave economic stagnation the dynamic of a crisis. The crisis had driven many toward structural adjustment, both IMF- and World Bank–supervised and self-taught. The prevailing mood was that globalization was inevitable and economic reform essential, but Muslim states remained wary about fundamental changes. Even if reform led to a more successful private sector, most ordinary Muslims would take years to benefit from any new prosperity. Meanwhile, disrupting the existing state-led and patron-client basis of Muslim economics was bound to leave millions of people with a much more uncertain economic future. Liberal capitalism threatened to disembed many ordinary Muslims from their existing support networks, and quite understandably, many were reluctant to see this happen. Political instability stalked the reform of economic relations, and there was no obvious way around this dilemma. For the foreseeable future, the crises of economic failure and cultural change would rack Muslim societies with political instability.

Notes

1. Halliday, "Globalization and Its Discontents," in *The World at 2000,* 2001, 66.

2. Ayubi, "Withered Socialism or Whether Socialism? The Radical Arab States as Populist-Corporatist Regimes," *Third World Quarterly* 13, no. 1, 1992, 103.

3. Ehteshami and Murphy, "Transformation of the Corporatist State in the Middle East," *Third World Quarterly* 17, no. 4, 1996, 761.

4. See Scholte, "Global Capitalism and the State," *International Affairs* 73, no. 3, July 1997, 427–452.

5. Ibid., 441–442.

6. Julius, "Globalization and Stakeholder Conflicts: A Corporate Perspective," *International Affairs* 73, no. 3, 1997, 468.

7. Scholte, "Global Capitalism and the State," 449; see also Sridharan, "G-15 and South-South Cooperation: Promise and Performance," *Third World Quarterly* 19, no. 3, 1998, 357–373.

8. Thomas, "Where Is the Third World Now?" *Review of International Studies* 25, Special Issue, December 1999, 233.

9. Cameron, "The World Trade Organisation and Globalisation," paper presented at the Annual Conference of the BISA, Southampton, 18–20 December 1995.

10. Wilkin, "New Myths for the South: Globalisation and the Conflict Between Private Power and Freedom," *Third World Quarterly* 17, no. 2, 1996, 235.

11. Weiss, "Globalization and National Governance: Antinomy or Interdependence," *Review of International Studies* 25, Special Issue, December 1999, 59.

12. Charlotte Blum, "The Middle East Adapts to GATT," *Middle East Economic Digest (MEED)* 39, no. 10, 10 March 1995, 2–3.

13. Claire Doole, "U.S. Blocks Iran WTO Application," BBC News Online, World: Middle East, Wednesday, 9 May 2001, http://news.bbc.co.uk/hi/english/world/middle_east/newsid_1320000/1320334.stm.

14. Joffé, "Relations Between the Middle East and the West," *Middle East Journal* 48, no. 2, Spring 1994, 265.

15. Higgot and Phillips, "Challenging Triumphalism and Convergence: The Limits of Global Liberalization in Asia and Latin America," *Review of International Studies* 26, no. 3, July 2000, 359–379.

16. Ibid., 371–373.

17. Hinnebusch, "The Politics of Economic Reform in Egypt," *Third World Quarterly* 14, no. 1, 1993, 161.

18. David Butter, "Reform Effort Needs to Shift Up a Gear," *MEED* 42, no. 23, 5 June 1998, 8.

19. David Butter and Peter Kemp, "Getting There," *MEED* 43, no. 10, 12 March 1999, 2–3.

20. David Butter, "Egypt Gets Rumbled," *MEED* 44, no. 28, 14 July 2000, 4.

21. Hinnebusch, "The Politics of Economic Reform in Egypt," 164.

22. David Butter, "New Impetus for Egypt's Reformers," *MEED* 43, no. 42, 22 October 1999, 2–3.

23. Ehteshami, "Islamic Governance in post-Khomeini Iran," in Abdel Salam Sidahmed and Anourshiravan Ehteshami, eds., *Islamic Fundamentalism*, 1996, 158.

24. Vahe Petrossian, "Hiatus at Half-time," *MEED* 43, no. 30, 30 July 1999, 3.

25. Mahdi, "Responses to Globalization in the Gulf Countries," paper presented at the Conference on Globalisation and the Gulf, 2–4 July 2001, Institute of Arab and Islamic Studies, University of Exeter, 2.

26. Owen, "The Politics of Economic Restructuring," in *State, Power and Politics in the Making of the Modern Middle East,* 2000, 135–136.

27. From an address given by Jan Kalicki (counselor to the U.S. Department of Commerce) to the American Businessmen of Jidda and the Jidda Chamber of Commerce, 5 March 1997. Reproduced in Kalicki, "A Vision for the U.S.-Saudi and U.S.-Gulf Commercial Relationship," *Middle East Policy* 5, no. 2, May 1997, 77.

28. James Gavin, "The Walls Come Down," *MEED* 44, no. 20, 19 May 2000, 4.

29. Tom Everett-Heath, "The Saudi Quickstep," *MEED* 43, no. 44, 26 November 1999, 4.

30. Mahdi, "Responses to Globalization in the Gulf Countries," 11.

31. Peter Kemp, "Hard Times, No Easy Way Out," *MEED* 43, no. 1, 8 January 1999, 2–3.

32. Everett-Heath, "The Saudi Quickstep," 4.

33. See Elmusa, "Faust Without the Devil? The Interplay of Technology and Culture in Saudi Arabia," *Middle East Journal* 51, no. 3, Summer 1997, 345–357.

34. Brohman, "Economism and Critical Silences in Development Studies: A Theoretical Critique of Neoliberalism," *Third World Quarterly* 16, no. 2, 1995, 298.

35. Ibid., 314.

36. Tétreault, "Individualism, Secularism, and Fundamentalism," paper

presented at the Annual Conference of the BRISMES, Birmingham, 5–8 July 1998, 4.

37. See Tomas Gerholm, "Two Muslim Intellectuals in the Postmodern West: Akbar Ahmed and Ziauddin Sardar," in Akbar S. Ahmed and Hastings Donnan, eds., *Islam, Globalization and Postmodernity,* 1994, 198–202.

38. Wilson, "Markets Without Capitalism: An Islamic Economic System?" Paper presented at the BRISMES Annual Lecture, London, 1998.

39. Ibid., 7–8.

40. See Beblawi, "The Rentier State in the Arab World, *Arab Studies Quarterly* 9, no. 4, Fall 1987, 383–398.

41. Roy, "The Islamic Economy: Between Illusions and Rhetoric," in *The Failure of Political Islam,* 1994, 145.

42. From comments made by the rapporteur of the Majlis Commission for Islamic Culture and Guidance, Zadsar, and broadcast on "The Nation's House" (weekly), Voice of the Islamic Republic of Iran Network 1, in Persian, 1200gmt, 18 December 1994. Reproduced in the BBC's *Summary of World Broadcasts (SWB),* MED/2183, 20 December 1992, [5], MED/2–3.

43. David Butter, "Getting Caught Up in the Net," *MEED* 42, no. 26, 26 June 1998, 2–3.

44. Barber, *Jihad vs. McWorld,* 1996.

45. Ibid., 81.

46. Barber, "Disneyfication That Impoverishes Us All," *The Independent,* 29 August 1998.

47. Parekh, "When Religion Meets Politics," *Demos,* no. 11 (Quarterly), 1997, 6.

48. Turner, *Orientalism, Postmodernism and Globalism,* 1994, 12–14.

49. Ibid., 17.

50. See Kamrava, "Social Change," in *Politics and Society in the Developing World,* 2000, 110–111.

51. Roberto Aliboni, "The Islamic Factor in International Economic Co-Operation," in Laura Guazzone, ed., *The Islamist Dilemma,* 1995, 298–299.

52. Halliday, *Islam and the Myth of Confrontation,* 1995, 129.

PART TWO

MUSLIM RESISTANCE AND ADAPTATION IN THE LIBERAL INTERNATIONAL ORDER

5

The Islamic Revolt and the Politics of Paralysis

F ew places have become so associated with political and social instability as the Muslim regions of the Middle East, North Africa, and southwestern Asia. At the end of the twentieth century, the story of the Muslim heartland was one of unfulfilled potential that perhaps can only find parallel in the failure of the Soviet Union. Muslims struggled to make the secular state and its economics work, and the attempt to engage with global capitalism from the 1970s on brought yet another crisis. Most Muslims knew that something had gone horribly wrong with their history, but there was little consensus about cause of the crisis or how to go about putting it right.

Amid the crisis and disillusionment, Islam articulated the one voice that stood out from the malaise. For millions of Muslims, Islam was the alternative to despair. Islamic revivalism had many manifestations, but the most important was the rise of a political Islam that aimed to institute an Islamic state and enforce a conservative social philosophy. Islam has a long history of puritanical revivals, but the Islamic resurgence that took hold of the Muslim world in the 1970s was notable because it was so widespread and lasted for so long. In almost all Muslim societies, resurgent Islam came to dominate the discourse about politics, society, and culture. The new Islamists soon fell into conflict with the established order, but Islam still focused some of the big debates about how Muslim societies should govern themselves and how they should deal with the outside world.

The Islamic phenomenon was not a monolithic one and produced many different experiences across the Muslim world. Political Islam met the conservative Islamic monarchies of Morocco and Saudi Arabia; the limited reformism of Algeria, Egypt, and Tunisia; and the belligerent modernism of the Iraqi and Syrian regimes. What many of the experiences shared, though, was that the rise of political Islam inaugurated a new phase in the Muslim crisis: almost all Muslims were caught between an uninspired authoritarian secular state and an Islamic rebellion that posed more questions than it answered. The standoff between authoritarian state and Islamists dragged on because the state was not so moribund as to prevent it holding a line against the Islamic rebellion. Only in Iran and Sudan did Islamists take the state, and although these cases were important developments, neither solved the modernization crisis. The Muslim world was further crippled. The politics of the Islamic revival were also the politics of paralysis.

The Crisis of Modernization in the Middle East

Pioneered in the West, modernization combines an industrial and technological revolution with a political and social revolution. The revolutions in technology and ideas brought enormous and permanent changes to Muslim societies in the twentieth century. For a time, modernization offered great hope. Muslims were freed from European colonialism following World War II, and many headed toward independence under nationalist and socialist regimes that mobilized the state to engineer a degree of social and economic progress. In important Middle Eastern states, modernity was aggressively pursued with secular ideologies that excluded religious ideas and organizations from positions of political and social authority. Although the Arab state did not sit comfortably with the ideology of pan-Arab nationalism, the territorial state became the vessel of politics and societies. In Turkey, Iran, Egypt, Iraq, Syria, Algeria, and other lesser countries, the secular state seemed to offer the way to a better life and a new degree of independence and prestige in the world.

The model of progress offered by the secular modernizers was to fail. The limitations of the Middle Eastern state were all too apparent. Beset with domestic and international conflicts, secular regimes remained authoritarian and were loath to take the risks involved in real programs of transformation. Muslim countries suffered from the same deficiencies as all state-run economies. Bureaucracies quickly became bloated, corrupt, and incompetent. Bureaucrats were not good at picking economic winners, and they were unable to manage existing projects successfully. The strategy of protectionism and import substitution further undermined economic development in the long run, as investment was misdirected and productive efficiency fell off. With low levels of productivity, states slid toward debt and balance of payments shortfalls. The oil boom of the 1970s aided most Middle Eastern states for a time, but the structural problems could not be addressed by simply consuming an oil windfall. By the 1970s, state planning had taken modernizing societies about as far as it could. The state remained the principal social and economic force in Middle Eastern societies, but it could no longer generate real hope.

The front line in the failure of the modernizing state was the disaster that was unfolding in the Middle Eastern city. Modernization had produced rapid population growth and a wave of rural-to-urban migration. Middle Eastern cities—Casablanca, Algiers, Tunis, Cairo, Damascus, Baghdad, Tehran, and others—were characterized by urban sprawl, decaying fabric, and poor services. At the same time, economies had failed to provide sufficient employment, even for the new high school and university graduates. The educated expected to do much more than menial work, and most dreamed of Western levels of prosperity. The aspirations of many educated people were out of reach. For far too many Middle Easterners, modernization meant poverty, overcrowding, idleness, long days traveling, and feelings of deprivation and frustrated expectations. Economic failure disembedded the hegemony of the modernizing secular state and inevitably produced a counterhegemonic force in Muslim societies.

For a time, the reaction to the fading dream of modernization was tempered by the ideological appeal of nationalism and by the absence of a plausible alternative. Gamal Abdul Nasser in Egypt, the Baath in Iraq and Syria, and the Front de Libération Nationale (FLN, National Liberation Front) in Algeria continued to ride the wave of Arab nationalism. In Iraq and Syria, nationalist ideology was even strong enough to allow minority groups—the Sunnis in Iraq and Alawites in Syria—to permanently entrench their influence in the state. However, by the 1970s, the connection between elites and frustrated masses was coming under strain. The defeat of the Arab states by Israel in the Six Day War of 1967 was a psychological blow from which Arab nationalism would not recover. The secular nationalists had staked everything on the defeat of Israel, and they had failed. Jerusalem had been lost. The era of Arab nationalism and of genuinely popular Arab leaders had passed.

The attempts of secular regimes to revive the modernity project further alienated popular opinion. The *infitah* reforms initiated by Anwar Sadat in Egypt and adopted in some measure by most Middle Eastern states sought to engage private and foreign capital. More exposure to capitalism helped little. Reform was patchy, and the benefits did not extend into society. The new markets were rigged for the benefit of an emerging capitalist class that had close personal relations—often through marriage alliances—with senior officials of the state. A burst in speculative business activity in land, tourism, and consumer goods made only a few rich and quickly raised the specter of social inequality. Few young educated Egyptians could look forward to upward social mobility, as the state retreated and as the new class of oligarchs carved up the private sector.

The new Egyptian elites were little interested in the old populism of Nasser, instead aspiring to Western lifestyles that were far removed from the lives of ordinary people. The masses watched an outbreak of conspicuous consumption and Western-style "moral degeneration." As the secular elite essentially abandoned the masses to their poverty and backwardness, a gulf between haves and have-nots opened. Disdain and envy for the rich is a pervasive mood in the Middle Eastern city. The final disaster for secular nationalism began in 1977, when Sadat flew to Jerusalem to make peace with what most Muslims still regarded to be the irredeemable enemy. Many ordinary people were no longer prepared to trust their lives and their history to the failed secular elites.

The sense of betrayal and victimhood was particularly evident among the young. A youth revolt against the state, private capitalists, and foreign interests was in the making.[1] A number of states experienced periodic bouts of urban unrest after the mid-1960s. The urban rage building up became startlingly clear in Egypt in January 1977, when cuts in subsidies on basic goods produced spontaneous urban rioting in Cairo and other cities on a huge scale.

Popular dissatisfaction was the basis for more than spontaneous opposition: it was the basis for the Islamic revival. At first, leaders like Sadat and, later, Algeria's Chadli Benjedid thought that they could harness the emerging Islamic mood against the leftist opponents of economic reform; it was a dangerous game, and they were wrong.[2] Islam began to articulate the voice of protest. Islamists talked of things that ordinary people wanted to hear: about better jobs, housing, health, and education. Where states failed, Islamists often moved to fill the material and ideological vacuum. In the neighborhoods of Middle Eastern cities, thousands of local mosques offered worship and community—and benevolent Islamic organizations moved to offer local health, education, welfare, and even banking services. The flow of money from the oil-rich conservative Gulf states helped to create the Islamic subsector, but much of its work was supported by the enthusiasm of a large number of committed volunteers.

The Islamic revival caught the imagination of alienated urban groups.[3] Doctors, lawyers, engineers, and educators—some tired of the stifling ineffectiveness of the bureaucratic state—gave their time and prestige to the Islamic cause. Small-scale traditional businesspeople and traders, who were losing out to modern systems of retail commerce, were a bulwark of Islamic activism. Islam struck a chord with young educated people who could not find fitting employment or the means to begin a family life in the city. Finally, Islam appealed to the urban poor as a provider of social support and of a vision of hope where there had seemed to be none. In a world of bureaucrats and private oligarchs, Islam offered a return to the equality and self-worth of the believer community. The Islamic revival, then, was not merely the revolt of the dispossessed but was a broadly based rejection of the politics and culture of the *infitah* oligarchy. The combination of the idle educated and the impoverished partially educated masses looked particularly dangerous. Indeed, the young, educated, lower-middle classes led the urban poor into violent political conflict.

On the face of it, militant Islam was antimodern, but for many of its new adherents, it was more a way of demanding that modernization be made more accommodating to their interests. Many of the Islamic revivalists of the 1970s supported the modernization of industry and education as well as material prosperity, but under an entirely new social contract. Islamic revivalism demanded a political and cultural revolution that put Islam at the center of everything, which could only be achieved by excluding secular Muslims and foreigners from commanding positions in Muslim society. For existing governments, the challenge of Islam to their authority was clear, and a prolonged period of contestation was inevitable.

The Fundamentalist Orthodoxy of the Islamic Revival

Islamic revivalism was a pervasive phenomenon across the Muslim world and had implications in almost every corner of Muslim society. Ordinary people reaffirmed their connection to Islamic faith. More men went to mosque, more women covered themselves with the *hijab,* and religious celebrations were more fully observed. Intellectual life was reshaped, and for those Muslim intellectuals who did not leave for the

West—and many did—Islam increasingly impinged on what they thought and what they could say. Muslim intellectuals who had once thought the socialist path to modernity the best option now turned to the priorities and language of Islam.

The Islamic revival also witnessed a battle within Islam. The intellectual currents of the traditional ulama (Islamic clergy or scholars), Sufis, modernists, and fundamentalists battled for the heart and soul of the Islamic revival. A tolerant Islam emerged in some places. Mystical Sufi Islam remained strong in particular localities, especially in North Africa, Turkey, and Central Asia. Elsewhere, Islamic modernists synthesized Islam and socialism and aimed to incorporate essentially Western notions of democracy, economic justice, and human rights. The modernists were most influential in Iran, where Ali Shariati and Abolhassan Bani-Sadr were important voices in the Iranian Revolution of 1978–1979.[4] In the end, though, Muslim publics were resistant to modernist reformulations of Islam. Modernists were often accused of heresy, sometimes with fatal consequences. The Islamic thinker Mahmud Mohammad Taha, for instance, was executed in Khartoum in 1985 for suggesting that adherence to Islam could be more religious than political and that a strict application of *sharia* law was not necessary.[5]

The Islamic revival was not monolithic, but the dominant voice of the revival was that of traditionalists and fundamentalists. They shared a vision of a society ruled by a rigorous Islamic order, and ties existed between them, but significant differences in emphasis were also clear. Traditionalists were immersed in the classical and medieval heritage of Islam and Islamic jurisprudence and largely opposed further doctrinal adaptation. The heart of traditionalism was the established clergy and members of the ruling elite in Arab kingdoms, and so many traditionalists were hostile to the use of Islam as an instrument of political mobilization. The fundamentalists, in contrast, had emerged from the frustrated social milieu of the modern urban landscape. Most fundamentalists were as much political ideologues as Islamic scholars and were interested in what Islamic politics could do for them in the modern world. In fact, fundamentalists were often hostile to the established clergy, which they condemned for its political passivity. Fundamentalists were prepared for doctrinal innovations that made the idea of rebellion against existing authority more thinkable.

The term *Islamic fundamentalism* is not without its critics, but it has stuck because it approximated what fundamentalists wanted: to purge the infidel and the deviant from Muslim society and to construct a proper Islamic order based on God's injunctions set down in the basic texts of Islam, the Quran and the sunna (the words and deeds of the Prophet). Religion and politics were united under an Islamic state that enforced God's will through *sharia* (Islamic law). The Islamic state had a duty to make humanity good, and it could only do this by enforcing *sharia* across all aspects of human life. Fundamentalists pressed for a conservative interpretation of *sharia,* with the Islamization of education and the veiling of women becoming the totems of the new Islamic correctness. However, even as fundamentalists focused on re-creating the essentials of the Prophet's perfect Islamic government of the seventh century C.E., they were also interested in adopting modern technology. Unlike the traditionalists, the fundamentalists sought a better modernity.

Fundamentalist doctrine was shaped by a number of prominent Islamic thinkers, the most important of which were Sayyid Qutb (d. 1966) in Egypt, Abu al-Ala al-Mawdudi (d. 1979) in Pakistan, and Ruhollah Khomeini (d. 1989) in Iran. The new ideologues drew on Islamic doctrine and past thinkers, notably that of Ahmad Ibn Hanbal (d. 855) and Ahmad Ibn Taymiyya (d. 1328), to outline a conservative vision of society and to forge a political revolution to realize it. Coexistence with unbelief and unbelievers was not possible, and Islamists could no longer put up with imperfect government, or wait for any gradual re-Islamization of society. The moral corruption and tyrannical government of the modern world—for Qutb, a new age of ignorance *(jahiliyya)*—must be overcome by all means possible. The fundamentalists spoke in the language of revolution, martyrdom, and jihad. Indeed, jihad was said to be the sixth pillar of the faith. The enemies of Islam were secular Muslims, Islamic modernists, and the West and Israel.

Across the Muslim world, fundamentalist vanguards set about mobilizing Muslims for political ends. In universities, Islamic groups asserted themselves in faculties and student unions. Islamic influence grew in professional associations, and where elections were allowed, scientists, engineers, lawyers, and doctors began to choose Islamic-inclined representatives. The mosque, and especially the tens of thousands of small religious meeting places that exist in Muslim countries, were places where the new politics was promoted. Where secular oppositions had found nowhere to hide from the authoritarian state, Islamists at least could find some shelter in Islamic language, communities, and institutions. Islam gradually emerged as the principal political opposition everywhere in the Muslim world.

The Islamic movement sought to create a parallel society at the local level, but it also organized across national and international spaces. The branches of the Muslim Brotherhood organization, established in Egypt as far back as the 1920s by Hasan al-Banna (d. 1949), was the principal transnational network in the Arab world. The main Islamic movements in Algeria, Egypt, Jordan, Sudan, Syria, and the Israeli Occupied Territories claimed connections to the Muslim Brotherhood. Groups that were even more militant than the Muslim Brotherhood also transcended international borders. Many of these radical Islamists met in a number of places of relative safety, notably in Pakistan and Sudan, as well as certain cities in the West. For the militants who faced death or torture at the hands of the secular state in Algeria, Egypt, Syria, Tunisia, India, the Philippines, and elsewhere, the structure supporting the anti-Soviet jihad in Afghanistan in the 1980s was a key haven. Saudi money and Pakistani support were real boons to the cause of Islamic struggle, as was the assistance of Afghan and Pakistani Islamists.

The potentially violent nature of both the Islamists and the authoritarian secular state did not bode well for the future of Middle Eastern politics. Although much of what Islamic movements did was essentially peaceful, from the outset, Islamic politics involved violence. In the 1970s and 1980s, a wave of Islamic-inspired instability swept across the Middle East.

Egypt's Gama'a al-Islamiyya was perhaps the archetypal revolutionary group.[6] Qutb was the inspiration, and from its base in the towns and university campuses of deprived southern Egypt, especially in al-Minya and Asyût, Gama'a quickly took to killing local officials and police, as well as Coptic Christians. Gama'a eventually directed its violent attentions toward the central government and its associated elites in Cairo. Gama'a's struggle with the Sadat regime would culminate in the spectacular assassination of Sadat at a military parade in October 1981. The war between Islamic militants and the Egyptian state that followed saw many of the militants imprisoned or killed, although the state could never quite finish them off. Nevertheless, the activities of the security services contained and splintered the Islamic opposition. In northern Egypt, a distinct cadre of urban militants had emerged as the al-Jihad group, but it was effectively broken there by the security services. Militants of both Gama'a and al-Jihad fled the country, and many traveled to the Islamic milieu of Pakistan and Afghanistan.[7] Al-Jihad militants in Pakistan led by Ayman al-Zawahiri—briefly imprisoned in a general roundup after Sadat's assassination—formed Gama'at al-Jihad and forged a close relationship with Saudi militant Usama Bin Laden and his followers. More widely spread abroad, the Gama'a al-Islamiyya leadership continued to support a campaign of violence in Egypt that killed significant numbers of state officials. Western tourists also became targets, most notoriously with a dreadful massacre of fifty-eight tourists in Luxor in November 1997.

The political turbulence across the Muslim world was fired by the epic moment of the Iranian Revolution in 1978–1979. The rebellion against the modernizing Pahlavi monarchy in Iran arose from the tensions generated by the expanding modern economy. The values and practices of the secular elite and its centralized capitalism ran into the interests of the traditional merchant class and the Shia clergy. Shah Mohammad Reza Pahlavi was overthrown by a populist coalition that included Islamic traditionalists, Islamic modernists, Marxists, and Islamic liberals, but it was the militant Shia clergy led by Grand Ayatollah Khomeini that emerged as the most dynamic force. Khomeini's religious organization captured the urban enthusiasm for change and eventually enabled it to win the battle on the streets. In a struggle for power from 1979 to 1983, the clergy eliminated their colleagues in the rebellion against the shah and went on to construct an Islamic state that enforced a socially conservative Islam.

The real Revolution in Iran entrenched the power of the militant clergy in a constitution that included the institution of the *velayat-e faqih* (the guardianship of the jurisconsult). The most senior Islamic expert was to hold almost absolute political and religious authority and had the last word in worldly rule. Khomeini himself became the Supreme Leader. The Revolution also took on the contemporary world in a way reminiscent of other Third World populisms; it sought to dismantle exploitative capitalism, achieve social equality, and resist Western cultural and economic penetration. The new order meant "Islam and austerity," but it was not some mindless traditionalism. The Revolution purposely synthesized the traditional and the modern and set about reeducating Iranians to think both Islamic and modern thoughts.

The Iranian Revolution had limited appeal to Sunni Muslims; indeed, most Sunni fundamentalists were committed to purging the kind of deviancy from Islam that Shi'ism represented. What happened in Iran, though, was a powerful example for all Islamic militants. One of the most formidable secular states in the Middle East had been overthrown by popular willpower. What had seemed impossible had been done. The regimes of the Middle East were shaken by Iran, and there was a sense that political turbulence could overtake the entire region.

However, a great Islamic uprising was not about to sweep across the Middle East, although in a few places there were some fearful outbreaks of violence.

In Saudi Arabia, an Islamic sect led by Juhayman al-Utaiba tried to promote a *madhi*—a man whose historical moment Juhayman thought had come—and to re-create the Prophet's ideal community by taking over the Grand Mosque in Mecca in 1979. In the fighting that followed in the basement of the Grand Mosque, scores of people were killed. The Saudis moved to tighten up on their Islamic credentials: the king restyled himself as the Guardian of the Two Holy Places of Mecca and Medina, and the religious police—official and unofficial—were allowed to roam more freely.

In Syria, the Muslim Brotherhood took on the Alawite-dominated regime of Hafiz al-Asad, and a spiral of violence eventually led to full-scale rebellion in the city of Hama. In the fighting, parts of Hama were demolished by the heavy guns of the Syrian Army. In Bahrain, Kuwait, Iraq, and Lebanon, Iranian-inspired Shia militants were the most serious threat to existing regimes. The battle between Saddam Hussein's Iraqi regime and the militants of the al-Da'wa movement had the greatest consequences, as it helped to precipitate the outbreak of the Iran-Iraq War in September 1980. Islamic militants and their revolution had not swept all before them, but they had had an enormous impact on political and social stability across the Middle East.

The Politics of Paralysis

The Islamic resurgence continued to flow, but in every part of the Arab world, the authoritarian state was too strong and the Islamic opposition too divided for revolution to take place. In the sectarian fiefdoms of Iraq and Syria, the regimes were capable of deploying such violence that the Islamic opposition was effectively smashed. Elsewhere, the Islamic challenge rumbled on. In Sudan, as in Pakistan before it, an Islamic state replaced a parliamentary system in the latter 1980s, but only as a result of a military coup in search of some mantle of legitimacy. In most places, the state could not be overthrown, but neither could it fully control the Islamists. Thus, what emerged was chronic and seemingly unending crisis.

A political dynamic soon became clear right across the Muslim world. The forces of political Islam were broadly united over ends—an Islamic state and the implementation of the *sharia*—but they differed over means, with the mainstream Muslim Brotherhoods far more reluctant to wage war with the secular state than the smaller, more militant groups. Mainstream Islamists wanted to conduct a dialogue over gradually extending Islamic values into societies. Keeping mainstream Islamic opinion away from the smaller, more radical groups was the key task of political management for the state. Differing combinations of re-Islamization, political reform, and coercion were the means by which states controlled their Islamic movements. The carrot and the stick was applied everywhere.

In most places in the Arab world, the state applied rather more stick than carrot, but all made concessions to the Islamic mood, and most accepted that the future would look more Islamic. State elites were not averse to clothing themselves in the language of Islam—no matter how insincere they really were—for such tactics were enough to conciliate some mainstream Islamic opinion. Governments bought up clergy and other Islamists and tried to control small mosques and meeting places by licensing and by insisting that they incorporate government imams and state money into their worship. Traditionalist clergy helped governments out. The prestigious clergy of the al-Azhar mosque and university in Cairo, Egypt, and of the Saudi religious establishment were not always precisely controllable, but they were generally supportive of the status quo.[8]

Whenever it was convenient to do so, states moved to demonstrate their concern for Islamic preferences. Few Muslim leaders now proclaimed the separation of religion and politics. Concessions to the *sharia* were made, especially in the area of family law. Secular states were sometimes reluctant to be seen supporting secular thinking. In Egypt, for instance, the al-Azhar was given a role in censoring all books published locally. Writers were censored, threatened, and even imprisoned for work that challenged Islamic sensibilities. On occasion, the new mood led to the voice of secularism being extinguished altogether, most infamously in the case of the writer Farag Fuda, murdered in June 1992 for speaking up too loudly against the influence of organized Islam. The consequences of being ruled *takfir* (excommunicated as an apostate) by Islamic authorities cast a shadow over all Muslim intellectuals who tested Islamic conventions, even in countries where the *sharia* and its death penalty for apostasy were not applied.[9] Popular forms of entertainment also accommodated themselves to the Islamic mood, especially in the much greater degree of modesty now required of women performers.

In some places, Islamists were even given a limited stake in the system, although the experience with inclusionary strategies varied widely. In Egypt, the Muslim Brotherhood was allowed to operate under tight supervision. In 1984, the Muslim Brotherhood was allowed to gain representation in parliament in coalition with the Wafd Party, and in 1987 with the Socialist Labor Party and the Socialist Liberals. Participating in subsequent national elections proved increasingly difficult, though, and the organization moved on to other electoral fields. In September 1992, Muslim Brotherhood candidates won the elections of the Egyptian Bar Association and took it over.

The Muslim Brotherhood had constantly to battle the Mubarak regime's efforts to frustrate its progress. The strides made by Islamists in professional associations, especially in medicine, law, and engineering, caused consternation among the secular elite, although it was important, Carrie Wickham argued, not to overemphasize the breakthroughs, because these victories were often based on elections in which much less than half of the membership voted.[10] The regime again moved to apply a bit more stick, and a law passed in February 1993 voided all elections to professional associations unless 50 percent of the membership voted in any first round of elections and 33 percent in second rounds. More of the stick also became evident with new emergency laws in 1997. In fact, in the course of the 1990s, as Eberhard Kienle observed, Egypt underwent a "substantial degree of political deliberalization."[11]

In the last analysis, Egyptian politics continued to be rigged in favor of the regime's National Democratic Party (NDP). Not even the intervention of the judiciary in parliamentary elections in October–November 2000 could stop the rigging of polling. Candidates and party workers were arrested, papers and party buildings closed, and voters prevented from polling. The harassment of the Muslim Brotherhood was reportedly stepped up significantly. In the end, official and unofficial members of the NDP won some 388 seats in the 444-member parliament, compared to seventeen independents representing the Muslim Brotherhood.[12] Of note, the first woman candidate representing the Muslim Brotherhood, Jihan Abdel-Latif el-Halafawy, was elected in Alexandria, although her husband and many of her party workers were reported arrested before polling began.[13]

In Jordan, the Hashemite monarchy went much further in allowing Islamists to operate openly, The monarchy faced its Islamic revolutionaries, with groups like Hizb al-Tahrir al-Islami (Islamic Liberation Party) and Mohammad's Army (formed by Afghan returnees), but the king retained a degree of traditionalist credibility with mainstream

Muslim opinion.[14] Reform was an option, and the pressure to do something was growing. In April–May 1989, an austerity program led to rioting. King Hussein dismissed his government and, amid the democratization sweeping the world at the end of the Cold War, initiated reforms that allowed Islamists to participate in local and national elections.[15] Elections were contested in November 1989. Most candidates were independents, but Islamists formed the largest grouping in the eighty-seat parliament, with over twenty owing allegiance to the Muslim Brotherhood and at least ten to other Islamic tendencies. Islamists went on to gain five cabinet positions in January 1991, controlling the ministries of education, religious affairs, justice, social development, and health.

For the king, bringing the Muslim Brotherhood into the political process was a successful tactic. The compromises necessary to enter the political process did divide mainstream Islamists from the more militant. Despite periodic disagreements, the Muslim Brotherhood got behind the king. At the same time, mainstream groups found politics to be a tricky game. The regime began to play with the system in ways that hindered the progress of the Islamists. The introduction of the National Charter in 1992 allowed the formation of political parties but also introduced a new first-past-the-post electoral law that favored clan and tribal groups. In the subsequent election of November 1993, the number of deputies under the Islamic Alliance Party fell from the midthirties to only sixteen.[16] The Muslim Brotherhood's speaker of the parliament, Abdel Latif Arabiyyat, lost his post. Islam had not swept all before it and became one among a number of interests that vied for influence in Jordanian politics.

A successful balance between the inclusion and exclusion of the Islamist opposition was a difficult one to strike. Governments could make concessions to Islam, but they might never be able to really satisfy even moderate Islamists. Even when included in a political process, some Islamists—and not just the very militant ones—were inclined to make claims to a superior legitimacy that challenged the authority of the state and its capacity to govern, including its monopoly on the use of legitimate violence. Political processes that included Islamists were liable to be unstable and marked by fluctuating degrees of enmity, repression, and violence between the secular state and the various Islamic groups. The actions of militant groups almost always cast a shadow over the regime's willingness to accept a role for Muslim Brotherhoods in society. The politics of inclusion was a troubled one in many places, but it was in Algeria that the ultimate disaster took place.

The riots that swept through Algeria's cities in 1988 may have resulted in the deaths of hundreds as the Algerian Army put down the unrest. Algerians were shocked, and the legitimacy of the one-party FLN state and the army was gone. The FLN had failed to give the rapidly growing urban population even a glimmer of hope since the fall in oil prices in mid-1980. Fundamental changes were needed, but the reforms initiated by President Chadli Benjedid from late 1988 were so rapid that they unleashed an impatient and revolutionary politics that was soon out of control. The secular opposition was weak, and it was Islam that became the vessel of the popular zeal for change. For the urban youth, Islam not only represented the chance of a new start, free from the stifling inertia of the FLN bureaucracy, but a chance to recapture the lost ideals of the great war of independence.

With astonishing speed, the Front Islamique du Salut (FIS, Islamic Salvation Front), led by Abbasi Madani, emerged from its small mosques and meeting places to transform itself into the principal political force in the country and into a government-in-waiting. Following constitutional reforms that opened the way for multiparty democracy in early 1989, the FIS made great strides, including sweeping gains in local elections in June 1990. The FIS held most of Algeria's cities and large towns. The moment of truth came with national parliamentary elections, scheduled in two stages for December 1991 and January 1992. Turnout was very low, but the FIS vote was close to a majority after the first round in December 1991. For those of the old secular regime, the prospect of militant Islamists ousting the FLN and taking the state had implications that could not be entertained. With the FIS clearly on the way to victory, the Algerian Army moved in before the second round of voting in January. The elections were annulled, martial law was declared, the FIS was banned and its leaders were imprisoned, and demonstrators were shot down.

The injustice of what the Algerian Army had done was so glaring that mainstream and extremist Islamists came together, and a savage civil war ensued. The outpouring of rage was terrible, and the response of the regime equally violent. Tens of thousands died in a struggle that seemed to have no end. The FIS soon had the company of smaller and even more violent Islamic groups, notably the Groupe Islamique Armé (GIA, Armed Islamic Group). Islamists took to killing officials, journalists, foreigners, ordinary villagers, and anybody else who strayed into their path, in ways that sometimes defied belief. The toll included President Muhammad Boudief, assassinated in June 1992. The loss of life was great, with the count in some massacres numbering in the hundreds. The response of the security services and of agent provocateurs completed the circle of horrors. According to the Algerian government, Islamists murdered over 26,000 people in the first five years of the civil war, although some estimates put the figure much higher.[17]

For Algeria, it was difficult to see a way out of its torment, for the divisions were deep and irreconcilable. The nation had been destroyed. The secular regime represented significant numbers of people—bureaucrats, army officers, journalists, intellectuals, the determinedly secular, and sometimes Berbers—who simply could not afford to be defeated because the prospects were so very horrendous. Thus, there would be no loss of regime-nerve in Algeria. Meanwhile, even as the Islamic movement fragmented under the coercive pressure of the state, the rage was so real and the Islamic impulse so widespread that the revolt could not be put down by force alone. The regime fostered a political process and even made overtures to the FIS leadership, but it would be a long road back, and it seemed unlikely that the GIA militants and the like could ever be incorporated.

Following Abdelaziz Bouteflika's appointment as president in May 1999, a new political initiative was launched by referendum (with 85 percent approval) that included a six-month amnesty—ending in January 2000—for Islamic activists not directly implicated in murders.[18] The government claimed that 1,500 Islamists surrendered, but the FIS leadership abroad rejected the moves.[19] Violence had been subsiding, but with subsequent massacres, Islamists sent out the message that the war was not over. As Algeria moved into the twenty-first century, the country was tired of the long civil conflict, but there was no resolution in sight. Civil war had left very little political legitimacy for anyone.

The Revolution Forestalled

Islamic movements were the principal political opposition everywhere in the Muslim world, but making it just that one step further into government proved illusive. After Iran in 1978–1979, there were no more moments of triumphant revolution. Only in peripheral Afghanistan and Sudan did Islamic fundamentalists come to power, and the extraordinarily parochial Islam that emerged in the Taliban's Afghanistan was not an example that anyone wanted to follow. In Egypt, Iraq, Syria, Tunisia, and Algeria, the prospect of an Islamic takeover had been averted. In Morocco, Libya, Jordan, the Gulf states, and Yemen, there was never a realistic chance of Islamic oppositions overturning existing regimes.

Life for the Islamic fundamentalist was also not getting any easier. States had moved to control Islamists across borders by means of bilateral arrangements and through the councils of the interior and justice ministers of the Arab League. A set of rules adopted by the Arab League in 1996 framed the rejection of Islamic terrorism by almost all its members. Finding a safe haven where they could operate openly or with a significant degree of freedom was increasingly difficult for Islamic militants, with Afghanistan, Pakistan, and, ironically, the West left as the best refuges. European states, notably Britain and Germany, were among the most favored sanctuaries. Indeed, the rather odd tolerance of Western states for militant Islamists in their midst was a source of some exasperation for the Egyptian and Algerian governments in particular. In fact, it was not really until the wave of horror that swept the world following the 11 September 2001 attacks on the United States by the al-Qaeda group that these last refuges came under a significant degree of attack or scrutiny. U.S. military action following 11 September aimed to shut down the Afghanistan and Pakistan refuges, and enhanced scrutiny and policing of Islamic groups in Europe and North America were also initiated. The shakedown of Islamic militants in the West and their global financial networks was one of the most important things that the post–11 September war on terrorism did to contain the threat of Islamic terrorism in the West and the Middle East.

By the 1990s, Islamic militants had largely met their match in the Middle Eastern state. For all the thunder of the Islamic revival, Arabs could not quite summon the enthusiasm for yet more rebellion. The failure to make the breakthrough took its toll on political Islam, and by the 1990s, Islamism seemed to be changing. Grand dreams of seizing the state were fading and were gradually being replaced by more localized social struggles: what French author Olivier Roy referred to in his book, *The Failure of Political Islam,* as the drift from political Islamism to neofundamentalism.[20] Political Islam was a mixture of the traditional and modern, but as the horizon narrowed, it was the reinvention of the traditional that came to preoccupy Islamists. What emerged was a form of militancy that had a highly conservative social vision but was also less political. Neofundamentalists were less immediately interested in taking the state and more in puritanical preaching aimed at re-Islamizing individuals and society from below. The ultimate objective of neofundamentalist Islam was to re-create the ideal community of the Prophet wherever Muslims lived.

For the neofundamentalist, Islam was everything. Neofundamentalism, as Roy observed, was a corpus of knowledge that could speak with equal authority on any matter.[21] As with all dogmas, it was a system that isolated itself from the world and gave the mediocre and the ignorant a way of claiming knowledge. Neofundamentalism was little interested in adapting Islam to modernity, which was reflected in its vulgar adherence to traditional cultural totems. The *sharia* was an unchanging absolute that must be applied, not discussed, and it negated the need for any real politics in society. Neofundamentalists also tended to have an ultraconservative attitude toward women and, unlike the political Islamists of the 1970s and 1980s, were loath to allow women any public role whatsoever. Finally, foreigners and infidels had nothing to offer. Western culture was anathema. Tourists were the spreaders of corruption and were liable to be purged. Neofundamentalists discarded Western dress and favored traditional styles only.

The neofundamentalist was typically a young man who imagined some austere authenticity and sought to impress such visions on his community with propagandizing and, if necessary, with coercion. Pious youths cast a shadow across many Muslim communities, and in some places the violence was so terrible that it shook society to its core. The violence of the neofundamentalist often seemed extreme and pointless, but it was born of the urge to demonstrate faith and was rationalized in terms of the righteousness of purifying society for God. By the mid-1990s, the violence of Gama'a in Egypt and the GIA in Algeria had little to do with taking on the state. Rather, young men took their knives, axes, and chainsaws into villages and schools to show what they were prepared to do for God. The righteous knew no limit.

Neofundamentalist violence was a lesser threat to the state, but it represented an endemic insecurity in the lives of many ordinary people. Such violence was difficult to control. Making concessions to appease neofundamentalists was simply irrelevant—the state could never do enough—and repressive measures were not easy to apply. Neofundamentalists were often, as Roy observed, a kind of "vagabond intellectual" operating on the fringes of society and were not particularly well integrated into any Islamic organization.[22] A low-level conflict between the state and neofundamentalists seemed likely to grind on indefinitely.

Dreams of Islamic revolution were dead by the mid-1990s, as was an era of Islamic political thought. A large part of the Islamic movement, the neofundamentalists and traditionalists, had united to go off down an ultraconservative dead end. The mainstream Muslim Brotherhoods had also reconciled themselves to the long haul of reforming Muslim societies from below. Muslim Brotherhoods now focused on gradually gaining influence in civil society, and doing their best to ease a way into electoral politics.

The one ray of light was that there were signs that some of the most militant were tiring of the endless struggle. In Egypt, for instance, a group within Gama'a renounced violence in 1998 and went on to pursue a political strategy in the form of the al-Sharia and al-Islah political parties, although both the Egyptian government and many of their former colleagues, especially the Gama'a leadership abroad, totally rejected what they were trying to do. Such developments pointed a way to the end of endemic conflict, although it was unclear how far any new politics could go and to what extent it might spread to militants in other Muslim countries.

Stuck Between a Rock and a Hard Place

The Islamic revival of the 1970s made Islam the dominant political and cultural presence in Muslim societies. Yet it is important to be circumspect about the power of Islam, because an all-embracing Islamic hegemony has not taken over the Muslim world. Most Muslim states remain essentially secular. Muslim societies were more Islamic in the 1990s than two decades before, but that did not mean that most Muslims wanted militant Islamists to run their lives. Quite simply, most Muslims were not supporters of militant Islam, and it was a mistake to overemphasize its influence. Islamism was a significant force, but almost nowhere did Islamists actually form a political majority, and their electoral performance in Morocco, Jordan, Turkey, and Yemen seemed to show this. Indeed, where Islamists had made an initial electoral breakthrough, they had often lost ground later, damaged by the emergence of divisions within their own camp and by the absence of a credible set of policies.[23]

By the 1990s, Muslim societies had reached an impasse. States had contained the Islamic challenge. Even where the Islamic threat was very great, as in Algeria, the state had won, although the victory was incomplete and most definitely pyrrhic. At the same time, states had struck bargains with Islamic opinion. The language of social life was now more Islamic, and Islamic groups were an influential lobby on such matters as the law, education, welfare provision, and moral standards. The problem was that Muslim politics had become a halfway house, stuck between pressing on to a better modernity and returning to tradition. The bargain forestalled revolution, but it was so delicate a balance and embodied so many contradictions that it brought Muslim societies to a standstill. Muslim politics was the politics of paralysis.

In the short to medium term, it was difficult to see a way out of the politics of paralysis. A reasonable future required social and economic development, and most people knew this, but modernization inevitably came with the cultures of modernity. Neither the state nor the Islamic opposition really knew what to do about the cultures of modernity. The secular state scrabbled along, but its room for maneuver was limited. For the Islamic opposition, "Islam was the solution," but the clock could not be turned back, and Islamists were really unable to tell Muslims how best to solve their worldly problems. Nor was Islamism necessarily compatible with all the aspirations of most Muslims, even its own supporters. The youth of Algiers, Cairo, and Tehran had gravitated to an austere Islamic banner, but it seemed unlikely that in the long run young people really wanted cinema, satellite television, the Internet, sports, travel, music, and dancing to be totally controlled by their elders or to disappear altogether. Whether politicized Islam could ever be successful beyond the realm of opposition, though, remained to be seen. For the time being, all political Islam had to do was rebel. Only in Iran did political Islam actually have to find new ways of entertaining the population.

Finding a better way forward was clearly going to be a prolonged process. Fouad Ajami perceived of Arab societies that

> the middle ground has been scorched in the two decades behind us. The ruler claiming everything, the oppositionist dispensing with all that has been built and secured by those who came before. On pain of poverty and decay, nations can persist with ruinous ways. An encrusted tradition has its own ways, a thicket of consolations and alibis shelter it from the world. Beyond economic repair (really a precondition of it), a modernist impulse will have to assert itself if rescue is to materialize.[24]

Between the rock of the authoritarian state and the hard place of the Islamic militants, Muslim politics had known too little of compromise, and even a minimum level of consensus was barely visible. For Ajami, a post-Islamist era was in sight, with a stubborn patrimonial tradition of monarchs and army officers "outwitting and outgunning" their Islamic opponents, but the victory of such a tradition was hardly the route to a better future. Ultimately, if Muslims were to progress, compromises and proper politics were necessary. The authoritarian state would have to admit its flaws, and political Islamists had to make a greater accommodation with modernity. At some point, both sides needed to accept that the other had legitimate rights and fears and that a political system that mediated everyone's aspirations was the best way forward. Truly representative government was the only real option for a resolution to the politics of paralysis.

At the beginning of the twenty-first century, the Muslim crisis was continuing, but there were a few rays of light. Muslims were beginning to think in innovative ways, and it was dawning on some states and Islamists alike that the idea of democracy and human rights might have a real value to them. From a rather unexpected root, Iran had emerged in the 1990s as a place that might become an important model for a new Islamic politics. The Islamic Republic's accommodation with the worldly had proved unsustainable, and both the Rafsanjani and Khatami governments sought a new balance between the traditional and modern. In the Arab world, too, a number of Islamists and Muslim states had begun to talk of democratic change. The voices of synthesis were sometimes hushed, but they could still be heard, and they pointed to a fundamental change in the direction of Muslim politics and society.

Notes

1. Remy Leveau, "Youth Culture and Islamism in the Middle East," in Laura Guazzone, ed., *The Islamist Dilemma,* 1995, 265–287.

2. Abdel Salam Sidahmed and Anoushiravan Ehteshami, "Introduction," Sidahmed and Ehteshami, eds., *Islamic Fundamentalism,* 1996, 7.

3. Roy, *The Failure of Political Islam,* 1994, 48–59.

4. Husain, *Global Islamic Politics,* 1995, 11.

5. Maurice Borrmans, "Cultural Dialogue and Islamic Specificity," in Gema Martin Munoz, ed., *Islam, Modernism, and the West,* 1999, 91.

6. See Fandy, "Egypt's Islamic Group: Regional Revenge?" *Middle East Journal* 48, no. 4, Autumn 1994, 607–625.

7. For insight into the life and views of an Islamic exile in Egypt's Gama'a al-Islamiyya group, see Tal'at Fua'd, "What Does the Gama'a Islamiyya Want? Interview with Hisham Mubarak," in Joel Beinin and Joe Stork, eds., *Political Islam: Essays from the Middle East Report,* 1997, 314–326.

8. See Barraclough, "Al-Azhar: Between the Government and the Islamists," *Middle East Journal* 52, no. 2, Spring 1998, 236–249.

9. Salwa Ismail, "Democracy in Contemporary Arab Intellectual Discourse," in Rex Brynen, Bahgat Korany, and Paul Noble, eds., *Political Liberalization and Democratization in the Arab World,* 1995, 106–107.

10. Carrie Rosefsky Wickham, "Islamic Mobilization and Political

Change: The Islamic Trend in Egypt's Professional Associations," in Joel Beinin and Joe Stork, eds., *Political Islam,* 120.

11. Kienle, "More Than a Response to Islam: The Political Deliberalization of Egypt in the 1990s," *Middle East Journal* 52, no. 2, Spring 1998, 220–235.

12. David Butter, "Young Leaders and Hard Fought Elections," *Middle East Economic Digest (MEED)* 45, no. 1, 5 January 2001, 4–5.

13. David Butter, "Open Season," *MEED* 44, no. 44, 3 November 2000, 4.

14. Beverley Milton-Edwards, "Climate of Change in Jordan's Islamist Movement," in Abdel Salam Sidahmed and Anourshiravan Ehteshami, eds., *Islamic Fundamentalism,* 123–142.

15. See Robinson, "Can Islamists Be Democrats? The Case of Jordan," *Middle East Journal* 51, no. 3, Summer 1997, 373–387.

16. Michael Hudson, "Arab Regimes and Democratization: Responses to the Challenge of Political Islam," in Laura Guazzone, ed., *The Islamist Dilemma,* 239.

17. From an Algerian Foreign Ministry statement to the Algerian News Agency. Broadcast on Algerian radio, Algiers, in Arabic, 1700gmt, 2 February 1998. Reproduced in the BBC's *Summary of World Broadcasts (SWB),* MED/3142, 4 February 1998, [71], MED24-25, MED/25.

18. Catherine Richards, "Algeria Awakes," *MEED* 44, no. 11, 17 March 2000, 2–3.

19. Reported by Algerian radio, Algiers, in Arabic, 1130gmt, 14 January 2000, Reproduced in *SWB,* ME/3739, 17 January 2000, [49], MED/17.

20. Roy, *The Failure of Political Islam,* 1994, 25.

21. Ibid., 97.

22. Ibid., 95.

23. Ehteshami, "Is the Middle East Democratizing?" *British Journal of Middle Eastern Studies* 26, no. 2, November 1999, 214–215.

24. Ajami, "The Arab Inheritance," *Foreign Affairs* 76, no. 5, September–October 1987, 144.

6

Islam and the Liberal Idea

T he Muslim world has never had a tradition of democracy and liberal human rights. Even as some Muslims embraced modernity in the
twentieth century, they did it minus the liberalism that was part of
Western modernity. The missing liberalism had much to do with the fact
that modernity was handed to Muslims by imperial masters, as well as
with the strength of illiberal ideologies in the Muslim world. Islam
embodied the rule of law and had often shown itself to be a humane culture, but at no time in its history had it ever been liberal or democratic.

Muslim societies had always been dominated by authoritarian state
elites. The relative weakness of an independent bourgeoisie and other
nonreligious civil society groups reduced many of the political demands
associated with Western modernity. Institutional politics was not developed, and to the extent that there was politics in the Muslim world, it
was largely that of the patrimonial hierarchy or localized fiefdom.
When the fiefdom and modernity were joined in the twentieth century,
political systems of great intolerance emerged, as the ultimate examples
of Iraq and Syria demonstrated. Western colonial powers left weak parliamentary systems, but they did not endure because the modern ideologies that succeeded were nationalism and socialism. Patrimonial and
sectarian hierarchies absorbed nationalism and socialism to produce the
modern authoritarian state.

The Muslim world's experience of authoritarian modernization—as
detailed in Chapters 4 and 5—was not a particularly successful one.
Muslim economies struggled to achieve sustainable development.
Muslim politics was characterized by violence and instability and eventually by the paralyzed politics of the conflict between the authoritarian
state and Islamic opposition. The authoritarian state lacked legitimacy,

with regimes hanging onto power long after they had ceased to be backed by any popular enthusiasm, but the Islamic opposition also put forward an illiberal alternative. Amid all this authoritarianism, though, there was a body of Muslim opinion, and not just secular intellectuals, who believed that the absence of democracy was a problem.

During the Cold War and the crisis of the Islamic revival, the possibility of real democratic reform was a distant one. The end of the Cold War changed the conditions for politics. The West made the liberal idea the dominant ideology of its global hegemony. Adhering to a standard of democracy and human rights became necessary for a state to be accorded full membership in the international community. The global economy also conveyed liberal imperatives. Although it was possible to engage with global capitalism without being fully democratic, Western states and companies often linked trade, direct investment, and development assistance to "good governance," and this connection was associated with the rule of law and open government. Moreover, the power of the hegemonic idea was such that non-Western states sometimes initiated political reforms because that was what they thought the West wanted and that in some way it was the route to future benefits. Most Muslim states felt themselves to be under a democratization spotlight after the Cold War, and although many did not welcome it, they often felt the need to respond.

The response of Muslim states as a whole to the liberal idea was one of limited accommodation. As a group, Muslim states often tried to point out that although some of the West's universal human rights could be found in Islam, there were legitimate differences. Having two universal codes of rights on the same planet was indeed difficult to reconcile. The Universal Declaration on Human Rights (1948) was accepted only in part by many Muslim states, with clauses relating to the freedom of religion and equality between all men and women especially problematic. At the UN Conference on Human Rights in Vienna in June 1993, Muslim states banded together with Asian states to criticize the West for the way it used its universal human rights to judge and condemn others.[1] Instead, the Muslim world referred to the Organization of the Islamic Conference's (OIC) Cairo Declaration on Human Rights, derived from God's law, not just from human law. At the OIC's Doha summit in November 2000, the conference of Muslim states

> expressed its deep concern over the repeated and wrongful linkage between Islam and human rights violations, and over the use of the

written and audiovisual media to propagate such wrongful concepts. It called for an end to the unjustifiable campaigns waged by certain non-governmental organisations against a number of Member States to demand the abolition of *Sharia* laws and sanctions in the name of protecting human rights, stressing the right of states to hold fast onto their religious, social and cultural specificities, which constitute their heritage and spring source for the enrichment of common universal conceptions of human rights. It called for the universality of human rights not to be used as a pretext to intervene in the internal affairs of states and undermine their national sovereignty.[2]

Liberal democracy has been a sensitive matter in the Muslim world, then, but the voice of democratic reform has gradually been heard in Muslim politics. In the aftermath of the Cold War, a wave of reform measures did sweep through the Middle East. Although some of the reforms were passing or imaginary—as in Algeria, Tunisia, Iraq, and Syria—in other places, more lasting changes were implemented. In Morocco, Egypt, Jordan, Yemen, Saudi Arabia, Kuwait, Oman, and Iran, authoritarian states made some effort to build new institutions and practices that bore the imprint of democracy. Human rights were also on the agenda, especially the rights of women to participate in politics and society.

The Islamic movement also joined the discourse about democracy. Most Islamists had far to travel before they could credibly talk about democracy, but some were beginning to make the journey. If Islamists became more democratic, it would at least be possible to liberalize political systems. Muslim states might or might not be inclined to pursue democratic reforms, but without a degree of consensus with Islamic opposition, no democracy could ever work. An Islamic acceptance of democracy was the necessary and sufficient condition for real democratic reform to take place in the Muslim world.

Progress toward democracy would be slow, partly because of doctrinal restraints but also because of the paralyzed politics of the Muslim world. Governments could not risk pushing democratic reform too far, with Algeria standing as the ultimate example of the risks of democratization. The one exception to the paralyzed politics of the state-Islamist conflict was Iran. In Iran, political Islamists had established an Islamic state with some legitimacy, but by the 1990s Iranians were talking about reforming it. Iran was a fairly strict Islamic state, but it also had quasi-democratic institutions that were the basis for a new politics. The Islamic Republic seemed to be a key test case for the future of Islamic democracy.

The Task of Reconciling Islam and Liberalism

Liberalism owes much to the Enlightenment. By way of the primacy of reason, the Enlightenment made the breakthrough idea that all humans were equal by virtue of their humanity alone and so entitled to certain rights and freedoms. The theorizing of individual liberty, religious freedom, democratic government, and free markets stemmed from the assertion of human equality. The toleration of differences of opinion and association—that is, pluralism—in the liberal society was necessarily implied. Although neither Europeans nor Americans ever quite lived up to their Enlightenment philosophy, the equality and rights ideal eventually became the core of Western civilization. Liberalism was promoted as a universal philosophy and system of government that was the only real route to a better future for all of humanity. The West had a liberal mission, and in the aftermath of the Cold War, all those who sought to engage with it had to take liberal concerns on board.

The world did become a more democratic place after the Cold War. The liberal guru of the time, Francis Fukuyama, observed that for

> a very large part of the world, there is now no ideology with pretensions to universality that is in a position to challenge liberal democracy, and no universal principle of legitimacy other than the sovereignty of the people. . . . Even non-democrats will have to speak the language of democracy in order to justify their deviation from the single universal standard.[3]

Everyone's right to have a say in the running of society and not to be arrested, imprisoned, tortured, or killed for trying to do so is at the heart of Western liberalism. To the extent that the West represented the universal civilization, it was in the truly global recognition after the Cold War that liberal goods were good for everyone. Moreover, Western power and prosperity reinforced the universal appeal of the liberal idea. Unelected rulers could no longer shield themselves behind the Cold War priority for order. In many places, too, the link between democratization, political stability, and economic prosperity was understood. Democratic revolutions swept through Eastern Europe, South America, and parts of Asia, and some of the most repressive regimes in the world were replaced by liberal democratic systems.

In the Muslim world, the tide of democracy did not sweep all before it, but Muslims did make concessions to the global mood. In a few cases, reform was a total sham. Saddam Hussein's constitutional reforms in Iraq in 1989 purported a new era of democratic freedoms, but they were meaningless. Elsewhere, democratization was limited but significant. In Morocco, Egypt, Jordan, Yemen, Kuwait, and Iran, elections and parliaments were made freer, and a greater plurality of views was allowed to be articulated. In Tunisia and Algeria, sweeping reforms were planned, although this led to such instability that most of the progress was clawed back. In Saudi Arabia and Oman, traditional dynastic despotisms were finally persuaded to widen the institutional basis of their rule, with new local and national-level assemblies set up for the first time. The Muslim world was a more democratic place in 1995 than it had been in 1985, but democratization was extremely patchy and incomplete, and in the Muslim Middle East, a genuine democracy was yet to appear.

The reasons for the slow progress lay deep in the political culture of Muslim societies. Muslims had an almost unbroken history of authoritarian rule, patrimonial social relations, and weak economic classes. In the twentieth century, endemic domestic and international conflicts and oil windfalls that made states more autonomous from their societies did not help matters. Wherever democratic experiments had taken place—in Iran, Turkey, Egypt, Iraq, Syria, and Pakistan—they were always deeply flawed and dogged by the ambitions of patrimonial groups and the military. The continuing influence of Islam on political culture was also a brake on democratic politics. Islam is a vision of religious community and social control, whereas the liberal idea is one of secularism, equality, individual autonomy, and economic liberation. The edicts of God govern social life in the Islamic ideal, but individual choice, self-interest, and contingent social contracts do so under liberal governance. Islam and liberalism differed over what constituted the rights of the individual and over the parameters of the community and how it should be run.

In Islamic theory, God rules man, rather than man ruling man. Sovereignty—that is, the ultimate locus of power and authority—resides with God. Human government existed to ensure submission to God, and so there could be no separation of religion and state. The eternal principles of God's good life had been written down in the Quran and other texts and subsequently distilled into codes of *sharia*. The *sharia* represented the perfect worldly constitution. Humanity was simply not entitled to claim the right to legislate in a way that superseded God's will, and thus the idea of majoritarian democracy was essentially heretical. At some point, the will of God—or rather, those who claimed to be the judges of it—could say what was and what was not permissible in an Islamic society. Thus, too much human politics was bad.

Political pluralism was not only irrelevant, it was sinful, and the promotion of such things as political parties or class-based interest groups was impermissible. The Islamic community must be united as one under God.

The sovereignty of God also had major implications for the nature of human rights in Islamic theory. Western liberalism tempered the sovereignty of the majority by endowing individuals with certain "natural rights": the rights to life, liberty, property, and due process of law and the freedoms of speech, association, and religion. The majority should not interfere with these rights unless the common good was significantly threatened by their misuse. The West has established these liberal rights and freedoms as an ideal in the international system, especially with the Universal Declaration of Human Rights (1948).

Muslim states had trouble signing up these liberal rights because Islamic rights were not based on the natural rights of the individual but on those outlined in Islamic texts and the *sharia*. The *sharia* represented a rule of law that established rights against arbitrary rule, but it also limited individual rights and freedoms and froze a system of punishments that looked anachronistic by the twentieth century. Where the *sharia* was fully enforced, transgressors could still expect public beheading, stoning, amputation, or whipping for a number of crimes, including apostasy, adultery, theft, and drinking alcohol. The practice of the punishments had lapsed in many Muslim countries, but in parts of North Africa, Sudan, the Gulf states, Iran, and Pakistan, they had either never disappeared or were restored by Islamic regimes.

Islamic law did not allow for the political and social freedoms taken for granted by liberals. Individual Muslims might have a personal relationship with God, but the faith was obligatory, and other Muslims were there to make sure that it was obeyed. Islamic doctrine did not accept the individual's right to choose alternative political, social, or religious visions. Unbelief and apostasy were not options for anyone born a Muslim. To renounce Islam in an Islamic state, to be a member of a heretical sect, or to cross certain boundaries of adherence, as Salman Rushdie did with *The Satanic Verses,* was to risk the ultimate punishments of the *sharia*.

Specific Islamic traditions also contradicted liberalism's ideal of universal human equality. Islam was a vision of equality, but not of universal equality. Women and unbelievers were not the legal or social equals of Islamic men. The *sharia* accorded superior rights to men wherever it was implemented or influential. In some Muslim societies, most notably in Afghanistan and Pakistan, women were the prisoners of male-dominated families, and even the *sharia* often failed to protect them from parochial interpretations of Islam that permitted arbitrary social violence. In such places, for a mother or daughter to transgress the moral code or sense of honor of the husband and son was to risk a violent death. Women were also veiled in most Muslim societies. The veiling of women was a more complex issue than it sometimes appeared, and modern Muslim women have used it to empower themselves in public life, but, in the last analysis, it was a form of social control that robbed women of public individuality. Across the Muslim world, women have been impelled to put the veil on since the 1970s. In Islamic states, not to wear the veil was a crime. In a few places, such as Algeria, the absence of full covering could mean death at the hands of unofficial Islamic enforcers.

In short, Islam and liberalism differed over the equal status of humanity and the human rights to which individuals were thus entitled. Liberal equality had to be universal, whereas Islamic equality is partial.[4] The freedoms of speech, association, and religion do not exist under the *sharia,* and in the Islamic state, it was only possible to speak and associate to the point where it did not challenge the supremacy of Islam or those who enforced it.

Islamic Thinking and the Idea of Representative Government

Islamic political theory could not sustain genuine liberal democracy or pluralism, but there was a slender tradition that gave some opening for representative politics. From the time of the Prophet Mohammad, Islamic doctrine referred to *shura,* or the rights of the Islamic community to be consulted by its leaders. The nature of consultation had always been rather informal and optional. Typically, *shura* involved a monarch consulting with officials, local leaders, and religious figures but also ordinary people. To this day, Saudi Arabia and other Gulf monarchies retain this kind of informal system of petitioning, with kings and provincial governors regularly making themselves available to their subjects.

The practice of consultation remained rather arbitrary because Islamic political theory did not develop an authoritative model of what the institutions of the Islamic state should look like. Historically, the Islamic orthodoxy had come down on the side of order, with the resulting preoccupation for strong government. Authoritarian states prevented political development. Parliaments were never brought into the picture. Political parties and other civil society groups were not encouraged or were banned outright. The idea of the caliphate, the political and religious head of the Muslim community, remained the principal focus of Islamic thought. Although the caliph and his representatives, such as sultans and other local strongmen, were expected to consult with the community, as long as they enforced the *sharia* their rule was legitimate, whether they listened to the community or not.[5]

In practice, Muslims have rarely known a functioning Islamic state of any kind. The original and universal caliphate had lost much of its power by the ninth to tenth centuries C.E., although Islamic political theory remained extremely durable, resisting the kind of innovations concerning the location of sovereignty that took place in the West following the Enlightenment. The inertia of the caliphate idea continued to endorse personalized authoritarian rule, with rulers nominally governing in the caliph's name with little regard to any consultation with anyone. Local autocrats derived their legitimacy as guarantors of law and order. In fact, it was not until Atatürk abolished the Ottoman Caliphate in 1924 that Islamists had to modify their theory of government, since it was soon clear that another pan-Islamic caliphate was a very distant prospect. Even so, caliphate principles remained influential.

The idea that legitimate worldly government had to stem from a person or institution that unified politics and religion was one perpetuated in a number of Islamic states and movements. The monarchies of Jordan, Morocco, and Saudi Arabia all claim in one way or another to be the successors of the Prophet Mohammad's personalized religious rule. The Islamic opposition also continued to advocate personalized systems of rule. The founder of the Muslim Brotherhood, Hasan al-Banna, referred to the caliphate, and the Front Islamique du Salut (FIS, Islamic Salvation Front) in contemporary Algeria advocated its return. Many modern Islamists, though, have moved away from the caliphate's classical association with the Prophet's Quraish tribe and from its claims to universal jurisdiction by referring to their particular local primate as the emir, or in Shi'ism as the *faqih*. The Taliban's Afghanistan had an emir, Mullah Mohammad Omar, who pronounced edicts from Kandahar. The system of the *velayat-e faqih* (guardianship of the jurisconsult) in Iran stems from a different root than that of the Sunni caliphate, but the most senior political figure of the state is also the principal religious leader.

What is noticeable about the advocacy of personalized religious rule in modern times is that Islamists have recognized the benefits of making the emir less despotic by formalizing the institutions of *shura*. From the nineteenth century, liberal Muslim thinkers like Muhammad

Abduh and Rashid Rida tried to build *shura*'s part in Islamic political thought. In the twentieth century, *shura* councils were formed and formalized. The Islamic Republic of Iran went furthest in formalizing a *majlis al-shura* that was not only consultative but also representative. In fact, Iran's parliament had a significant say in how Iran was run, with its role really going beyond consultation and into what amounted to legislation. From the late 1980s, the more conventional Sunni Islamic states also moved to make greater concessions to *shura*. In Morocco, Jordan, Kuwait, and Yemen, parliaments with formally elected representatives were allowed and began to share in the business of government. In some places, the Islamic opposition was absorbed into the new parliamentary politics quite successfully, although in Sudan, Tunisia, and Algeria, the experiments in democratization broke down.

The case of the Gulf states put the issues into particularly sharp focus. All the Gulf states were essentially absolute monarchies. For years, most of the Gulf monarchies had either refused to formalize the consultative systems around royal courts or to develop the moribund institutions that were in place. By the early 1990s, though, a number of factors were coming together to persuade Gulf elites that a degree of reform was necessary.[6] The end of the Cold War increased the exposure of Gulf citizens to the new globalization, as it did everyone else, and the global discourse of liberal reformism was really the only game in town. The Kuwait crisis of 1990–1991 stoked up local political demands. The depressed price of oil since the mid-1980s had put the Gulf states and their welfare policies under financial pressure. Some of the regimes were even beginning to think more about taxation. Gulf elites were aware of the economic case for liberalization and for giving citizens a greater stake in the country and economy. The reform process in Iran also gave impetus to the local reform discourse. Arab leaders were conscious that Iran had elections, representative institutions, and women as candidates and voters. Reform in the Gulf states would be measured, but significant political development was to take place in all the Gulf states, except the United Arab Emirates.

Reform in Saudi Arabia came after the Gulf War amid an unusual degree of political agitation. A new kind of urban and educated Islamist was articulating criticisms of Saudi rule, and the kingdom saw the emergence of a number of opposition groups, such as the Committee for the Defense of Legitimate Rights (CDLR).[7] The CDLR sought to tap into the international discourse about democracy and human rights, although not entirely credibly, bearing in mind the group's own commitment to a rigorous *sharia*. The CDLR and its like were eventually squashed, but the Saudi government clearly thought it time to make concessions. In March 1992, King Fahd unveiled a package of reforms that included a basic law of government that formalized provincial-level and national-level consultative councils. The national Shura Council was composed of sixty members (raised to ninety in 1997), who served for four years, although, crucially, members were appointed by the king.[8] In any event, the king gave greatest representation to businesspeople, senior officials, and academics.

The reforms did not represent a fundamental change in the basis of government or the rights of Saudis. The regime itself was eager to emphasize that the changes were a minor adjustment. Article 23 of the Shura Council's statute allowed for the initiation of draft legislation and the amendment of executive legislation, but the primary function of the council was not legislative but consultative. King Fahd made the situation clear in an often cited interview in late March 1992, in which he pronounced that

> the prevailing democratic system in the world is not suitable for us in this region; our people's composition and traits are different from the traits in the world. We cannot import the way other peoples deal [with their own affairs] in order to apply it to our people; we have our own Muslim faith which is a complete system and a complete religion. Elections do not fall within the sphere of the Muslim religion, which believes in the consultative system and the openness between ruler and his subjects and makes whoever is in charge fully answerable to his people. . . . Free elections are not suitable for our country.[9]

For the king, Islam negated the need for a fuller democracy.

Yet the reforms were an important step beyond court politics and marked a move away from the absolutism of the Saudi religious monarchy. The practice of government was codified and institutions of real politics were created. The Shura Council was not an elected legislature, but it did fulfill a "representative, deliberative and symbolic function" and was there to be deepened and widened in the future.[10] Members of the Shura Council had links with the executive and could expect a say in government.

Whether further democratization would happen in Saudi Arabia depended on the mood of the regime and of the people of the country. Modern politics was some way off, but a broader modernity was penetrating the kingdom. According to the government's own Saudization plans, far more Saudis were due to enter the labor market to take wage-earning jobs at all levels. The status of women was also a key marker of change. Saudi women remained shackled by discriminatory legislation—they were not supposed to mix with men in public, and they were banned from driving—but some significant developments were taking place in the economy. Saudi women were becoming managers of their own businesses, and in Saudi universities, hospitals, and ministries, women were being groomed for management positions. Important social changes like these must eventually produce demands for political and social reforms. Murmurs of discontent could be heard in Saudi Arabia. Some Saudis were frustrated by the nature of Saudi society and the political and economic policies of their government. Poor economic performance fostered the unhappiness, with the unemployment and underemployment among young Saudi males a particular problem. Saudi Arabia had changed. It was a growing urban society, and at some point its politics would have to significantly change to reflect this development.

Developments in some of the smaller Gulf states might also feed a mood for change in Saudi Arabia. In these states, elites were beginning to move further in responding to the reform debate. Starting in Kuwait and Oman after the Gulf War, there was a significant opening up of political systems, and the new mood would spread to Qatar and Bahrain by the end of the 1990s.

In Kuwait, a limited parliamentary system was reestablished after the Gulf War that was far from under the control of the al-Sabah regime, with parliament agitating on such matters as openness and corruption. Indeed, the emir even dissolved parliament and called new elections in May 1999 in the hope of getting a less troublesome lot. The Kuwaiti government also pressed the National Assembly to approve a draft law allowing the vote for women, although to the cheers of many of the men present, the proposal was voted down. The government remained committed to extending the franchise, but clearly, democratic reform in the Gulf states did not necessarily mean more liberal politics.

In Oman, a system of local and regional councils created institutions of politics where none had existed. A national Shura Council was devised under the principle of universal suffrage. In Qatar, the government abolished censorship rules in 1996, allowing an unknown level of information and comment to be published on matters that had been beyond media comment.[11] The al-Jazeera satellite network represented an unprecedented experiment in a freer speech and was viewed across the Muslim world. Qatar moved toward democratic elections at the municipal level in March 1999, and constitutional reform leading to a national assembly was planned for mid-2002. Women would be allowed to vote and to stand as candidates.

One of the most encouraging developments in the Gulf states took place in Bahrain. The first Bahraini parliament had been suspended in 1975, and there had been a long-running situation of civil unrest among the majority Shia community against the ruling Sunni family. An upsurge in unrest after 1994 gave the Bahrain government a terrible human rights reputation. Yet the unrest was managed with bold moves by Shaikh Hamad bin Issa al-Khalifa after he assumed power in 1999. The shaikh made good on commitments to reform. Women and non-Muslims were brought into the existing nominated parliament, political prisoners released, and emergency laws dating back to 1974 abolished. The relaxation was deepened. A referendum in February 2001 gave the government overwhelming backing for a new national charter that was set to establish a representative parliament with real legislative powers, make the judiciary independent, and define a clear system of political and human rights for all Bahrainis.[12] Women voted in the referendum itself and were set to have equal political rights in future institutions. The new national charter promised an unknown level of democratic politics for the Arab Gulf, although it might not come into full effect until 2004.

Clearly, there were some important things happening in the smaller Gulf states, although whether any of the Gulf states would evolve into genuine democratic monarchies remained to be seen. Much was still to be done in moving Gulf state societies from absolute monarchical rule and the informal court politics that went with it to proper constitutional politics. Reforms would be paced. However, some of the smaller Gulf states especially seemed likely to have a real brush with constitutional government.

Democracy and the Islamic Opposition

The other obstacle Islam put in the way of democratization was its role in the political conflict between the authoritarian secular state and Islamic opposition. The politics of paralysis was illiberal politics. Moreover, although political Islam may have been the principal opposition to the authoritarian state, its own attitude to democracy vetoed any chance for political reform. The thought of the Islamic revival was substantially hostile to democracy, and to any version of human rights other than that defined by the *sharia*. The revivalist Islam of Abu al-Ala al-Mawdudi and Sayyid Qutb insisted that democracy was merely a reflection of the worldly vanity of the infidel.

For the influential Qutb, the sovereignty of God *(hakimiyya)* was absolute and exclusive, and his oneness meant that the only political distinction that could be made was between *Hizb Allah* (Party of God) and *Hizb al-Shaytan* (Party of Satan). Democracy was not only irrelevant to God's purpose, but any discussion between the parties of good and evil was wrong. Disagreeing with the Islamic state meant questioning God's edicts, and this was simply impermissible. The Islamic state was to leave Muslims in no doubt that Islam required a unity of belief and practice and that there was nowhere to hide in Muslim society from Islamic submission.

In fact, modern fundamentalists were so intolerant of any autonomous political or social life that they represented something of a departure in Muslim history and threatened to bring a rather novel Islamic totalitarianism. The *sharia* did not apply itself, so much of this fundamentalist thinking was really the prescription for the authoritarian rule of an emir and his Islamic jurisprudents. Sunni fundamentalists remained rather unclear about what exactly they wanted to do with the institutions of the state, but whatever it was, it did not look good for liberals.

The position of some Islamic fundamentalists, however, was not as straightforward as some of the doctrine suggested. Notwithstanding claims that Islam was an eternal and unchanging faith, as time passed the practice of politics had some effect on militants. Some Islamists responded to contingent needs with a more accommodating approach to democracy and human rights. The need to look at democracy stemmed from two pressures. First, there was an urge among large numbers of ordinary Muslims for greater democracy. Islamists themselves adapted to elections and democratic systems in such places as Morocco, Egypt, Jordan, Yemen, Turkey, Iran, and Pakistan. Second, many Islamic groups found themselves facing ruthless authoritarian states that were exerting a great deal of coercive pressure on them. For obvious reasons, some Islamists began to tap into the language of human rights, speaking of the need for the rule of law and of greater toleration in civil society. In Egypt, for instance, the Muslim Brotherhood talked of the need for freedom of speech, for protection against torture, and for the due process of law as defined by the *sharia*. Islamic movements shared such moderating experiences across the Muslim world, from the Nahda Party in Tunisia to the Refah Party in Turkey and to Jamaat-i-Islami in Pakistan.

Islamic doctrine gave all fundamentalists plenty of scope to justify drifting back to authoritarianism, but the Islamic discourse about democracy did appear to be more than tactical and held out the prospect of an alternative course for revivalist Islam. Indeed, even having a debate about democratic principles made it part of Muslim political culture, something that had to be considered even by the most militant. The recent emergence of a much more complex and diverse world, James Piscatori has argued, has speeded the development of more varied Muslim thought.[13] Piscatori noted that Islamic doctrine was broadly uncomfortable with pluralism, but there is a de facto diversity of opinion among Islamists about right and wrong interpretations of Islam. No one could speak for Islam with complete authority, so different Muslims tended to work out different political and social formulations from the faith according to what they found useful and justifiable in their own setting. Indeed, there are big variations in what Islamists—let alone Muslims more generally—are prepared to think and do with respect to enforcing the *sharia*, and thus the scope left for politics and social life differs.

What may emerge from all these slightly differing Islamic perspectives is difficult to plot. Islam has not had a great theorist-personality since the death of Grand Ayatollah Ruhollah Khomeini in 1989, or Sunni Islam since Abu al-Ala al-Mawdudi's passing in 1979. No one has given a clear voice to the Islamic mood since the 1980s, and so it remains difficult to pin down the developments in Islamic political theory. In making an assessment of opinions within Arab Muslim Brotherhoods as well as those of particular Muslim authors, such as Muhammad Imara, Muhammad Salim al-Awwa, Fahmi Huwaydi, and Fathi Uthman, Gudrun Kramer has identified some of the important avenues that contemporary Islamic thought may be taking.[14] According to Kramer, the likes of Qutb continue to set the tone for the most militant and the oppressed urban poor, but the influential middle class of the Muslim Brotherhood was beginning to articulate more thoughtful alternatives. Kramer recognized that there was no real groundswell of Islamic opinion for democracy but thought that "a growing number of Muslims, including a good many Islamist activists, have called for pluralist democracy, or at least for some of its basic elements: the rule of law and the protection of human rights, political participation, government control, and accountability."[15]

A distinction that Kramer perceived some Muslims now making was between the unalterable rules of religious duties *(ibadat)* and the rules covering political, economic, and social life *(mu'amalat)* that could be revised in the context of time and place. The core principles of Islam were sacrosanct, but the community could govern itself with a system of justice *(adl)* and consultation *(shura)* that might not be that far from a system of electoral democracy and human rights. The key debate was over whether the *sharia* was a detailed and rigid canon, or whether it could be regarded as a more flexible roadmap from which new rules and practices could be imputed according to time and place.

Kramer perceived that some mainstream Muslim opinion was gradually coming around to the idea that worldly government was in the realm of *mu'amalat* and that new rules could be produced according to the Islamic principle of the common good of the community *(maslaha)*. Government was really a matter of technique, and so democratic practices were possible as long as they did not contradict the fundamental principles and practices of worship. In other words, there was no doctrinal objection to the elected representatives of the Muslim community limiting, checking, or removing a political and religious leader.[16] Indeed, some Muslim thought tended to view political participation itself as a religious duty and asserted that the fuller realization of *shura* could even be regarded as an act of allegiance to God. Kramer argued that

> modern positions mark a definite shift of emphasis away from the person of the ruler and the duty of obedience and acquiescence for the sake of peace and order, even under unjust rule, to the authority of the community and the responsibility of every individual believer. This shift no doubt reflects the impact of modern political ideas as well as the decline and final abolition of the historical Caliphate.[17]

Islam could not support unfettered liberal democracy, and for some Islamists, no amount of theorizing could mask its association with Western infidels, but *shura* was a potential basis for the development of a more democratic Islamic political theory. Much was still to be formulated and accepted about the terms of an Islamic democracy—such as what powers *shura* gave the *majlis* in relation to the executive and whether political parties were permissible—but Islamic thinkers and practitioners were beginning to do this by the 1990s. Developments in practice were to indicate that Islam did allow for elections, parliamentary rule, the separation of powers, and an independent judiciary. *Shura* was credibly Islamic, and those Islamic thinkers developing it seemed more likely to command greater acceptance from more Muslims than the reforming efforts of the secular thinkers and Islamic modernists who had gone before them. However, only time would tell whether all the possibilities of *shura* could be realized in the theory and practice of Islamic politics.

The Islamists and Democracy in Practice

By the 1990s, then, Islamic thinking presented mixed evidence about the likely direction of Islamists. A highly authoritarian branch had developed out of the Islamic revival, but it was tempered by a discernible shift in mainstream Muslim opinion. Islamists had started to move beyond the rage of al-Mawdudi and Qutb and, with time to reflect, were considering democracy. Given the chance, it was possible that *shura* could lead to an acceptance of elections and parliaments.

The problem was that Islamic politics was not being given the chance. The great divide between the "politics of paralysis" and real political development was still to be bridged, with progress frustrated by the conflict between the secular state and Islamic opposition. Gauging how serious Islamists were about democracy and human rights was very difficult, and ruling elites could not afford to get it wrong. In fact, many Islamists may not have been entirely clear themselves about their commitment to democracy, since few in the Islamic opposition had ever been tested by holding power or by having to give it up. If the democratic process went against God, could Islamists really hand over the state to infidels? It looked unlikely to secular Muslims. Until the divide in trust was closed and Islam's commitment to democracy was tested, it was difficult to see how political development could take place.

The weight of experience did little to suggest that the democratic gap could be bridged. The case of Sudan in the 1990s, for instance, was not encouraging. The leading Islamic thinker and practitioner, Hasan al-Turabi, looked to be relatively moderate, and his Sudanese National Islamic Front (al-Jabha al-Qawmiyya al-Islamiyya) participated in the parliamentary system after 1985. Yet following a military coup led by General Umar al-Bashir in 1989, both al-Turabi and his party acquiesced to the dismantling of the multiparty parliamentary system in favor of a fairly rigid Islamic state. Only later did al-Turabi fall out with al-Bashir.

Elsewhere, notably in Algeria and Turkey, Islamists seemed to be close to the moment of truth, only to be denied the final test by entrenched secular elites. In Turkey, after a brief period of toleration, the Turkish establishment moved to prevent talk of Islamization and banned the Islamic Welfare Party in 1997. The result was that Turkey had increasingly to deal with the militants of its own Hizballah organization. In Algeria, the collapse of the reform process was catastrophic by any standards. The intolerant streak in Algerian political Islamism, most notably articulated in the rhetoric of Ali Belhadj, was enough to persuade secular Algerians that they faced a future of Islamic totalitarianism that must be stopped at any cost. Judging by what happened in the civil war after 1992, the fears of secular Muslims were not unwarranted. Algeria became *the* nightmare scenario for both secular Muslims and Islamists.

The Algerian reform process was such a disaster because it unleashed an urban rage that was totally incompatible with democracy. Where the rage was less violent, the prospects for democratization were probably better. Perhaps a more viable lost opportunity for real politics occurred in Tunisia after late 1988. Islamists were offered a place in a reformed political system by the Zayn al-'Abidin Ben 'Ali government, only to have that offer withdrawn.

The leader of the Islamic party, Hizb al-Nahda (Renaissance Party), Rachid al-Ghannoushi, was one of the most prominent advocates of Islamic democracy in the Muslim world. Ghannoushi had explicitly tried to reassure secular Muslims that al-Nahda did not mean a future of *sharia* punishments, veiling, austerity, clerical supremacy, and isolation from Europe.[18] For Ghannoushi, Islam and democracy were far from antithetical; indeed, Islam and democracy had only been separated because history had conspired to stop Muslims from appreciating democracy. Al-Ghannoushi was reported to advocate majority rule, freely conducted elections, a free press, and the political and legal equality of women. Nevertheless, in 1989–1990, the Ben 'Ali regime clearly underwent a change of mind about the reform process. Al-Nahda was refused registration, and amid claims of plots to overthrow the government, the regime moved on the Islamists with force. Al-Ghannoushi got no nearer to parliament, let alone to political power. With events degenerating in neighboring Algeria, only a number of small secular political parties were allowed to operate.

In a number of other places—Morocco, Egypt, Jordan, Yemen, and Kuwait—the authoritarian state raised the option of more democracy, and although progress was made in some, the ruling regimes had no intention of relinquishing their grip on the real reins of power. The levels of coercion differed from place to place, but in the last analysis, fundamental challenges would be resisted by force. In particular, organized Islamic political parties were not welcomed and were either prohibited or severely restricted everywhere.

In short, Muslims in the Middle East had yet to experience anything approaching real democracy. Meaningful democratic reform could not take place until the politics of paralysis were broken across the Muslim Middle East: that is, until ruling regimes were fully prepared in principle and fact to give up political power and Islamists were prepared to tolerate the existence and rights of people who disagreed with them.

The Struggle for Democratic Reform in Iran

Iran seemed a notable exception to the paralyzing standoff between the authoritarian secular state and Islamic opposition. In Iran, the Islamic opposition had won and was given the chance to move beyond the politics of protest. The Islamic Republic was an important test case of whether a modern Islamic state could be devised and successfully run.

The Shia clergy who led the overthrow of the shah's modernist regime embodied some very authoritarian tendencies. In the cultural revolution that followed the clergy's ascendancy, political and social deviants were punished, women forcibly veiled and discriminatory family laws restored, and *sharia* punishments reintroduced. However, the Islamic Republic was forged in practical revolutionary politics, and there was much more going on than first appeared. The revolutionary clergy had appealed to the population with a mix of the traditional and modern, and most agreed that the oppressed people must be consulted in the business of government. The outcome was the formulation of a political system that synthesized theocratic institutions with a democratic structure that bore more than passing resemblance to the French Fifth Republic. Democratic principles were accorded their own worth.

The supreme office in the Islamic Republic was intended to be occupied by the senior religious figure of the country. The Supreme Religious Leader made many of the key appointments to the government, judiciary, and armed forces and stood at the apex of a system of representatives and supervisory committees that monitored almost every aspect of Iranian government and society. Grand Ayatollah Khomeini was the natural choice as the first Supreme Leader, but any candidate for the post had to be approved by the Assembly of Experts (Majlis-i Khubregan), an elected body of eighty-three expert clergymen that met to make authoritative judgments on matters related to the constitution.

Below the theocracy, as set out in the Constitution of 1979, was an elected president who appointed a prime minister to run the cabinet. The cabinet and its business were to be extensively monitored by the elected parliament, the Majlis al-Shura. A body of learned clergymen, the Council of Guardians (Shura-i Negahban)—six members appointed by the Supreme Leader and six by the Majlis—made sure that legislation conformed with Islamic injunctions. Significantly, the Majlis was elected on the basis of universal suffrage. Women had taken a step back in many respects, but they were given the right to vote in elections and to stand as candidates for the Majlis, although they could not hold the highest offices of the state or be judges. The religious minorities, Zoroastrians and Jews, were also given citizenship and the right to be represented in the Majlis, although they too were barred from leadership positions. Universal suffrage was a breakthrough in such a rigorous Islamic state.

The system outlined in the 1979 Constitution gave considerable scope for real politics. Theocratic institutions had the last say, but, in practice, neither the Supreme Leader nor the Council of Guardians could dominate policy outcomes. The Majlis was more than a rubber stamp and within limited bounds was a forum for the representation of different beliefs and interests. It regularly shaped its own legislation, voted to reject government proposals, and threw out cabinet ministers. Indeed, politics was highly contested. In the first decade of the Islamic Republic, the disagreements over policy between the government, Majlis, and Council of Guardians often reached gridlock. Radicals in the Majlis sought to extend the powers of the Islamic state, whereas the Council of Guardians took the contrary view. With Khomeini declining to intervene decisively in disputes, a supreme arbitrating council was established in early 1988. The Council for the Determination of Exigencies (Shura-i Mashlahat-i Nezam) was made up of thirteen senior figures, and Khomeini framed its powers in terms of the Islamic principle of *maslaha* (common interest).[19]

The implications of Khomeini's use of *maslaha* were significant and became clear in an exchange of letters between Khomeini and President Ali Khameini. The president voiced concerns that the state was in danger of taking upon itself almost unlimited powers that could justify the overriding of quite basic Islamic tenets. In response, Khomeini was clear: the needs of the Islamic state were supreme. The idea that the Islamic state could do what it felt to be in its best interests opened the door to all sorts of political innovations, although Khomeini subsequently retreated from his opinion, and the full implications of what he had said were not developed. Getting things done in Iran still required consensus building across the political system.

Constitutional politics was established, then, but the real limitation on its democratic operation lay in the repression of views outside the Islamic consensus. Political parties were banned, and even the clergy's own Islamic Republican Party had been disbanded in the mid-1980s. Secular Muslims, Islamic modernists, and members of the Bahai sect were defined as unacceptably deviant and faced high levels of repression. The conflict between the Islamic regime and the armed Islamic modernists of the Mojahedin-e Khalq (the People's Combatants) was particularly violent. Special revolutionary courts executed thousands for plotting against the state and for being "hypocrites" and "corrupters on earth." Even the clearly benign Islamic liberals of Mehdi Bazargan's Iran Freedom Movement faced considerable coercive pressure. Bazargan was Khomeini's first prime minister, and although he himself continued to receive a degree of leeway, the tolerance for criticism was very low. Bazargan died in January 1995 and was succeeded as head of the Freedom Movement by Ebrahim Yazdi. The harassment of the organization was stepped up. In July 2001, for instance, the Tehran Revolutionary Court issued a warrant for Ebrahim Yazdi's arrest for failing to return to a court summons while he was away having cancer treatment in the United States.

The Islamic state and its courts rigorously repressed other alternative political viewpoints, but dissenters also faced intimidation from local Islamic groups organized around mosques, Revolutionary Guards units, and other organizations. The self-appointed upholders of the Islamic order were everywhere, always prepared to organize pro-revolutionary demonstrations, judge the morality of public behavior, censor the press, bully the opposition and break up their meetings, and take women to task for bad *hijab*. Iran was a place where a woman could be dragged off the streets to be flogged and fined for what a religious zealot regarded as immodest dress. The Iranian political system was not a totalitarian one, but a kind of arbitrary archaic totalitarianism existed across Iranian society. For opponents of the regime, the politics of the Islamic Republic could be arbitrary and violent.

Yet, for all its intolerance, the Islamic Republic had democratic potential: it was a constitutional system that gave scope for real politics. The end of the Iran-Iraq War in 1988 and the death of Khomeini in 1989 afforded the opportunity for progress.[20] A committee set up to reform the constitution sat between April and July 1989 and made a number of recommendations that were later approved by the Assembly of Experts and by national referendum. Two key changes emerged. First, the qualifications for the position of *faqih,* or Supreme Leader, were reduced. The Supreme Leader no longer had to be the highest religious authority *(marja taqlid)* but could be just an ayatollah. The elected Assembly of Experts also assumed the right to debate and vote on the competence of the Supreme Leader while he was in office, and this change potentially made it the ultimate arbiter of political authority in a way that it had not been during Khomeini's time. After some debate by the Assembly of Experts, President Ali Khameini was promoted to the rank of ayatollah and made Supreme Leader. The second crucial change following the 1989 reforms was the creation of a new executive presidency, effectively combining the offices of president and prime minister. The new president was to be elected in a national vote, and in August 1989, Hashemi Rafsanjani won the election.

The changes to the constitution were extremely significant. The downgrading of the Supreme Leader's religious qualifications and the popular legitimacy of the new executive presidency did devalue Khomeini's theocratic ideal of the *velayat-e faqih*. The new Supreme Leader, Ali Khameini, represented political experience but not religious seniority. Khomeini's idea of a state ruled by the most senior clergymen had disappeared in the absence of appropriately qualified candidates for the highest offices of the state.

The new leadership moved to do something about the highly intolerant nature of the political culture. The Rafsanjani presidency (1989–1997) cultivated a slightly more relaxed atmosphere. Private and foreign business interests were encouraged to invest in Iran, the freelance activities of the most rigorous Islamic enforcers were discouraged, and greater participation for women in society was mooted. The atmosphere may have relaxed during Rafsanjani's period in office, but a real break with intolerance was not made. The Majlis was controlled by hard-liners, and it countered the reformist mood by refusing to pass legislation, by vetoing the appointment of cabinet ministers, and by initiating campaigns against bad *hijab* and satellite television. In the end, Rafsanjani resorted to introducing tougher qualifying criteria for candidates to the Assembly of Experts and the Majlis in an effort to disqualify his ultraconservative critics as being too incompetent to hold office. Not surprisingly, the heat of the debates got higher, but eventually many of the most prominent conservatives were sidelined.

Rafsanjani stood down in 1997 after the maximum two terms allowed by the constitution. The presidential election in May 1997 was another landmark of political development, witnessing a landslide of nearly 70 percent of the vote for the reforming cleric, *Hojjatoleslam* (a religious rank below ayatollah; literally, "proof of Islam") Mohammad Khatami, over the establishment candidate, Nateq Nouri. Not since the fall of President Abolhassan Bani-Sadr and his Islamic modernism in 1981 had Iranians been offered such stark choices. Khatami was elected by a coalition of those frustrated by the status quo, including many young people, students, women, the middle class, and even some of the poor. Khatami fronted a politics that was partly rooted in the Islamic revolution's own philosophy of activism and of the widening of political and social participation. Individuals were now participating, but not necessarily in ways that the clerical establishment had expected. One interesting phenomenon was that the reform movement included a number of notable "converts," such as Saeed Hajarian, Abbas Abdi, Moussavi Khoeiniha, and Akbar Ganji, who had been at the heart of the Islamic revolution and its security apparatus before being purged.[21] Moussavi Khoeiniha, for instance, was prominently involved in the seizure of the U.S. embassy in Tehran in 1979. It seemed that the Islamic revolution might have had some quite unanticipated modernizing effects.

The Khatami government certainly heralded a change in the political atmosphere in Iran and led a wave of reformists into government, the Majlis, and state companies. Reformists also moved into a new system of local councils. In the first instance, new publishing permits were granted, and a flood of free-speaking newspapers, magazines, and books soon appeared. Writers got down to publicizing some of the excesses of the security apparatus, as well as the graft going on within the Islamic state. In the absence of political parties, Vahe Petrossian observed, newspapers had an unusual importance as the poles of politics, airing policy discussions and rallying individuals around positions.[22] In the universities, too, academics—Abdol-Karim Soroush was the best known—were also making their contribution to a more modern definition of Islam. For Soroush, Islam and democracy were not only compatible but actually inevitable: one without the other was not perfect.[23] Islam was a faith in which interpretations legitimately changed, and all Muslims, not just the learned clergy, had the right to make new interpretations.

Many Iranians clearly wanted more political and social freedom. Others were determined to stop their having it. The hopes of liberals ran into the conservatism of the revolutionary generation. The conservatives had socioeconomic empires to run and privileges to protect, so they were not about to take all the criticism now coming their way. The conservatives were deeply entrenched in a state in which elected authority could be trumped by religious authority. The *faqih* was at the top of the nonelected institutions of the state that still held the reins of real power in Iran. The conservatives were dominant in the judiciary, police, Revolutionary Guards, *Basiji* militia, local Islamic committees, and state-run television and radio. War veterans and members of martyrs' families—many dependent on the subsidies and handouts of the state and religious sector—also formed a larger constituency that were committed to the original idea of the revolution and were often prepared to roughly crowd out the voices of liberal reform. The reformists were not nearly so well organized or so well located in the Islamic state. Reformers held the presidency, cabinet, and Majlis, but it was very unclear whether this was enough to transform Iran.

Holding the ring was Ayatollah Khameini as the Supreme Leader, and Rafsanjani as chair of the Expediency Council. Khameini and Rafsanjani were more conservative than Khatami, and each was prone to very illiberal language, but both accepted that some degree of reform was necessary. The support of these two figures was crucial to Khatami, but because he especially walked such a fine line between conservatives and reformers, the leadership's preference appears to have been to temper very limited reforms by constantly giving something else back to the conservatives—a case of one step forward and at least one step back. Thus, Khatami's room for actually implementing significant changes in Iran was very limited.

The ensuing struggle between reformers and conservatives saw heightened conflict over almost every aspect of politics and society. Reformers who spoke too loudly and women who looked too good were favorite targets of the Islamic enforcers. For young women, a touch too much makeup or a pair of sunglasses could attract attention. Getting caught at a party could result in a flogging and forcible virginity test.[24] Real violence was never far away. Reformers were commonly assaulted by the police and by Islamic vigilantes, including senior ministers. In 1998, there were even a series of murders of academics and writers. In the resulting row over the murders, Ayatollah Khameini intervened. A number of people working for the Information (Intelligence) Ministry were arrested, and the information minister, Dorri Najafabadi, was forced to resign. Conservative members of the judiciary also took to imprisoning the opposition. The major of Tehran, Gholamhossain Karbaschi, was an early target of conservative judges. Karbaschi was detained in early April 1998 on corruption charges, although Khameini would again intervene to release him from prison. With the police admitting the torture of municipal officials in search of confessions, the Karbaschi case fell apart, and he was eventually discharged with a fine. In December 1999, the former interior minister, Abdollah Nouri, was not so lucky before a special clerical court, winding up in prison on charges of political and religious dissent.

When hard-liners turned their attention to students, an even more dramatic confrontation unfolded in the form of a remarkable explosion of protest in Tehran and other major cities over six days in July 1999. Tired of restrictions on the freedom of the press, notably a court order banning the newspaper *Salam,* and enraged by a number of violent attacks by police and vigilantes on campus, large numbers of students took to the streets, causing the biggest civil disturbances since the revolution.[25] A heavy-handed crackdown by the security forces, including the mass mobilization of Islamic vigilantes, contained the protests, but few Iranians politicians can have been happy to see the brightest and the best of the country meeting the Islamic state quite in this way. The leadership was mindful to publicly listen to student complaints after quashing the riots, and there was a public debate about the importance of the rule of law. The leadership joined calls for the strict adherence to proper procedures. The activities of judges, the police, and Islamic vigilantes were questioned. Indeed, having been under pressure for some time, the conservative chief justice, Ayatollah Mohammad Yazdi, stepped down, although his replacement was another conservative, Ayatollah Mahmud Hashemi-Shahrudi.

In an important subsequent test, reformers swept to victory in the Majlis elections of February and April 2000, reportedly taking over 200 of the 290 seats.[26] Khatami's brother, Mohammad Reza Khatami, won a seat and was soon appointed deputy speaker. Hard-liners were reduced to a rump by the election, but again they were able to strike back through their dominance of the judiciary, especially of the special revolutionary courts. Reformist papers and magazines were closed, and journalists and other reform figures, including members of the Majlis, were harassed, arrested, and imprisoned. Ayatollah Khameini, too, swung back to favor the conservatives. Khameini moved to support the judiciary and to stall a number of the civil liberties proposals concerning the powers of police on university campuses being considered by the new Majlis.

The harsh sentences given to seven intellectuals and journalists in January 2001 for attending a conference in Berlin in April 2000 also indicated the way things were going.[27] Among those imprisoned was the investigative journalist Akbar Ganji, who had made enemies for his reports on official corruption and violence. Ganji was initially given ten years in prison and a further five in internal exile, although the issue of Ganji's sentence was a political football that was to run on; it was later reduced to six months, and then raised again to six years.[28] Two translators, including one who worked for the German embassy in Tehran, were also given nine and ten years at the January 2001 trial. The conservatives were ruthless men, prepared to do almost anything to make sure that their grip on society remained tight.

The frustrations of trying to maneuver around the entrenched establishment were great. Indeed, Khatami was reported to be so fed up that he was even considering not standing in the presidential elections in June 2001.[29] Khatami did stand and won another landslide, reportedly raising his share of the vote to 77 percent of the 28 million votes cast.[30] The electoral mandate for change was unequivocally there, but there was subsequently little sign of any real breakthrough in the business of politics and government. The conservative judiciary continued unabated their repression of the reforms and democratic movement.

Khatami's problems were entirely predictable because all Islamic experiments with democracy had a fundamental barrier to pass: the fact that the people and their representatives were not really sovereign. At any moment, Islamic authorities were liable to step in to say what was permissible and what wasn't permissible, no matter what the majority thought. Until the religious establishment essentially gave up its claims of superior political authority and deferred to the will of the majority of ordinary Muslims, the moment of democratic transition could not really come. The democratic barrier to reform was particularly difficult to pass in Iran because it had a well-organized and interest-orientated clerical bureaucracy. The political struggle between conservatives and reformers was not just about religion but also about socioeconomic interests. The religious bureaucracy had jobs, status, and incomes to protect against the more pluralistic organizing principles of the reformers. The struggle was over who ran what socioeconomic hegemony in Iran. Until the religious authority and huge socioeconomic system that supported the conservative bureaucracy became ineffective or unsustainable, it was difficult to see how the reformers could dismiss the conservatives.

Much rested on the Supreme Leader, Ayatollah Khameini, taking Iran over the reform barriers, but it was far from clear that he wanted to do so. If Khatami succeeded, the Islamic order that Khameini had helped found and now presided over could be further devalued. A more liberal Iran might find less use for much Islam in politics and so many clergymen in political power. Khameini had the last word in Iranian politics but, like his predecessor, was more than reluctant to make the definitive judgments to resolve key disputes.

The paralysis of political thought and action at the top could doubtless go on for a considerable period, but the longer it did, the more serious were the risks. The clergy ran Iranian politics, and if its politics could not meet the rising social and economic expectations of the population in the global age, it would be likely face the judgment of the people in the same way as any other political class. Economic failure stalked the political system. The prestige of the governing clergy had doubtless already been worn down by its association with worldly government. In elections, most Iranians were clearly trying to say that they were tired of the religious bureaucracy's mismanagement, restrictions, and corruption. The frustrations building up in Iran's sprawling cities were clearly strong, and the country had already witnessed outbreaks of urban unrest. If Khatami failed, Iran was likely bound for trouble.

Iran was a mass Islamic society—not just an oil-rich microcosm— and for that reason it seemed to be an important case study for Muslims everywhere. Until Khatami was elected, the Iranian Revolution had failed to provide the Muslim world with a useful model, but he represented another chance. Khatami promised to experiment with a new liberal Islamic model, and Muslims everywhere might be able to draw on the results. The conservative resistance to reformism was strong, but, as Ali Abootalebi has argued, the creation and consolidation of participatory politics in the Islamic Republic looked nearly unstoppable in the long term.[31] The religious establishment might not be able to hold back this tide of reformism forever. From unpromising roots, it seemed possible that the Islamic Republic might one day define what a mass Islamic democracy could look like.

Democracy and the Future of Muslims

The Muslim world has not been a hospitable place for liberal democracy and human rights. The reasons for Muslim authoritarianism are many and varied: the tradition of patrimonial rule that weaves its way from village to capital city; the historic weakness of the bourgeoisie and labor movement; the strength of well-organized sectarian and tribal minorities; the experience of Western colonialism; insufficient levels of economic, social, and educational development; failed modernization; the prevalence of destabilizing international conflicts; and the divisions of the Cold War and its aftermath. Few leaders and elites have been prepared to willingly relinquish the prize of the state, and many remain determined to hold on to power until the absolute bitter end.

The importance of Islamic thinking has also been a block to democratic progress. Far from all Muslims live in Islamic states, but the influence of Islam resonates in all Muslim political cultures. Islamic political theory does not separate religion and politics, and Islam has been accorded a supreme status that inhibits the absorption of other political and social ideas. In all Muslim societies, the rights of the individual remain disproportionately subordinate to the state and the idea of the community. For the time being, the Muslims who enjoy the greatest democratic freedoms and standards of legal justice are those who live in the West. The result is that moving to Europe, North America, and Australia is a dream for millions of Muslims.

The failure of the Muslim world to create sustainable democratic systems is not without cost in the contemporary world. The relationship between democracy and development is the subject of a disputed debate—capitalists will do business where markets and a stable order exist—but it is hard to avoid the fact that the most successful places in the world are also the home of the liberal idea. In the long run, the dynamism of any society is stifled by an authoritarian and bureaucratic system of government. Where a certain level of liberty, reward, and information exchange is possible, both individuals and society are much more likely to fulfill their full potential. Indeed, the Western societies that are clearly best able to freely use capital, information, and people are those that run the world.

Islamic theory cannot produce the kind of liberal democracy familiar to the modern Westerner, but that does not mean that Muslim countries cannot absorb liberal democratic ideas over time. As a number of Muslim countries have shown, the effort to take on democratic practices has been made in both secular and Islamic states. Islam and liberalism are not easily compatible, but the force of Western hegemony and the new globalization has created a powerful imperative to get on with synthesizing Islam and liberal ideas. Liberalism may lack the moral foundations and communal solidarity of the Islamic faith, but to avoid it is to court a pious isolation that is the road to backwardness and, ultimately, to being dominated by the less moral. Such is the dilemma facing all Muslims today.

Notes

1. Huntington, *The Clash of Civilizations and the Remaking of the World Order,* 1996, 195–197.

2. From the Final Communiqué of the Ninth OIC Summit Conference in Doha, Qatar, 12–13 November 2000 (Legal Affairs Section, Point 113). Text reproduced on Homepage of the Permanent Delegation of the OIC to the UN Offices in Geneva and Vienna, http://www.oic-un.org/english/is/9/9th-is-sum-final_communique.htm#int.

3. Fukuyama, *The End of History and the Last Man,* 1992, 45.

4. As Fukuyama puts it, "the liberal state . . . is rational because it reconciles competing demands for recognition on the only mutually acceptable basis possible, that is, on the basis of the individual's identity as a human being. The liberal state must be universal, that is, grant recognition to all citizens because they are human beings, and not because they are members of some particular national, ethnic, or racial group. And it must be homogeneous insofar as it creates a classless society based on the abolition of the distinction between masters and slaves. . . . the authority of the state does not arise out of age-old tradition or from the murky depths of religious faith, but as a result of a public debate in which the citizens of the state agree amongst one another on the explicit terms under which they live together." Fukuyama, *The End of History and the Last Man,* 201–202.

5. Bill and Springborg, *Politics in the Middle East,* 1994, 48–49.

6. Ehteshami, "Political Change in the Era of Globalisation," paper presented to the Conference on Globalization and the Gulf, 2–4 July 2001, Institute of Arab and Islamic Studies, University of Exeter, 1–3.

7. Dekmejian, "The Rise of Political Islamism in Saudi Arabia," *Middle East Journal* 48, no. 4, Autumn 1994, 640–641.

8. See Dekmejian, "Saudi Arabia's Consultative Council," *Middle East Journal* 52, no. 2, Spring 1998, 204–218.

9. Comments made by King Fahd in an interview with the Kuwaiti publication *Al-Siyasah.* Reported by the Saudi Press Agency, in Arabic, 28 March 1992. Reproduced in *SWB,* ME/1342, 30 March 1992, [13], A7–A9.

10. Dekmejian, "Saudi Arabia's Consultative Council," 205.

11. Angus Hindley, "Special Report Qatar: Breaking the Mould," *Middle East Economic Digest (MEED)* 44, no. 10, 10 March 2000, 7.

12. "Festive Vote for Bahrain Democracy," BBC News, World: Middle East, Wednesday, 14 February 2001, 1743gmt, http://news.bbc.co.uk/hi/english/world/middle_east/newsid_1154000/1154501.stm.

13. Piscatori, "Religious Transnationalism and Global Order, with Particular Consideration of Islam," in John Esposito and Michael Watson, eds., *Religion and Global Order,* 2000, 85.

14. Kramer, "Islamist Notions of Democracy," in Joel Beinin and Joe Stork, eds., *Political* Islam, 1997, 73.

15. Ibid., 71.

16. Ibid., 75.

17. Ibid., 75–76.

18. Abootalebi, "Islam, Islamists, and Democracy," *Middle East Review of International Affairs Journal* 3, no. 1, March 1998, 5–6.

19. Bakhash, "The Politics of Land, Law, and Social Justice in Iran," *Middle East Journal* 43, no. 2, Spring 1989, 196; Katouzian, "Islamic Government and Politics: The Practice and Theory of the Absolute

Guardianship of Jurisconsult," paper delivered to the Symposium on the Postwar Arab Gulf, 12–14 July 1989, Centre for Arab Gulf Studies, University of Exeter, 14–17.

20. Murden, *Emergent Regional Powers and International Relations in the Gulf: 1988–1991,* 1995, 51–56.

21. Vahe Petrossian, "Reformers Set for Victory," *MEED* 44, no. 8, 18 February 2000, 2–3.

22. Vahe Petrossian, "Hiatus at Half-time," *MEED* 43, no. 30, 30 July 1999, 2–3.

23. Abootalebi, "Islam, Islamists, and Democracy," 6.

24. New Year parties for 2000–2001 were reported to have resulted in hundreds of arrests and many floggings. Jim Muir, "Analysis: Backlash Gathers Pace," BBC News, World: Middle East, 14 January 2001, 0001gmt, http://news,bbc.co.uk/hi/English/world/middle_east/newsid_1116000/1116367.stm.

25. Gary Sick, "Mullahs in Full Cry to Turn Back Time," *Sunday Times,* 18 July 1999, 23.

26. Vahe Petrossian, "It's the Economy," *MEED* 44, no. 26, 30 June 2000, 5.

27. "Conference That Created a Furore," BBC News, World: Middle East, 13 January 2001, 0858gmt, http://news.bbc.co.uk.hi/english/world/middle_east/newsid_1115000/1115171.stm.

28. "Iran Sentences Spark Row," BBC News, World: Middle East, 15 January 2001, 1246gmt, http://news.bbc.co.uk/hi/english/world/middle_east/newsid_1117000/1117881.stm; "Iran Reformist Jailed for Six Years," BBC News Online, Monday, 16 July 2001, http://news.bbc.co.uk/hi/english/world/middle_east/newsid_1441000/1441707.

29. Vahe Petrossian, "Khatami's Test," *MEED* 44, no. 47, 24 November 2000, 4–5.

30. Abootalebi, "State-Society Relations and the Prospects for Democracy in Iran," *Middle East Review of International Affairs* 5, no. 3, September 1991.

31. Abootalebi, "State-Society Relations and the Prospects for Democracy in Iran."

7

Islam in the International System: A Future of Conflict or Cooperation?

At the beginning of the twenty-first century, Muslims made up over 1 billion of the world's population and were a majority in over forty states. Stretching from West Africa to the Philippines, the Muslim heartland occupies the land at the center of the Eurasian landmass that is a bridge between Africa, Europe, Central Asia and Russia, India, China, and the Pacific. Following the end of the Cold War, Muslims began to reassert their distinctive identities in southeastern Europe and across six new Muslim republics of Central Asia. The Muslim diaspora in Europe and North America also numbered in the millions.

The power of the Islamic religion to shape beliefs and behavior across the Muslim world has confounded expectations associated with the Western experience of modernization. Secularism had not yet pushed Islam into a shrinking private realm. In the midst of modernization, Islam remained the principal factor in the politics and culture of many Muslim countries. Whether the realm of Muslims could be characterized as the realm of Islam was another matter, but it was an idea that featured prominently in the discourses of both Muslims and Westerners in the 1990s. Muslims were aware of a common heritage and consciousness, but the extent to which this translated into international politics was debatable. The international role that Islam played or might play was difficult to assess because Islam was not a monolithic faith or political ideology but was divided by the differing interpretations of sects, ethnic groups, and states. Islam was used to both legitimate states and to rebel against them, to support localized tribalisms and nationalisms as well as to condemn them. Yet, although Muslims differed, most were united by a core of doctrine and practice and by a heightened political consciousness reinforced by the Islamic revival.

The stream of Islamic information passing around the Muslim homeland and diaspora was creating a truly global community whose members identified with each other.

Muslims experienced the pressure of enormous changes in the twentieth century. Few Muslims felt content about the recent past or the likely future. Modernization was difficult, and the new globalization threatened an even greater tide of uncertainty and foreign influence. The Muslim world lived in the shadow of the vastly more advanced West, and it was widely believed by Muslims to be indifferent or hostile to their development and welfare. Scratch the surface, and most Muslims were unhappy about the world. Frustration and rebellion were the dominant idioms of revivalist Islam.

The obvious tensions between Muslims and the West were the basis of a prominent discourse common to both civilizations that suggested that Islamic and Western cultures were so different and incompatible that international conflict was inevitable. The governments of both Western and Muslim states may have dismissed the applicability of Samuel Huntington's *Clash of Civilizations,* but his thesis was enormously influential in framing the post–Cold War debate about Muslim-Western relations. In both the Muslim and Western worlds, Huntington set a marker in the discourse, with his worst-case scenarios to be either avoided or embraced, depending on one's point of view. Certainly, many Islamists were all too anxious to reproduce, in word and deed, the stereotypes coming out of the West portraying Muslims as an intolerant, hostile, and violent people. A simple refutation of these ideas of conflict was not possible.

Understanding the direction in which Muslims are going will clearly be an important part of the study of international relations in the twenty-first century. Muslims make up a large part of the world's population and occupy great areas of land, much of it strategically central to the human world. The study of Islam is a truly global study. Moreover, at its most dynamic, Islam contests not only the West's domination of the international political and economic systems but also those very systems themselves. The 11 September attacks on the United States by Islamic-inspired terrorists were the most dramatic example of the kind of challenge that some Islamists wanted to make to the West, but the friction in Muslim-Western relations is far broader and more complex than the threat posed by a relatively small cadre of Islamic terrorists. The continued strength of Islamic religion, especially among a very large numbers of ordinary people in Muslim societies, suggested that Western liberal hegemony is not about to sweep all before it. To what extent the counterhegemonic potentials of Islam are realized in the twenty-first century, or whether Islam leads Muslims in a more cooperative direction, is a matter of real significance to the entire world.

Islam and the International System

Islam does not have a tradition of complex theorizing about the international system. In the millennium that followed the life of the Prophet Mohammad, Islamic international relations constructed the world as a simple division between good and bad, them and us: specifically, between the realm of Islam/peace *(dar al-Islam)* and the realm of war *(dar al-harb)*. In the realm of Islam, Muslims were united by their submission to God's will and could have no just cause for conflict with each other. The unification of the Muslim community, the *umma*, under a proper Islamic government was the principal ideal of Islamic theory. Meanwhile, those inhabiting the realm of war could not be accorded equal respect, nor was the Islamic state to grant legal recognition to the infidel. Indeed, it was incumbent on Muslims to pursue jihad (religious struggle) to convert or subdue nonbelievers. The Islamic ideal was to make all humans Muslim. Thus, the boundaries of the *umma* were entirely provisional and could be expanded as means allowed. The possibility of permanent conflict hung over the realm of Islam's relations with its neighbors. For much of Islam's history, Muslims were in a state of cold war or actual war with neighboring Christendom.

As time passed, though, Muslims had to be pragmatic about the reality of distinct territorial jurisdictions developing within the realm of Islam itself and about relations with non-Muslim powers. A categorization often referred to as the realm of truce *(dar al-sulh)* was applied to relatively benign neighboring powers. Treaties could be signed, and doing so represented a de facto recognition of other ways of life. Peaceful coexistence was accepted, and by the end of the seventeenth century, Muslims had reconciled themselves to their own borders. The perpetual jihad against unbelief was over. Although Muslim states may have adapted to the conditions on the ground, Islamic ideals did not change. The division between believers and nonbelievers remained the definitive understanding of international relations.

Islamic theory was sustainable as long as a certain degree of unity existed across the Muslim *umma* and as long as the realm of Islam was basically a world unto itself. A number of hegemonic Islamic states sustained the ideal of *dar al-Islam,* but the increasing superiority of

European powers from the eighteenth century on made it increasingly difficult to reconcile Islamic theory with reality.[1] The Ottoman Empire was the last Islamic hegemon that could sustain the idea of Muslim unity.

The creation of the modern state and international system by Europeans—and its subsequent globalization—fundamentally challenged Islamic theory and left Muslims without a plausible way of looking at the world. In the modern state system, the nation and its territorial jurisdiction were the basis of sovereignty and international relationships, not any religious or ideological distinctions. The logic of the state system implied that territorial sovereignties were legally separate and equal, and this logic essentially demanded that states accept that the system was secular. The boundaries of the various states, and those boundaries only, defined what was inside and what was outside the jurisdiction of the community. Alternative communities might exist, but they did not have a legal basis in the modern state system. Religious authorities in one place could not make legitimate political claims over the citizens of another state, and transnational communities like the Islamic *umma* no longer had any recognition in international legal theory. In short, modern states could not really tolerate independent religious authority either in the domestic or international setting.

Muslims could do little more than be pragmatic in response to the founding of the modern state system in the Muslim world. The collapse of the Ottoman Empire at the end of World War I led to a period when Muslim peoples were divided and funneled into territorial states. The new states were either the creations of European colonial powers or were the fiefdoms of local elites anxious to use the modern state for their own benefit. The Ottoman Caliphate was abolished in 1924, and a radically modernist Turkish state replaced it. Meanwhile, Arab lands were broken up into the Arab states of the Levant that exist today. The new states suffered from low levels of legitimacy, but over time, they made their own realities. New states made new societies. Iraq, Syria, Jordan, Saudi Arabia, and others built their bureaucracies and armies, as well as roads, ports, schools, hospitals, and factories. Subjugating and absorbing alternative forms of authority and identity, the new states made themselves permanent, and even Islamic purists could scarcely imagine a world without them.

The modern Muslim state was here to stay, and of the more than forty that exist today, almost all are willing participants in the main conventions of the international system. When signing up to various international agreements, notably the United Nations and Arab League (both in 1945), Muslim leaders explicitly recognized the principles of territorial sovereignty, noninterference in the internal affairs of others, and the peaceful resolution of international disputes. Without formulating a change in Islamic ideals, Muslims had de facto accepted the formal division of the *umma*. A conceptual chasm had opened between Islamic ideals and Muslim realities. Islam no longer had a workable theory of international law, and it was not easy to see how it ever could. To this day, the fundamental reformulation of Islamic theory on international law and relations has not really begun.[2]

Muslims had subscribed to a game that weighed against their Islamic ideals and collective power. The Muslim *umma* was divided and without coherent institutional support in the international system. Meanwhile, secular Muslim nationalisms and parochial Islamic nationalisms were promoted by the states. Muslim states all had their own *raison d'état,* and most were almost as prone to compete as much with each other as with non-Muslim states. Buying into the modern state also tended to mean buying into the Western-made theoretical baggage of realism and neorealism, and these theories did not discriminate between Muslims and non-Muslims. In realist theories, the security of the state was the principal concern, and it was only rational to consider all other states a potential threat.

Although Arabism and Islamism offset the full implications of the modern state and its unbridled *raison d'état* in the Muslim world, the pursuit of self-interest quickly took Muslim states in different directions. In the 1950s and 1960s, Arab nationalists questioned the state system and even moved to do away with some of its borders, but pan-Arabism was insufficiently persuasive to offset the powerful attractions of the new state to localized interests and identities. The collapse of the Egypt-Syria union in 1961 was an important moment of failure. The territorial states defined by Europeans in the Middle East had triumphed, and their demise could not be envisaged.

To the extent that Muslim states continued to pursue their Islamic identity, it was through the conventional means of interstate alliances and multilateral bodies. In August 1969, an overenthusiastic Christian tried to burn down the Al-Aqsa mosque in Jerusalem. Amid the outrage that swept across the Islamic world, a group of Muslim countries resolved at a summit in Rabat, Morocco, in September 1969 to create the means of collective action. The result was the creation of the Organization of the Islamic Conference (OIC), designed to bring Muslim states and peoples together in an international organization (see Map 7.1). Non-Muslim states with a significant Muslim minority also

Map 7.1 The Organization of the Islamic Conference

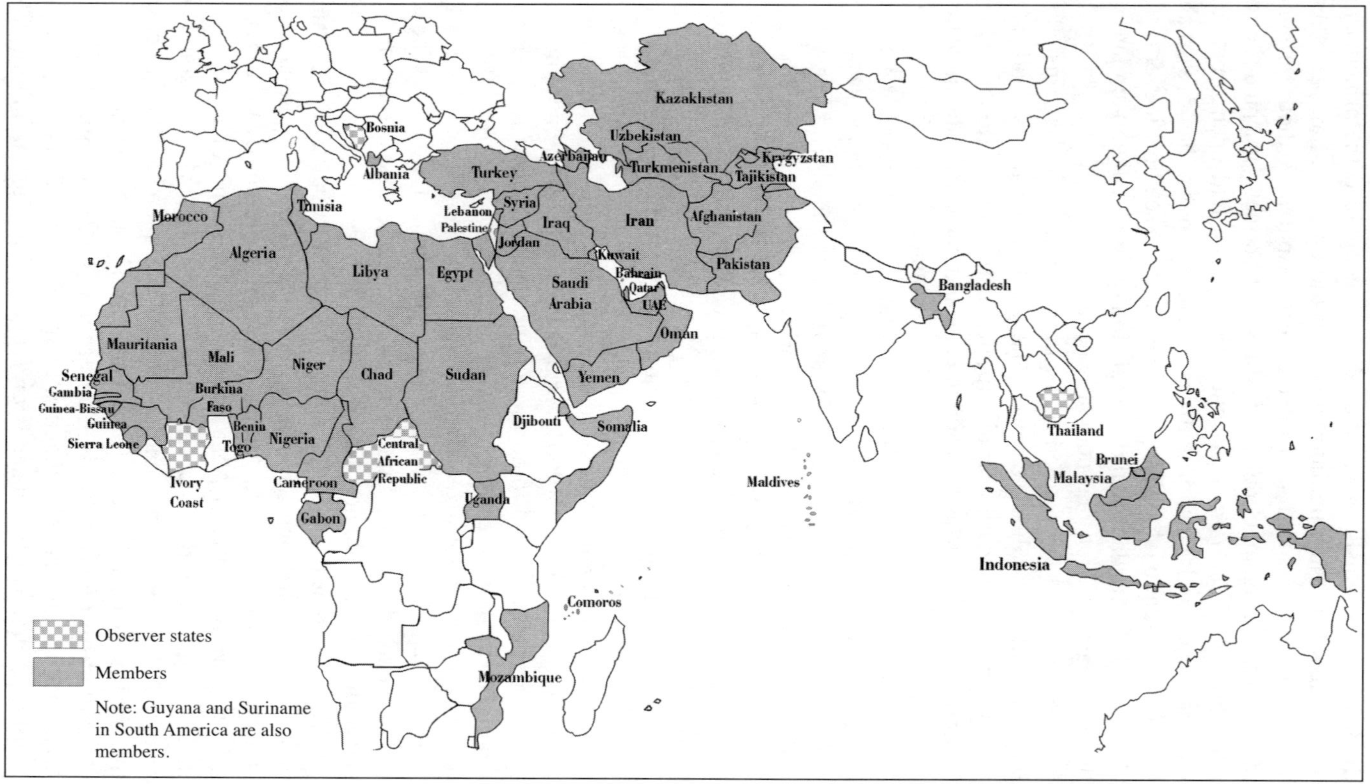

Observer states

Members

Note: Guyana and Suriname in South America are also members.

joined. The signatories to the OIC agreed that meetings of their heads of state should take place once every three years and meetings of foreign ministers once every year. A permanent headquarters and bureaucracy was set up in Jidda, Saudi Arabia, to promote a permanent stream of pan-Islamic dialogue.

The OIC was an important step forward for Islamic representation in the international system, but it was a limited intergovernmental alliance. The OIC Charter of 1972 affirmed its commitment to the UN Charter, and Article II(B) made it clear that the principles of sovereign equality, noninterference in the domestic affairs of other states, complete respect for the sovereignty of members, and the peaceful resolution of all disputes were recognized as the foundations of the OIC.[3] The OIC was a forum in which common Islamic responses might be formulated, but it had no power to define a consensus or to implement decisions beyond that agreed by all members. The institution itself was limited.

An even more significant limitation of the OIC's capacities stemmed from the divisions that were immediately apparent within its own ranks. The big Muslim states differed over their interpretations of Islam, as well as about what role the OIC should have in international crises. General foreign policy hostilities between Muslim states were transferred into the OIC. In the 1970s, Saudi Arabia jousted with Nasserist and Baathist states, and in the 1980s, the kingdom was on the defensive against the Islamic Republic. The Saudi-Iranian cold war paralyzed the OIC and made it a forum for a conflict over the stewardship of the hajj. In sum, the OIC was a body in which the states were sovereign and so were their interests. Despite first appearances, the OIC was essentially a secular institution.

Islamic Militants and the International System

By the 1970s and 1980s, the modern Muslim state was practically immovable, but the Islamic revival also meant that Islamists still contested it. For the dissidents of the Islamic revival, the idea of a unified *umma* was the focus, and many instinctively insisted that Islam was the only source of worldly legitimacy. Sayyid Qutb and his followers quite simply believed the nation and the state were heresy; they were vestiges of the corruption that Europeans had brought to the Muslim world. For the fundamentalists, the West had purposefully plotted to undermine Islamic potential in many ways, but no more so than in dividing the

Islamic communities into nation-states. Groups like Jihad in Egypt and Islamic Jihad within the Palestinian community followed Qutb's view. Islamic fundamentalists advocated a war on the West and a war on the West's international system. The ultimate aim was to make the world fully Islamic.

By far the most important manifestation of the tensions between Islamic revivalism and the state system came after the Iranian Revolution. Khomeiniism ultimately looked forward to a new Islamic world order, but it also embodied a rather unusual mix of Shia Islam and Third Worldist concerns with nonalignment and capitalist exploitation: "them" and "us" were defined as the oppressors *(mustabarum)* and the oppressed *(mustazafin)*, rather than simply as Muslims and non-Muslims. Grand Ayatollah Ruhollah Khomeini himself was rather hesitant about the use of violent means to pursue world Islamic revolution. Nevertheless, it quickly became clear that the revolutionaries were largely indifferent to the conventions of the international system and were not averse to supporting acts of violent subversion. Iranian students seized the U.S. embassy in 1979 and held its diplomats hostage. For a number of years after the revolution, the Islamic state and "freelance" activists sent agents, money, and arms abroad to support the other Islamic struggles and to combat the influence of the "Great Satan" of the United States and its agents. Iran interfered in the politics of other Muslim states and supported activities that were quite clearly illegal under the domestic law of other states, as well as in international law.

The impact of the Iranian Revolution was most pronounced among the other Shia communities of the Middle East. The Gulf states faced serious sedition, particularly in Bahrain and Kuwait. The annual hajj in Saudi Arabia was the scene of constant political agitation, leading to violent demonstrations in Mecca, especially at the 1987 hajj in which hundreds were killed in rioting. In Iraq, a violent conflict between the Baathist regime and Shia militants eventually set Saddam Hussein on the path to the full-scale invasion of Iran in September 1980. The Iran-Iraq War dragged on for eight years. In Lebanon, Iranian support for the Shia activism of Amal and Hizballah, especially after the Israeli invasion in 1982, changed the balance of the Lebanese political system and went on to give Israel the most serious military setback in its history. Shia militants from Lebanon were also behind a wave of international terrorism in Europe and the Middle East directed at Israel, the United States, and the Gulf states. Hizballah kidnapped any Westerners it could get its hands on in Beirut.

Yet, ultimately, if the Islamic Republic proved anything, it was the effect of the enormous inertia of the modern state and state system on the practice of Islamic ideology. The war with Iraq after 1980 speeded the ascendancy of pragmatic forces, as did pressing economic problems. The costs of isolation were unsustainable. Efforts to bring the Islamic revolution to all Muslims were scaled down and increasingly focused on certain Shia communities in adjoining countries. Freelance Islamic revolutionaries were brought under the control of the Islamic state, a move involving the execution of the most radical. Then, Iranian activities abroad were instrumentalized: they became less about a general revolution and more about the interests of the Iranian state. The last gasp of the Islamic Republic's revolt against the international system came with Ayatollah Khomeini's *fatwa* (religious edict) on the British Muslim author Salman Rushdie in 1989. Khomeini's *fatwa,* which condemned Rushdie to death for apostasy, represented the widespread Muslim outrage against Rushdie's book, the *Satanic Verses,* but his implicit claim to extraterritorial jurisdiction across the entire Muslim *umma* was not backed by other Muslim states and organizations.[4] Khomeini's *fatwa* also made life more difficult for those trying to run the Iranian state, for it seriously disrupted their efforts to rebuild Iran's relationships in the world. The pragmatists did not have the religious authority to rescind Khomeini's command, but, before long, they were quietly indicating that the *fatwa* was a religious policy rather than an official government one.

The death of Khomeini in 1989 marked the moment when the Islamic Republic became a conventional state. Presidents Hashemi Rafsanjani and Mohammad Khatami did not advocate general revolution, even as an ideal. Iran restored relations with many states previously condemned as evil and largely stopped using violence abroad. The Islamic Republic continued to be accused by Algeria, Egypt, Saudi Arabia, and the United States of interfering in the affairs of others and of supporting international terrorism, but the accusations were increasingly difficult to pin down. In reality, most Iranian aid went into Lebanon and Sudan, and such aid was not inconsistent with normal practices in the state system. Iran was always likely to speak up for Muslim rights across the world—it had opinions about what was on at the cinema in Turkey, about the rights of schoolgirls in Egypt or France to wear the *hijab,* and about the massacres of Muslims in regional conflicts—but it was increasingly less prone to act on them, especially if international law defined such actions as illegal.

The Islamic Republic had basically come to accept the rules of the international system, including such things as the inviolability of borders and the principle of noninterference in the affairs of others. When tested in conflicts in Lebanon, Afghanistan, Azerbaijan, and the Gulf in the 1990s, Iranian foreign policy was limited, even moderate. The one case in which the Islamic Republic's policy aspirations were unlimited and unconventional was with respect to Israel, but even here, the position was rationalized in terms of international law. For Iranian leaders, the "Zionist entity" was simply not a legitimate state that was entitled to even a minimum of respect. Israel's status stood in contrast to that of the Great Satan itself, the United States, which was regarded as a legally constituted state that Iran, in principle, could have relations with, as long as a list of disputes was resolved. Although Iranian leaders continued to work against all aspects of U.S. influence in the Muslim world, little in what they did after 1989 was really revolutionary. In fact, Iranian governments were increasingly looking to engage with elements of the Western hegemony, especially capitalism and global markets.

Elsewhere in the Muslim world, militant Islam gave voice to a universal message, but most Islamists were contained within a state, and that is where their struggles were largely directed. In practice, Islamists wanted the state for themselves, and although many regarded the international system as problematic, they spent little time worrying about it. The universal revolution was consigned to the distant future, and Islamists made the appropriate rationales. As Sohail Hashemi observed,

> the ideal of a united Muslim world remains—however inchoate—a central aspect of the normative framework of Islamic activism. The question of how this pan-Islamic vision will be realized does not concern the activists because just as the socialist state was to have withered away, leaving the communist utopia, so will the triumph of truly Islamic regimes lead to the re-creation of the unified Muslim *umma*.[5]

Thus, should the likes of the Front Islamique du Salut (FIS, Islamic Salvation Front) in Algeria, al-Jihad and Gama'a al-Islamiyya in Egypt, or Hamas in the Palestinian National Authority ever succeed in their assault on the secular state, it seemed very unlikely that any would do more than assume the reins of government and be subjected to the same *raison d'état*. Even the internationally organized al-Qaeda group was really focused on achieving limited objectives within the state system rather than fighting the system itself. It must be said, though, that the assault that al-Qaeda mounted on the United States was the most powerful challenge to the dominance of the West in the international system ever attempted by a substate Islamic group.

The inescapable fact for militant Islamists was that their Islam could not really triumph without the modern state, yet the territorial state was bound to compromise Islamic doctrine. In the absence of a great Islamic hegemon restoring unity to the *umma,* it seemed very unlikely that this contradiction could ever be resolved. Islamic revivalists might replace governments, but it did not look like they would be replacing the division caused by states. Moreover, in David George's view, the problem went even further, in that

> an Islamic state is a contingent impossibility, a sheer contradiction in terms; Islam and the secular are mutually exclusive. . . . what is required to ensure the success of the Islamic enterprise is nothing less than the replacement of the present world order by an alternative Islamic one—an authentic *Pax Islamica.*[6]

Even the most radical of Islamists knew that the prospects for bringing down the entire international system were so incredible that it was not worth even considering. The contemporary Islamist seemed destined to be perpetually disappointed by the mismatch between Muslim realities and Islamic theory. Islam could not be a transnational actor in the state system, only a transnational community of thought.

The Experience of
Muslims in the Post–Cold War World

The end of the Cold War meant a better future for much of the world, but most Muslims had cause for mixed feelings. Soviet communism had gone, and the Muslim world could now embrace a new frontier of Muslim countries across Central Asia. However, some things about the new era looked more ominous. The United States was now an unrivaled superpower, and some Muslims foresaw that U.S. attention might turn toward them. Saddam Hussein was one of those pessimists. In the Middle East, Arabs had lost the political and military backing of the Soviet Union, and Israel now enjoyed an unknown level of military superiority. Israeli forces continued to suppress Palestinian opposition to its occupation of the West Bank and Gaza and to attack Lebanon in support of its illegal occupation of the south of the country. With U.S. protection, Israel did not have to bother too much about international law or the censure of the UN.

Then, within a year of the fall of the Berlin Wall came the Iraqi invasion of Kuwait and the disaster of the Gulf War. Muslim states joined the U.S.-led coalition to fight Iraq. Saddam Hussein appealed to the Muslim *umma* for support against the onslaught, but the response was ineffectual. Many Islamists and nationalists rallied to Iraq, for U.S. imperialism was deemed a greater enemy of Islam than even Saddam Hussein, but without the active support of Muslim states, they could not get into the war. The passions of ordinary Muslims were easily contained. Iraq was left to fight alone, and the Arab world's most dynamic state was demolished. Arabs were left deeply divided. The Gulf states had also become beholden to the United States for their security in a way not seen before: they backed a tough regime of sanctions against Iraq and accepted the permanent military presence of the United States in the Gulf. When the United States called for an Arab-Israeli peace process, few Arab states had the strength, will, or unity to go on resisting. The Arabs could not deploy a strong hand in the peace process, and for Palestinians, the reality of the pax Americana meant trying to adapt to an unequal and unjust peace.

If the emergence of a pax Americana in the Middle East was deeply depressing for many Muslims, at least it maintained a degree of international order. In many other places, Muslims were under violent attack. The reorganization of the borders of the Soviet Union led to a grim series of wars in Azerbaijan, Tajikistan, and Chechnya that pitted Muslims against Russia and its allies. Meanwhile, as the Yugoslav Republic fell apart, Serbian expansionism was not effectively met by the United States or European countries. The ineffectual Western response and paralysis in the UN Security Council was to the real disadvantage of Bosnian Muslims. The UN arms embargo on all sides left the Bosnians without the ability to properly defend themselves against the already well-armed Serbs. Tens of thousands of Muslims were killed, and terrible massacres were perpetrated in places such as Bihac and Srebrenica in front of a watching world.

With the UN blocking Bosnia's right to self-defense, Muslim states were limited in what they could do. Iran and Libya provided some military training and weapons, although even this was ended by the United States after it became more involved following the Dayton Accords in 1995. For most Muslim states, the supply of money and humanitarian aid was as much as they could be seen doing. The lifting of the UN arms embargo and the defense of Bosnian Muslims were beyond the powers of the Muslim world itself; they were really the responsibility of the West. The West failed to act in time, and decisive U.S. intervention came far too late. Bosnia left deep scars in the Muslim world, and many saw yet another conspiracy of Western indifference, double standards, and inaction.

In many other places, from West Africa to Kashmir to the Philippines, Muslims were also fighting the more powerful armies of adjoining states. Few Muslims met any real success on the battlefield or found much sympathy in the non-Muslim international community. The Muslim world noticed the different ways in which the West dealt with Iraqi aggression in Kuwait, as opposed to Israeli, Serbian, Russian, and Indian violence against Muslims. The charge of Western double standards was a cry heard in every conflict involving Muslims. In what was perceived to be the West's indifference and discrimination against them, large numbers of Muslims saw an age-old hostility to Islam, as well as a contemporary Western plot to beat them down. The sense of injustice was reinforced by the inconsistent way that the UN was deployed and the failure of Western rhetoric that this implied. When Muslims needed the protection of the UN, it was not often there for them, whereas the West had little trouble in using it to protect its own interests, sometimes against Muslims.

The Potential for Collective Action: The Significance of the Organization of the Islamic Conference

Muslims were under attack in the post–Cold War world. The question for the Muslim world as a whole was what could be done about it. Islamic faith was the basis of a self-conscious global-scale community, but divisions between the Islamic world's sects, ethnic groups, political systems, and international orientations negated the creation of an effective alliance of Muslim states. With fifty-six members by 2000, many of which had only a minority Muslim population, what could be expected of the OIC was limited.

What the OIC was able to do was forge recognizably Islamic common positions and then articulate them in an agreed way at an international level. Where the interests of Muslims were being challenged, the OIC position was at its most coherent. Muslim states disagreed about the strength of the language required and how far to blame the West for their troubles, but the OIC produced strongly worded documents that defined the Islamic position and often said who was right and wrong in any particular conflict. Using the cover of the OIC, Muslim states could more comfortably call for international action, promote conflict-related fund-raising in their countries, and send direct aid to besieged Muslim brethren. The OIC gave Muslim states confidence as international actors.

The OIC was also significant because it expressed an authoritative Islamic view on some of the big philosophical and legal debates going on in the post–Cold War international system. The Western hegemony was not only putting Muslim states under a democracy and weapons proliferation spotlight, but it was also beginning to fiddle with some of the most basic understandings about the state system and UN Charter. OIC positions represented authoritative Islamic arguments amid the intersubjective discourses going on in the international system. Ironically, the OIC was generally a defender of the modern state system. Muslim states had taken a long time to come to terms with the territorial state, and none welcomed the idea of a new round of normative contestation. The OIC nearly always argued that it was vital to stick to international law and UN Security Council resolutions as the basis for political positions. The Muslim states were essentially status quo powers.

Of course, the normative line that the OIC treaded between the principle of sovereignty and the rights of self-determination for Muslims was sometimes a fine one. Sovereignty was the priority in Bosnia and Iraq, but self-determination was the goal in Kashmir and Kosovo. In cases in which international law was very clear, as with the Chechen conflict, the OIC and its members backed oppressed Muslims with political and material support, but its official position accepted the legitimacy of existing structures and the need to negotiate with Russia.[7] Even when it came to the principal Islamic issue, that of the Arab-Israeli conflict and Palestinian rights, the OIC pinned the collective flag of Muslim states to international law. By the 1990s, Israel was still widely regarded as the enemy of Muslims, but the OIC consensus accepted the principle of a peaceful settlement under the land-for-peace formula defined by UN Security Council Resolutions 242, 338, and 425.[8] A number of the members did not agree with this moderate stance, but almost all were prepared to sign on to the OIC consensus because it reflected the majority mood.

The great limitation with the OIC as an organization was in the realm of action, and in this respect, the lowest common denominator tended to be the norm. Expressing Islamic ideals and sensibilities was one thing, but doing things in the state system was another. OIC summits looked and sounded impressive, but the consensus that they produced almost always precluded actions that might bring Muslim states into direct conflict with foreign powers or might challenge the principal role of the UN and of Western powers in international conflict management. An influential coalition of Muslim states, including Egypt,

Morocco, Saudi Arabia and the Gulf states, Turkey, Malaysia, and Indonesia, tended to keep a lid on the more ambitious aspirations of Islamic opinion, partly because of their ties to the United States. Even the Islamic Republic of Iran, which often called for more proactive responses and cared less about what the West thought, was increasingly pragmatic from the 1990s.

The kind of role that the OIC played was well demonstrated after the 11 September 2001 attacks on the United States. In the aftermath of the attacks, a wave of anxiety swept through the Middle East as Muslim states pondered what the United States might do in response. Muslim states moved to support the United States but quickly flagged a number of concerns. At an extraordinary meeting of OIC foreign ministers in Qatar on 10 October, OIC members "strongly condemned the brutal terror attack that befell the United States" and insisted that "such shameful terror acts are opposed to the tolerant divine message of Islam." The OIC underscored its support for bringing the perpetrators to justice "to inflict on them the penalty they deserve." The conference affirmed the commitment of all OIC members to combat international terrorism but called on the UN to take a more prominent role in defining the war on terrorism "without selectiveness or double standards." Fearing where U.S. unilateralism might lead, the OIC communiqué

> stressed its rejection of any linkage between terrorism and rights of Islamic and Arab peoples, including the Palestinian and Lebanese peoples' right to self-determination, self-defense, sovereignty, resistance against Israeli and foreign occupation; all of which are legitimate rights enshrined in the United Nations Charter and international law.[9]

Differences over the Arab-Israeli conflict represented a significant point of tension between Muslim states and the United States. As far as the OIC statement was concerned, Israel practiced state terrorism against the Palestinians, and resistance to it was legitimate. In short, the OIC's Qatar statement essentially supported the war against al-Qaeda's international terrorism, but the markers were clear. Al-Qaeda was a legitimate target, and—notwithstanding concerns for Afghan civilians—the Taliban was a sacrificial lamb, but if the United States sought to refocus its war on terrorism against those Arabs engaged in the Arab-Israeli conflict, it would meet the opposition of OIC members. The Arab-Israeli conflict was one of the very few issues where it was possible that the OIC consensus could weather the disapproval of Western states.

In the end, the OIC was reasonably good at representing the Muslim bloc and articulating the Islamic viewpoint but remained some way from being able to do things for the Muslim world. Until the majority of Muslim states could agree to coordinate significant common actions, the 1 billion people of the Muslim world would fail to actualize their potential in the international system.

The Significance of Muslim Opinion and Its Potential for Counterhegemony

For all the talk about civilizational politics in the post–Cold War world, Islam was far from a coherent actor. Muslim states were too diverse, too suspicious of each other, too tied up with non-Muslim powers, and too lacking in confidence. Yet, Islam was a force to be reckoned with at an international level. Islam was important because hundreds of millions of people identified with the idea of an Islamic identity. It was not a monolithic religion, but it was one of the great immanent preferences of the post–Cold War world. Muslims believed that the Islamic *umma* was significant, that they were discriminated against by other civilizations, that the West was arrogant and overbearing, and that East Jerusalem and the Al-Aqsa mosque should be restored to Islamic stewardship.

The connection between Islamic preferences and the behavior of Muslim states was rarely direct, but one did exist. In all the post–Cold War conflicts pitting Muslims against non-Muslims, Muslim states and organizations almost always sided with their Muslim compatriots. Muslims in conflict could expect political support, money, humanitarian aid, and sometimes arms from Muslim states. What Muslims in conflict could not expect was that Muslim states and organizations might band together to apply effective economic and military sanctions against non-Muslim adversaries. Few Muslim states were prepared to take on the costs and commitments of real alliances with other Muslim states, nor were they willing to accept the risks of going to war.

Living in the shadow of the Western hegemony was the principal issue facing Islam and Muslims. Most Islamic and secular Muslim states were tied up in Western-dominated political and economic systems, a fact reinforced by the increased pace of the new globalization in the 1990s. A few Muslim states aspired to be counterhegemonic, but doing so was a big game that had real costs, as Iran, Iraq, Libya, and Sudan found out. Even most of the discontents had now come to the conclusion that actually doing things that were counterhegemonic was unsustainable.

Iran was the most obvious example of an Islamic state beginning to stand down from its counterhegemonic watch. In his capacity as chairman of the eighth OIC heads of government summit in Tehran in December 1997, President Mohammad Khatami lamented the preponderance of Western civilization but was clear that the task of rejuvenating a "common Islamic home" could not mean "regression, rejection of scientific achievements, withdrawal from the modern world, or seeking conflict with others."[10] Khatami knew that Muslims could only succeed if they utilized the "scientific, technological and social accomplishments of Western civilization" and that this was "a stage we must inevitably go through to reach the future." The West did things that were bad for Islam and Muslims, but Muslims had to find some way of absorbing its achievements.

Muslim states were not a counterhegemonic force in the international system, nor were they likely to be so in the foreseeable future. The kind of grand Islamic alliance fighting for the geopolitical interests of Islamic civilization prophesied by Samuel Huntington was not on the horizon. To the extent that Islam was counterhegemonic, it was as a more diffuse force. The counterhegemonic potential of Islam really came in two forms: first in the violent activism of substate Islamic groups and second in the realm of cultural values.

The Islamic Militants

Islamic fighters and terrorists were a presence in international affairs, a fact dramatically highlighted by the events of 11 September 2001. The relationship between Muslim states and Islamic militants varied considerably: some states were direct sponsors, some indirect sponsors, and some outright opponents. Where Muslim states supported Islamic insurgency, it was most often as a substitute for their own direct participation in particular conflicts, most notably in the Arab-Israeli and Kashmir conflicts. In the conflict over the Israeli occupation of southern Lebanon, for instance, the militant Hizballah organization led Muslim resistance against Israel throughout the 1990s. Hizballah was the proxy of Iran and Syria, and although they ran some risks for their support of the organization, the risks were much reduced. With Hizballah as the lead force, the conflict was confined to southern Lebanon, and through a war of attrition, Hizballah went on to inflict a strategic defeat on Israel, forcing its military retreat in May 2000.

A network of Islamic activists played a role in almost every post–Cold War conflict involving Muslims. The Arab Muslim Brotherhood and Pakistani Jamaat-i-Islami were the principal organizations of the international network, but Muslim states were also quietly involved. A cadre of even more radical activists moved in and out of the mainstream framework, with some creating their own, more independent networks. In Sudan, the leading Islamic politician and thinker, Hasan al-Turabi, sought to organize an international caucus of militant Islamists and nationalists aimed at developing an alternative to the stewardship of the big states and mainstream Islamic organizations, which many militants thought had failed Muslims. The Popular Arab and Islamic Conference first met in Khartoum in 1991 and continues to bring a varied group of militants from all over the Middle East together for conferences.

The Islamic milieu of Afghanistan-Pakistan-Kashmir was a particularly important node for the more radical in the Islamist network. Al-Qaeda became the most important of these radical groups, but it was not the only one. Many of the militants that passed through or found refuge in Pakistan continued to focus on local struggles in their countries of origin, but the idea that Islamists were engaged in a collective global struggle was encouraged by some in the area, notably al-Qaeda. The conflict zones in adjacent Afghanistan and Kashmir were ready-made engines for basing, recruitment, indoctrination, and training. Moreover, the Islamic milieu increasingly slipped beyond the control of the key state sponsors, Pakistan and Saudi Arabia, especially after so many of the militants fell out with Saudi Arabia over the basing of U.S. troops in the kingdom after 1990. Pakistan and Saudi Arabia hung on to some of their leverage in the milieu, but the rise of the Taliban in Afghanistan in 1994–1996 gave the most radical further options for basing. Amid this milieu, al-Qaeda developed into a global phenomenon by the end of the 1990s.

The Islamic militants were a significant, if sporadic, security threat to U.S. forces and citizens. Of course, their moment of greatest success came with the al-Qaeda attack on the United States on 11 September 2001: thousands killed, tens of billions of dollars in costs, some of the nation's most important buildings damaged or demolished, and al-Qaeda propelled to enormous global prominence. The idea that such people might get their hands on various weapons of mass destruction was a frightening prospect indeed. Islamic militants also threatened the security and stability of some of the most important allies of the United States in the Middle East, and this threat seemed likely to grow in the aftermath of 11 September.

It is important, however, to get the threat posed by Islamic terrorism into some perspective. Short of an unlikely Islamic revolution in one of the major Middle Eastern states, the militants did not really pose a strategic threat to the power of the United States, much less to the Western hegemony. Meanwhile, Islamic militants might continue to fight it out with the Israeli, Russian, Indian, and Philippine armies, but these were long wars of attrition over limited tracts of land. On occasion, as with the major battles that took place between Islamists and the Indian Army in Kashmir between May and July 1999, local fighting threatened a more serious escalation into interstate conflict, but in none of these conflicts was a successful outcome in sight for Islamic militants.

The Palestinian terrorism of the 1970s and the Iranian-backed terrorism of the 1980s contributed to a much higher tempo of terrorist activity than was evident in the 1990s, even with the emergence of al-Qaeda. The global war on terrorism launched after 11 September 2001 seemed likely to suppress terrorist activity even further, especially if the Afghanistan-Pakistan-Kashmir sanctuary for Islamic militants was eventually closed down. The mood almost everywhere in the Muslim world had already hardened against the use of insurgency and terrorism. Many Muslim states had put increasing efforts into both bilateral and multilateral schemes to control, divide, and marginalize the most militant Islamic activists. The OIC was a forum for moderation, too, and the pressure on all member states to conform was considerable. At the OIC's Tehran summit in 1997, the OIC resolved to "declare that the killing of innocent people is forbidden in Islam," although it recognized the "rights of peoples under colonial or alien domination or foreign occupation for self determination."[11] The OIC called on everyone to "deny asylum to terrorists, assist in bringing them to justice, and take all necessary measures to prevent or to dismantle support networks helpful in any form to terrorism." The final communiqué of the summit specifically condemned the massacre of nearly sixty Western tourists at Luxor in Egypt as a "barbaric crime."[12]

Muslim states were principal targets of Islamic terrorism and most were extremely serious about tackling the problem of violent militancy, even before September 2001. Other than in a very few conflicts, notably with respect to Israel and Kashmir, violence was increasingly thought to be wrong, counterproductive, and damaging to the reputation of Islam and Muslims. For almost all Muslim states, attacking Westerners went out of bounds in the 1990s, and even Iran, Syria, and Libya were no longer really in the game of international terrorism. The contraction of the Iranian government's support for Islamic revolutionaries in the 1990s led to a significant falloff in terrorist activity. In the long run, most of the independent-minded Islamic groups probably had little choice but to defer to the big Muslim states or to the organizations linked to them. Moreover, notwithstanding the stunning impact of the 11 September 2001 attacks in the United States, insurgent warfare and terrorism were essentially the tools of the weak, not of the strong. Desperate acts of Islamic terrorism were almost a litmus test for the continuing weakness of Muslims in the international system.

The Diffuse Counterhegemony of Islamic Social Values

Islam was perhaps at its most significant as a counterhegemonic force not at the level of the international actor but as a social ideology; its significance was not so much in the realm of geopolitics as in the realm of culture and economics. Islam's power stemmed from the fact that millions of ordinary Muslims did not believe in the universality of the liberal idea, nor were they insensible to the challenge that global capitalism represented to their Islamic faith and traditions. Relations with Western states and global capitalists were widely problematized by Muslims, and Muslim governments had ultimately to take notice of Islamic sensibilities.

The battle for culture was being fought in the homes, streets, shops, mosques, and workplaces of the Muslim world, and it was on these battlefields that Islam was at its most powerful. The Western hegemony had arrived, to be sure, but Islam remained central in the political and cultural debates of the Muslim world, and it was widely agreed that the new globalization had to be tempered by Islamic values. The liberal politics and economics of the Western hegemony had an unprecedented ability to penetrate other societies, but in the Muslim world, the West met resistance from individual Muslims taking a myriad of day-to-day decisions and from Islamic social institutions and organizations, including the Muslim family. Islam's resistance could not really challenge the political and military supremacy of the Western hegemony, but it could act as a brake on its capacity to transform Muslim societies. In a world rapidly being swallowed by an all-pervasive global system, Islam was a diffuse grassroots counterhegemony.

Conclusion: Into the Twenty-First Century

The Muslim world saw enormous and unsettling events in the twentieth century. The Ottoman Empire finally faded into history. European colo-

nialism came and went. Israeli colonialism came and stayed. Nationalists led the way to independence but were tarnished by a troubled modernization and by military defeat at the hands of Israel. The oil boom
made some wealthy but more frustrated. Muslims were drawn into the
Cold War, while its end left the United States as an unrivaled hegemonic power. Muslims sought comfort in tradition, and the Islamic revival
came to dominate the politics and culture of Muslim lands, but it did
not significantly improve the lot of most Muslims. When in power, the
performance of Islamists was poor. When in opposition, Islamic
activism led to a paralyzed politics that went nowhere. Islamic civilization was essentially moribund at the end of the twentieth century.

Most Muslims know that they live in a world dominated by others
and, for the foreseeable future, that is how it will remain. All too
often—as the above history shows—Muslims were hapless parties in
someone else's game, their voices parried or dismissed. The forces of
the new globalization added to the uncertainty about where Muslim history was going. Having just about come to terms with the modern territorial state by the late twentieth century, Muslims now must readjust to
the decentralizing pressures of globalization. What the West had given,
it was now taking away.

The twenty-first century will doubtless witness similar great
changes and trials for Muslims. Of course, any futurology carries the
risk of disappointment, and the unforeseeable will occur, but a number
of things seemed predictable. The importance of Muslims will grow
significantly. The world's Muslim population is growing at an extraordinary rate: 2–3.5 percent per annum in many Muslim countries. By the
middle of the twenty-first century, Muslims will likely constitute over
one-third of the world's population, with countries such as Algeria,
Egypt, Saudi Arabia, Syria, Iraq, Turkey, Iran, and Pakistan doubling or
even tripling their populations. Such population growth will be a driver
of change and conflict.

Muslims sit on top of by far the world's largest reserves of oil. The
closing decades of the twentieth century were lean years in the world
oil market, but world consumption is bound to rise just as alternative oil
supplies will decline. Notwithstanding significant energy substitution
for oil fuels, the world will become more dependent on Middle Eastern
oil in the twenty-first century, and it seems inevitable that oil will again
bring great wealth into the Middle East. With Asia growing to demand
40 percent of the world's oil by 2020, the competition for secure and
reasonably priced oil between the West and Asia will be keener.[13]

Oil, money, and population size, even if poorly deployed, will increase the weight of Muslim states with significant consequences. Muslim states will continue to prioritize military security, and a few seem likely to follow Pakistan in acquiring nuclear weapons. Short of an acceptable Arab-Israeli peace, a profound crisis of security for Israel looms in the twenty-first century. Avoiding a calamity in the Middle East is one of the principal issues facing humanity. The renewed centrality of the Middle East is also likely to draw in other major actors. U.S. hegemony will likely have to deal with the emerging superpower interests of Europe, China, and possibly India.

Muslims will be more important in the world in the twenty-first century, but most cannot feel unreservedly optimistic about the future. The prosperity gap across the Muslim world is likely to widen. In some places, the incentives for Muslims to emigrate to somewhere better will heighten tensions with neighbors. The business and technology found in most Muslim countries are decades behind those in the most advanced countries, and it seems unlikely that Muslims will catch up soon. A few pockets of advanced economic activity may develop in such places as the Arab Gulf, but the global economic system will continue to leave most Muslims on the wrong side of profoundly unequal relationships.

Politicized Islam will go on casting a shadow across all Muslim societies, but it is unclear where Islamic militancy is going. Fundamentalists had triumphed in Iran, Sudan, and Afghanistan, but the next breakthrough could not be foreseen. Opinions differed, but many observers saw that fundamentalism had just about run its course. Fouad Ajami thought the strength of political Islam had always been exaggerated, and it had now passed its peak. For Ajami, all the fundamentalists could ever have done was "mount a rear-guard action against an encircling civilization they could neither master nor reject."[14] Fred Halliday believed that the Islamic challenge was a myth, confounded by the realities of states, economics, and unequal distributions of power in the world.[15] Olivier Roy argued that neofundamentalism had taken political Islamism into a dead end and had already disarmed Islam of its political power:

> The impact of Islamism . . . is essentially socio-cultural: it marks the streets and customs but has no power relationship in the Middle East. It does not influence either states borders or interests. It has not created a "third force." It has not even been able to offer the Muslim masses a concrete political expression of their anti-colonialism. Can it offer an economic alternative or deeply transform a society? The answer seems to be no.[16]

Samuel Huntington also thought fundamentalism a dead end but believed that it would continue to have power until Muslim population growth slowed sometime in the second or third decade of the twenty-first century.[17] According to Huntington, Muslims were likely to look back on the Islamic resurgence and see that "Islam is the solution to the problems of morality, identity, meaning, and faith, but not to the problems of social justice, political repression, economic backwardness, and military weakness."[18] Benjamin Barber foresaw that McWorld would eventually overpower jihad everywhere, although the likely persistence of "Jihad's microwars" would continue to make predictions about the end of history look "terminally dumb."[19] In the long run, McWorld would be unstoppable.

The voice of Islamic militancy will continue to be fired by the dissatisfaction of millions of ordinary Muslims with their lot and by the uncertainties of change. Fundamentalism will also be fed by the chronic conflicts that continue to beset Muslims, especially the Arab-Israeli conflict. That Islamic fundamentalism is a dead end, though, is clear. The rise of fundamentalism was a sign of just how little confidence Muslims had in themselves and their societies. Of course, every non-Western society must deal with the fact that the West made the modern world and still dominates it, but Islamic culture continues to make Muslims struggle more than most to come to terms with these facts.

Modernization and Westernization cannot be separated, only endured and accommodated, but this fact Islamism has yet to accept. The debates required to modernize Islamic politics have started in some places, but it remains unclear how far they can go. The cost of the cultural impasse is that the Muslim world is not very modern and not very competitive. Fundamentalists may express the rage of some Muslims about their situation, but if they can do no more than that, they will play little role in solving the many crises facing the Muslim world. Fundamentalists must provide solutions for the contemporary world, not just raise problems. In the meantime, Islamic fundamentalism means paralysis, and few Muslims really want more paralysis, parochialism, and backwardness.

More broadly, and notwithstanding some of the more alarmist predictions of civilizational warriors, one thing seems clear. The Muslim world is too divided to act as a coherent bloc in international politics, although Islam is a cultural power at work across Muslim societies. Moments of unity or common outrage may sweep across the Muslim world—there are issues such as that of the Al-Aqsa mosque in

Jerusalem that may produce explosive stirrings—but it is very difficult to see how Islam can be united or who can do it. The traditional methods of empire building embodied in Iraq's behavior toward Kuwait are hardly viable, especially with a giant hegemonic power watching so closely. The bodies of Muslim unity like the OIC will likely remain subordinate to the interests and immediacy of the state.

In the end, the only real option for Muslims in the twenty-first century is to make a better accommodation with the future rather than the past. Globalization is here to stay, and not to take full advantage of it is to leave the world to the stewardship of others with fewer moral qualms. Muslims have absorbed globalized ideas and practices, but there is little recognition that Islamic culture is being synthesized or that such change is a good thing. The result is distorted change. Muslims have taken up technology and consumerism without an acceptance of the individualism, public and private institutions, and democratic principles that make modernity in the West work so much better. Partial globalization represents a sight of the promised land without the means of really getting there.

If Muslims are to avoid the despair of the backwater or of some unsatisfactory halfway house, there must come a point at which cultural synthesis is genuinely embraced. Muslim societies cannot possibly develop to compete with Western and Asian countries as long as they are caught in the grip of authoritarian cliques and military rulers or of Islamic fundamentalists. Nor can Muslims compete as long as the potential of women is so contained by political and social restrictions. The unleashing of women was the most important social and economic phenomenon in twentieth-century Western society, and one that added enormously to its productiveness, especially in the United States.

At the beginning of the twenty-first century, most Muslim countries have failed to reconcile the global and the local. Malaysia is one of the few places that has found a working accommodation. The big Arab societies of Algeria, Egypt, and Syria remain paralyzed by political deadlock. A number of the smaller Arab states are making more headway, and it seems possible that such places as Jordan, Kuwait, Bahrain, Qatar, and the United Arab Emirates might slowly show the way toward a more liberal future, including political and social toleration and greater status for women. Saudi Arabia and Morocco lag in the conservative slow lane, but in the realm of commerce and the workplace, significant changes are coming into place.

Across the Gulf, the Islamic Republic of Iran also has a long way to go, but what is happening in Iran looks important. Iran has the position, size, and resources to be a major power in its own right, but unleashing that potential is about getting the politics of Islam right. Most Iranians know what debates they have to have, as well as what the likely outcome will be, but that does not stop the resistance of entrenched conservative interests. In Iran, Muslims are poised to modernize and democratize under their own ideological steam, and this would be an important development. Iran holds out the promise of being the first mass Islamic democracy.

Embracing globalized modernity does mean Westernization to some extent or other, but defensive and exclusionary responses can only perpetuate backwardness and failure. The future points to more complex Islamic identities, and that requires a leap of faith, but it does not mean the end of Muslim civilization. The capacity of the global to integrate is considerable, but Muslims will not merge seamlessly into some vast global culture. Muslims are distinct and will remain so, as they continue to identify with their own communities, as well as with over 1,400 years of Islamic faith and culture. Of course, the yet unanswered question is, can Islamic cultures effectively assimilate the best in global practices, and if so, when? Can Muslims mesh Islamic culture with the universal goods of the liberal idea? Muslims need to know, and their politics ought to find a way of telling them. Finding the path to a better modernity is the principal issue in Islamic politics and will substantially define the Muslim experience in the twenty-first century.

Notes

1. Hashemi, "International Society and Its Islamic Malcontents," *Fletcher Forum of World Affairs* 20, no. 2, Winter–Spring 1996, 13–29.

2. Ibid., 18.

3. "Charter of the OIC," reproduced on the Homepage of the Permanent Delegation of the OIC to the UN Offices in Geneva and Vienna, http://www.oic-un.org/about/Charter.htm.

4. Piscatori, "The Rushdie Affair and the Politics of Ambiguity," *International Affairs* 66, no. 4, 1990, 783–784.

5. Hashemi, "International Society and Its Islamic Malcontents," 24.

6. David George, "Pax Islamica: An Alternative New World Order?" in Abdel Salam Sidahmed and Anourshiravan Ehteshami, eds., *Islamic Fundamentalism,* 1996, 73.

7. From the text of the Final Communiqué of the Ninth Summit of the OIC, Abu Dhabi, 12–13 November 2000 ("The Situation in Chechnya," Point 51). Reproduced on the Homepage of the Permanent Delegation of the OIC to the UN Offices in Geneva and Vienna, http://www,oil-un.org/english/is/9/9th-is-sum-final_communique/htm#int.

8. Final Communiqué of the Ninth Summit of the OIC, Abu Dhabi, 12–13 November 2000 ("The Question of Palestine, *Al-Quds Al-Sharif,* and the Arab-Israeli Conflict," Point 40). Reproduced on the Homepage of the Permanent Delegation of the OIC to the UN Offices in Geneva and Vienna, http://www,oil-un.org/english/is/9/9th-is-sum-final_communique/htm#int.

9. Final Communiqué adopted by the Ninth Extraordinary Meeting of OIC Foreign Ministers in Doha, Qatar, 10 October 2001. Reproduced on the Homepage of the Permanent Delegation of the OIC to the UN Offices in Geneva and Vienna, http://wwww.oic-un.org/home/FQ.htm.

10. Address by Mohammad Khatami to the Eighth Islamic Summit Conference in Tehran, 9 December 1997. Reproduced on the Homepage of the Permanent Delegation of the OIC to the UN Offices in Geneva and Vienna, http://www.oic-un.org/8/ khatami.htm.

11. From the "Tehran Declaration," Eighth Islamic Summit Conference ("Solidarity and Security in the Islamic World," Point 10). Reproduced on the Homepage of the Permanent Delegation of the OIC to the UN Offices in Geneva and Vienna, http://www-oic-un.org/8/tehdec.htm.

12. Final Communiqué of the Eighth Islamic Summit in Tehran, 9–11 December 1997 ("Legal Affairs," Point 107). Reproduced on the Homepage of the Permanent Delegation of the OIC to the UN Offices in Geneva and Vienna, http://www.oic-un.org/8/fincom8.htm.

13. Peter Kemp, "The Tortoise and the Hare," *Middle East Economic Digest* 42, no. 32, 7 August 1998, 5.

14. Ajami, "The Arab Inheritance," *Foreign Affairs* 76, no. 5, September–October 1987, 139.

15. Halliday, *Islam and the Myth of Confrontation,* 1995, 119.

16. Roy, "The Geostrategy of Islamism: States and Networks," in *The Failure of Political Islam,* 1994, 131.

17. Huntington, *The Clash of Civilizations and the Remaking of the World Order,* 1996, 120.

18. Ibid., 121.

19. Barber, "Introduction," in *Jihad vs. McWorld,* 1996, 20.

Appendix I:
The History of the Liberal Idea

In the reign of Henry II of England (1154–1189), the "rule of law" was established in books of "common law." Arbitrary rule by King John I resulted in a baronial revolt and the signing of the *Magna Carta* in 1215. The king was obliged to maintain the rule of law and consult the barons. In 1258, Simon de Montfort forced Henry III to accept the Provisions of Oxford. A fifteen-man council elected by barons assumed the key sovereign powers of the king, and an assembly of four knights elected from each English county represented the grievances of the entire realm. A parliament with powers over taxation would eventually become well established in England.

Across northern Europe, the Protestant Reformation challenged the divine claims of kings and the ideology of Catholicism. In England, relations between Charles I and Parliament broke down into the Civil Wars (1642–1651). The king was deposed by parliamentary forces led by John Pym, Thomas Fairfax, and Oliver Cromwell. Radical republicans known as the Levellers pressed for equality, democracy, and religious tolerance, but were suppressed after "agitation" in the New Model Army. The Levellers were too far ahead of their time. Cromwell drifted toward military dictatorship. The English monarchy was restored in 1660, but political rights were reaffirmed in the "Glorious Revolution" against James II in 1688–1689. In 1689, joint monarchs William III and Mary II ratified the "Bill of Rights": it was the centerpiece of legislation that secured Parliament's primacy over taxation and the army, denied the Crown the right to suspend laws, and guaranteed certain rights and liberties, including religious toleration for all Protestants, elections every three years, and freedom of speech for parliamentarians. Britain led the world in the development of constitutional government.

The Enlightenment: Natural sciences led the way to reason from the late seventeenth century, especially in the work of Issac Newton and David Hume. In *Two*

211

Treatises on Civil Government (1690), John Locke proposed a social contract that included freedom of conscience and the right to property. Adam Smith theorized market economics in the *Wealth of Nations* (1776). In France, Voltaire and Jean-Jacques Rousseau attacked the traditional and argued for the rights of the common people. In Germany, Immanuel Kant advocated religious tolerance, and in his essay *Perpetual Peace* (1795) claimed that the spread of democratic nations might produce a "democratic peace" across the world.

▼

The American and French Revolutions: The kind of radical thought expressed by Englishman Thomas Paine in *Commonsense* (1776) and *The Rights of Man* (1791–1792) was taken up in a revolt over taxation in Britain's American colonies. Thomas Jefferson, Alexander Hamilton, and John Adams made liberalism a reality. The American Revolution (1775–1783) ended colonial rule and led to the U.S. Constitution (1789); its Bill of Rights amendments (1791) became the classic statement of liberal rights, including trial by jury and the freedoms of religion, speech, press, and assembly. In France, a bourgeois-led revolution overturned the *ancien regime* in 1789. Liberty, equality, and fraternity were promised, but the revolution was lost to the tyranny of Robespierre and Napoleon. European liberalism became inextricably associated with nationalism and the idea of national self-determination. In the Western world, democracy gradually became the norm; the franchise was extended for males, and, in 1893, New Zealand became the first Western nation to give women the vote in national elections.

▼

During the nineteenth century, the British Empire was at the center of the first truly global economic system. Britain was the most important economic and normative force in the world, although its hegemony waned as other powers caught up. The twentieth century saw an epic struggle within European civilization between the liberal West and authoritarian East. U.S. intervention was decisive in swinging the balance. World War I did away with absolute monarchy. World War II turned the tide on extremist nationalism. In August 1941, Britain and the United States signed the Atlantic Charter, outlining a future world based on the rule of law, self-determination, and freer trade. The Atlantic Charter underpinned the foundation of the United Nations in 1945 and the Universal Declaration of Human Rights in 1948. In 1950, the European Convention on Human Rights was agreed by the Council of Europe. The United States superseded Britain's global role and established a liberal system capable of resisting the Soviet alternative. In the 1980s, Margaret Thatcher and Ronald Reagan forged a liberal-capitalist revival that was to dominate the world economy. The Marxist-Leninist challenge was finally defeated in 1989. Francis Fukuyama's *The End of History and the Last Man* (1992) spoke of the global triumph of the "liberal idea" and the way in which it represented the ultimate political and economic system. Anglo-American liberalism was the ideological foundation of a globalized Western hegemony. Liberalism faced only localized resistance.

Appendix 2:
The History of the Islamic Faith

From 610 to 632 C.E., the Prophet Mohammad (570–632 C.E.) received revelations from God through the angel Gabriel. The Islamic era began in 622 C.E., when Mohammad migrated from Mecca to Medina (the *hejira*) to escape persecution and find a following. Mohammad's recollections of God's message were set down in the Quran, and its 114 chapters *(suras)* are the basis of Islamic faith and social life. God was one *(tawhid)*, and so must be humanity's submission. The aim of Muslims was to reach God's paradise, and each had to account for his or her life's deeds on a day of judgment. The perfect Muslim was the Prophet. Mohammad's words and deeds were the *sunna,* later collected as the *hadith.*

The "five pillars" of Islamic observance are (1) the *shahadah* declaration ("there is no god but Allah, and Muhammad is his messenger"); (2) *salah* (five ritualized daily prayers orientated to Mecca); (3) *zakat* (alms giving); (4) *sawn* (dawn to sunset fasting during the month of Ramadan); and (5) *hajj* (pilgrimage to Mecca). Muslims prayed to God directly, but mosques were built for community worship and learning. The midday prayer on Fridays—the *Jumah* prayer—is the most important act of weekly communal worship. All Muslims are equal under God.

The Islamic community *(umma)* was governed by the *caliph,* a ruler with both political and religious primacy. The era of the Four Rightly Guided Caliphs ended in civil war. In 661 C.E., Caliph Ali (Mohammad's cousin and son-in-law) was defeated and later murdered in a revolt led by the Ummayad family based in Damascus. With astonishing speed, Islamic warriors and merchants forged an empire from Spain to India.

▼

Sunni Islam

▼

Shia Islam

213

Sunni Islam.   Under the Ummayad (661–750 C.E.) and Abassid (750–1258 C.E.) Caliphates, the Quran and *sunna* were used to produce Islamic law *(sharia)*. The *sharia* included severe penalties for particular crimes, such as apostasy, adultery, theft, and drinking alcohol. Four schools of orthodox jurisprudence developed: the *Hanfi, Shafi, Hanbali,* and *Maliki.* Sunni Islam prioritized order and became traditionalist. The subordinate status of women was fixed. Islam was periodically revived by mystical Sufi cults and by funda-mentalist revivals.

▼

The Islamic empire fragmented, but Islamic civilization developed advanced philosophy and science, reaching a peak in Andalusia. Muslims came under attack. The First Crusade in 1096 inaugurated 150 years of conflict with Christendom in the Holy Land. Muslims were pushed back in the Mediterranean. In Spain, Islamic Granada was extinguished in 1492. In the east, the Mongols destroyed the huge Muslim empire of Khwarezm in the 1220s and went on to smash the Abassid Caliphate in Baghdad in 1258. Mamluk soldiers stopped the Mongols at Ayn Jalut in 1260 and led Islamic cul-ture from Egypt until the rise of the Ottoman Empire. In 1453, the Ottomans stormed Christian Constantinople and made it their capital. In 1517, the Ottomans defeated the Mamluks. The caliphate was transferred to the Ottoman capital. The failure of the Ottoman siege of Vienna in 1683 marked the end of Ottoman expansion. In India, Muslim soldiers of Mongol descent established the great Mughal empire in 1526.

▼

The Muslim empires were bureaucratic, and the Islamic world stagnated. Between the eighteenth and twentieth centuries, Europeans moved in. The last Mughal emperor was deposed by the British following the Indian Mutiny in 1857. Periodic attempts were made to revive Islam, including an effort to absorb liberalism. World War I ended the Ottoman Empire. Britain and France divided the Middle East into territorial states. Mustafa Kemal abolished the Ottoman Caliphate, and secular nationalism carried Muslims toward indepen-dence. Nationalism failed. Jerusalem was lost to Israel in 1967. A new militant Islam was forged by Hasan al-Banna, Sayyid Qutb, and Abu al-Ala al-Mawdudi. The Islamic revival took hold across the Muslim world from the 1970s, but paralyzed political and economic development.

Shia Islam.   In the line of Ali: Ali's son, Husain, was killed by Ummayad forces at Karbala in 680 C.E. Shia Islam fragmented into sects, such as the Ismailis and Zaydis, based on adherence to different religious personalities, known as *imans.* The most important sect, the Twelvers, adhered to the twelfth and final iman, who disappeared in 873 C.E. but was expected to return as a *madhi* at the end of history. The Shia developed the *Jaafari* school of jurispru-dence, as well as a far more hierarchical clergy than Sunnis.

▼

As a deviant minority, the Shia were pressed to more remote regions, and developed the pacific doctrine of *taqiyya* (concealing their faith). The center of Shia Islam was Najaf and Karbala (now in southern Iraq), but in 1501 the Persian Safavid Empire (1501–1736) declared Shi'ism its official religion. In 1639, the border between the Safavid and Ottoman empires was fixed, approximating the present-day Iran-Iraq border. Persia eventually superseded Najaf and Karbala as the heartland of Shia Islam. Qom, Isfahan, and Mashad were the principal centers of Shia Islam in Iran.

▼

In the early twentieth century, Iran experienced parliamentary politics, in which Shia clergymen were involved. In 1921, the Qajar monarchy was overthrown by Reza Khan, who established the modernizing Pahlavi dynasty. In the 1950s and 1960s, Grand Ayatollah Ruhullah Khomeini emerged as a key figure in the opposition to the Pahlavi state. Khomeini proposed the *velayat-e faqih* (the guardianship of the jurisconsult). Militant Shi'ism led the Iranian Revolution of 1978–1979. The new Islamic state in Iran had followers in other Shia communities, but its energy was exhausted by the Iran-Iraq War (1980–1988). Khomeini died in 1989. Conservatives and reformers battled over the future of Iranian politics. Mohammad Khatami was elected as Iranian president in 1997, with a reform agenda.

Bibliography

Abdel-Fadil, M., "Globalization and the New Economy in Gulf States," paper presented to the Conference on Globalization and the Gulf, 2–4 July 2001, Institute of Arab and Islamic Studies, University of Exeter, United Kingdom.

Abootalebi, Ali R., "Islam, Islamists, and Democracy," *Middle East Review of International Affairs Journal* 3, no. 1, March 1998 (MERIA online journal, distributed by the BESA Center for Strategic Studies, Bar-Ilan University, http://meria.biu.ac.il/; besa@mail.biu.ac.il/>/).

———, "State-Society Relations and the Prospects for Democracy in Iran," *Middle East Review of International Affairs* 5, no. 3, September 1991 (MERIA online journal, distributed by the BESA Center for Strategic Studies, Bar-Ilan University, http://meria.biu.ac.il/; besa@mail.biu.ac.il/>/).

AbuKhalil, As'ad, "The Incoherence of Islamic Fundamentalism: Arab Islamic Thought at the End of the 20th Century," *Middle East Journal* 48, no. 4, Autumn 1994, pp. 677–694.

Agnew, John, and Stuart Corbridge, *Mastering Space: Hegemony, Territory and International Political Economy,* London: Routledge, 1995.

Ahmad, Mumtaz, and William Zartman, "Political Islam: Can It Become a Loyal Opposition?" *Middle East Policy* 5, no. 1, January 1997, pp. 68–84.

Ahmed, Akbar S. *Post-Modernism and Islam: Predicament and Promise,* London: Routledge, 1992.

Ahmed, Akbar S., and Hastings Donnan, eds., *Islam, Globalization and Postmodernity,* London: Routledge, 1994.

Ajami, Fouad, "The Arab Inheritance," *Foreign Affairs* 76, no. 5, September–October 1987, pp. 133–148.

———, *The Arab Predicament: Arab Political Thought and Practice Since 1967,* Cambridge: Cambridge University Press, 1992, updated edition.

———, "The Summoning," *Foreign Affairs* 72, no. 4, September–October 1993, pp. 2–9.

Albert, Mathias, and Lothar Brock, "Debordering the World of States: New Spaces in International Relations," paper presented at the Annual

Conference of the British International Studies Association, Southampton, 18–20 December 1995.

Albrow, Martin, *The Global Age: State and Society Beyond Modernity,* Cambridge: Polity Press, 1996.

Amuzegar, Jahangir, "Iran's Economy and the U.S. Sanctions," *Middle East Journal* 51, no. 2, Spring 1997, pp. 185–199.

Anthony, John Duke, "The US-GCC Relationship: A Glass Half Empty or Half Full?" *Middle East Policy* 5, no. 2, May 1997, pp. 22–41.

Armstrong, Karen, "Fundamentalism," *Demos*, no. 11 (Quarterly), 1997, pp. 15–17.

Axford, Barrie, *The Global System: Economics, Politics and Culture,* Cambridge: Polity Press, 1995.

Ayubi, Nazih, "Withered Socialism or Whether Socialism? The Radical Arab States as Populist-Corporatist Regimes," *Third World Quarterly* 13, no. 1, 1992, pp. 89–105.

Azzam, Maha, "The Gulf Crisis: Perceptions in the Muslim World," *International Affairs* 67, no. 3, July 1991, pp. 473–485.

Bakhash, Shaul, "The Politics of Land, Law, and Social Justice in Iran," *Middle East Journal* 43, no. 2, Spring 1989, p. 196.

Barber, Benjamin, "Disneyfication That Impoverishes Us All," *The Independent* (Weekend Review Section), 29 August 1998.

———, *Jihad vs. McWorld: How Globalism and Tribalism Are Reshaping the World,* New York: Ballantine Books, 1996.

Barraclough, Steven, "Al-Azhar: Between the Government and the Islamists," *Middle East Journal* 52, no. 2, Spring 1998, pp. 236–249.

Baylis, John, and Steve Smith, eds., *The Globalization of World Politics,* Oxford: Oxford University Press, 1997.

Beblawi, Hazem, "The Rentier State in the Arab World," *Arab Studies Quarterly* 9, no. 4, Fall 1987, pp. 383–398.

Beinin, Joel, and Joe Stork, eds., *Political Islam: Essays from the Middle East Report,* Los Angeles: University of California Press, 1997.

Beyer, Peter, *Religion and Globalization,* London: Sage Publications, 1994.

Bienefeld, Manfred, "The New World Order: Echoes of a New Imperialism," *Third World Quarterly* 15, no. 1, 1994, pp. 31–48.

Bill, James A., and Robert Springborg, *Politics in the Middle East,* New York: Harper Collins, 4th ed., 1994.

Binder, Leonard, "The Changing American Role in the Middle East," *Current History* 88, no. 535, February 1989, pp. 65–68, 96.

Booth, Ken, "Huntington's Homespun Grandeur," *Political Quarterly* 68, no. 4, 1997, pp. 425–428.

Brohman, John, "Economism and Critical Silences in Development Studies: A Theoretical Critique of Neoliberalism," *Third World Quarterly* 16, no. 2, 1995, pp. 297–318.

Brown, Chris, "Cultural Diversity and International Political Theory," *Review of International Studies* 26, no. 2, April 2000, pp. 199–213.

———, "History Ends, Worlds Collide," *Review of International Studies* 25, Special Issue: The Interregnum: Controversies in World Politics 1989–1999, December 1999, pp. 41–57.

Brynen, Rex, Bahgat Korany, and Paul Noble, eds., *Political Liberalization and Democratization in the Arab World, Volume 1: Theoretical Perspectives,* Boulder, Colo.: Lynne Rienner Publishers, 1995.

Buzan, Barry, "New Patterns of Global Security in the Twenty-first Century," *International Affairs* 67, no. 3, July 1991, pp. 431–451.

Buzan, Barry, and Richard Little, "Beyond Westphalia? Capitalism After the 'Fall,'" *Review of International Studies* 25, Special Issue: The Interregnum: Controversies in World Politics 1989–1999, December 1999, pp. 89–104.

Byman, Daniel, Kenneth Pollack, and Matthew Waxman, "Coercing Saddam Hussein: Lessons from the Past," *Survival* 40, no. 3, Autumn 1998, pp. 127–151.

Cameron, Angus, "The World Trade Organisation and Globalisation," paper presented at the Annual Conference of the British International Studies Association, Southampton, 18–20 December 1995.

Cantori, Louis J., "The American Way: U.S. Development Policy in the Middle East," *Middle East Policy* 5, no. 1, January 1997, pp. 170–177.

Chan, Stephen, "Too Neat and Under-thought a World Order: Huntington and Civilizations," *Millennium: Journal of International Studies* 26, no. 1, 1997, pp. 137–140.

Chubin, Shahram, "Does Iran Want Nuclear Weapons?" *Survival* 37, no. 1, Spring 1995, pp. 86–104.

Chubin, Shahram, and Jerrold D. Green, "Engaging Iran: A U.S. Strategy," *Survival* 40, no. 3, Autumn 1998, pp. 153–169.

Clapham, Christopher, "Introduction: Liberalisation, Regionalism and Statehood in the New Development Agenda," *Third World Quarterly* 17, no. 4, 1996, pp. 593–602.

Cox, Robert, "Civil Society at the Turn of the Millennium: Prospects for an Alternative World Order," *Review of International Studies* 25, no. 1, January 1999, pp. 3–28.

— — —, "Thinking About Civilizations," *Review of International Studies* 26, Special Issue, December 2000, pp. 217–234.

Cumings, Bruce, "Still the American Century?" *Review of International Studies* 25, Special Issue: The Interregnum: Controversies in World Politics 1989–1999, December 1999, pp. 271–299.

Deegan, Heather, *The Middle East and the Problems of Democracy,* Buckingham: Open University Press, 1993.

Dekmejian, R. Hrair, "The Rise of Political Islamism in Saudi Arabia," *Middle East Journal* 48, no. 4, Autumn 1994, pp. 627–643.

— — —, "Saudi Arabia's Consultative Council," *Middle East Journal* 52, no. 2, Spring 1998, pp. 204–218.

Dervis, Kemal, and Nemat Shafik, "The Middle East and North Africa: A Tale of Two Futures," *Middle East Journal* 52, no. 4, Autumn 1998.

Deudeney, Daniel, and G. John Ikenberry, "The Nature and Sources of Liberal International Order," *Review of International Studies* 25, no. 2, April 1999, pp. 179–196.

Deutsch, Robert S., Anthony H. Cordesman, Hervé Magro, and William A. Rugh, "Symposium—The Challenge in the Gulf: Building a Bridge from

Containment to Stability," *Middle East Policy* 5, no. 1, January 1997, pp. 1–21.

El-Doufani, Mohamed M., "Regional Revisionist Client States Under Unipolarity," *Third World Quarterly* 13, no. 2, 1992, pp. 255–265.

Dowty, Alan, and Michelle Gawerc, "The Intifada: Revealing the Chasm," *Middle East Review of International Affairs* 5, no. 3, September 1991 (MERIA online journal, distributed by the BESA Center for Strategic Studies, Bar-Ilan University, http://meria.biu.ac.il/; besa@mail. biu.ac.il/>/).

Doyle, Michael W., "A More Perfect Union? The Liberal Peace and the Challenge of Globalization," *Review of International Studies* 26, Special Issue, December 2000, pp. 81–94.

Drake, Laura, "Hegemony and Its Discontents: United States Policy Toward Iraq, Iran, Hamas, the Hizbullah and Their Responses," paper presented at the 38th annual convention of the International Studies Association, Toronto, Canada, 18–23 March 1997.

Ehteshami, Anoushiravan, "Islamic Fundamentalism and Political Islam," Chapter 9 in Brian White, Richard Little, and Michael Smith, eds., *Issues in World Politics,* London: MacMillan, 1997.

———, "Is the Middle East Democratizing?" *British Journal of Middle Eastern Studies* 26, no. 2, November 1999, pp. 199–217.

———, "Political Change in the Era of Globalisation," paper presented to the Conference on Globalisation and the Gulf, 2–4 July 2001, Institute of Arab and Islamic Studies, University of Exeter, United Kingdom.

Ehteshami, Anoushiravan, and Emma C. Murphy, "Transformation of the Corporatist State in the Middle East," *Third World Quarterly* 17, no. 4, 1996, pp. 753–772.

Elmusa, Sharif S., "Faust Without the Devil? The Interplay of Technology and Culture in Saudi Arabia," *Middle East Journal* 51, no. 3, Summer 1997, pp. 345–357.

Esposito, John. "Clash of Civilizations? Contemporary Images of Islam in the West," in Gema Martin Munoz, ed., *Islam, Modernism, and the West: Cultural and Political Relations at the End of the Millennium,* London: I. B. Tauris, 1999, p. 96.

———, "Political Islam: Beyond the Green Menace," *Current History,* January 1994, pp. 19–24.

———, *The Straight Path,* Oxford: Oxford University Press, 1991.

Esposito, John, ed. *Voices of Resurgent Islam,* Oxford: Oxford University Press, 1983.

Esposito, John, and James Piscatori, "Democratization and Islam," *Middle East Journal* 45, no. 3, Summer 1991, pp. 427–440.

Esposito, John, and Michael Watson, eds., *Religion and Global Order,* Cardiff: University of Wales Press, 2000.

Fahmy, Ninette S., "The Performance of the Muslim Brotherhood in Egyptian Syndicates: An Alternative Formula for Reform?" *Middle East Journal* 52, no. 4, Autumn 1998, pp. 552–562.

Fairbanks, Stephen C., "A New Era for Iran?" *Middle East Policy* 5, no. 3, September 1997, pp. 51–56.

Faksh, Mahmud A., and Ramzi F. Faris, "The Saudi Conundrum: Squaring the Security-Stability Circle," *Third World Quarterly* 14, no. 2, 1993, pp. 277–293.

Fandy, Mamoun, "Egypt's Islamic Group: Regional Revenge?" *Middle East Journal* 48, no. 4, Autumn 1994, pp. 607–625.

Farsoun, Samih K., and Mehrdad Mashayekhi, *Iran: Political Culture in the Islamic Republic,* London: Routledge, 1992.

Féler, Alain, and Oussama Kanaan, "An Assessment of Macroeconomic and Structural Adjustment in the Middle East and North Africa Since 1980," *Middle East Policy* 5, no. 1, January 1997, pp. 102–110.

Frank, Andre Gunder, "Third World War: A Political Economy of the Gulf War and the New World Order," *Third World Quarterly* 13, no. 2, 1992, pp. 267–282.

Freij, Hanna Yousif, "State Interests vs. the Umma: Iranian Policy in Central Asia," *Middle East Journal* 50, no. 1, Winter 1996, pp. 71–83.

Friedman, Robert I., *The World Trade Center Bombing and the CIA,* New Jersey: Open Magazine Pamphlet Series no. 27, October 1993, p. 16.

Fukuyama, Francis. *The End of History and the Last Man,* London: Penguin Books, 1992.

Gause, F. Gregory, "Getting It Backward on Iraq," *Foreign Affairs* 78, no. 3, May–June 1999, p. 54.

———, "The Illogic of Dual Containment," *Foreign Affairs* 73, no. 2, March–April 1994, pp. 56–66.

———, *Oil Monarchies: Domestic and Security Challenges in the Arab Gulf States,* New York: Council on Foreign Relations.

Gerges, Fawaz A., "Washington's Misguided Iran Policy," *Survival* 38, no. 4, Winter 1996–1997, pp. 5–15.

Gerner, Deborah, ed., *Understanding the Contemporary Middle East,* Boulder, Colo.: Lynne Rienner Publishers, 2000.

Ghanea-Hercock, Nazila, "Diplomatic Efforts to Protect Human Rights in Iran," paper presented at the British International Studies Association Annual Conference, University of Sussex, 15 December 1998.

Ghoreishi, Ahmad, and Dariush Zahedi, "Prospects for Regime Change in Iran," *Middle East Policy* 5, no. 1, January 1997, pp. 85–101.

Guazzone, Laura, ed., *The Islamist Dilemma: The Political Role of Islamist Movements in the Contemporary Arab World,* Reading: Ithaca Press, 1995.

Hadar, Leon, "America's Moment in the Middle East," *Current History* 95, no. 597, January 1996, pp. 1–5.

———. "What Green Peril?" *Foreign Affairs* 72, no. 2, Spring 1993, pp. 27–42.

Al-Haj, Abdullah Juma, "The Politics of Participation in the Gulf Co-operation Council States: The Omani Consultative Council," *Middle East Journal* 50, no. 4, Autumn 1996, pp. 559–571.

Halliday, Fred, "The Gulf War and Its Aftermath: First Reflections," *International Affairs* 67, no. 2, April 1991, pp. 223–234.

———, *Islam and the Myth of Confrontation,* London: I. B. Tauris, 1995.

———, *The World at 2000: Perils and Promises,* Basingstoke: Palgrave, 2001.

Hashemi, Sohail H., "International Society and Its Islamic Malcontents,"

Fletcher Forum of World Affairs 20, no. 2, Winter–Spring 1996, pp. 13–29.

Hashim, Ahmed, "Iraq: Fin de Regime?" *Current History* 95, no. 597, January 1996, pp. 10–15.

Hawthorn, Geoffrey, "Liberalism Since the Cold War: An Enemy to Itself?" *Review of International Studies* 25, Special Issue: The Interregnum: Controversies in World Politics 1989–1999, December 1999, pp. 145–160.

Held, David, and Anthony McGrew, "The End of the Old Order? Globalization and the Prospects for World Order," *Review of International Studies* 24, Special Issue, December 1998, pp. 219–243.

Higgot, Richard, "Beyond Embedded Liberalism: Governing the International Trade Regime in an Era of Economic Nationalism," paper presented at the Annual Conference of the British International Studies Association, Southampton, 18–20 December 1995.

Higgot, Richard, "Contested Globalization: The Changing Context and Normative Changes," *Review of International Studies* 26, Special Issue, December 2000, pp. 131–153.

Higgot, Richard, and Nicola Phillips, "Challenging Triumphalism and Convergence: The Limits of Global Liberalization in Asia and Latin America," *Review of International Studies* 26, no. 3, July 2000, pp. 359–379.

Hinnebusch, Raymond A., "The Politics of Economic Reform in Egypt," *Third World Quarterly* 14, no. 1, 1993, pp. 159–171.

———, "State and Civil Society in Syria," *Middle East Journal* 47, no. 2, Spring 1993, pp. 243–257.

Honderich, Ted, ed., *The Oxford Companion to Philosophy,* Oxford: Oxford University Press, 1995.

Hoskins, Eric, "The Impact of Sanctions: A Study of UNICEF's Perspective," New York: Office of Emergency Programmes Working Paper Series, reproduced on UNICEF's Website, "Newsline: Iraq Surveys Show Humanitarian Emergency," http://www.unicef.org/newsline/99pr29.htm.

Hudson, Michael C., "After the Gulf War: Prospects for Democratisation in the Arab World," *Middle East Journal* 45, no. 3, Summer 1991, pp. 407–426.

———, "The Middle East Under Pax Americana: How New, How Orderly?" *Third World Quarterly* 13, no. 2, 1992, pp. 301–316.

———, "To Play the Hegemon: Fifty Years of U.S. Policy Towards the Middle East," *Middle East Journal* 50, no. 3, Summer 1996, pp. 329–343.

Hunter, Shireen, ed. *The Politics of Islamic Revivalism: Diversity and Unity,* Bloomington: Indiana University Press, 1988.

Huntington, Samuel, "The Clash of Civilizations," *Foreign Affairs* 72, no. 3, Summer 1993, pp. 22–49.

———, *The Clash of Civilizations and the Remaking of the World Order,* New York: Touchstone, 1996.

———, "If Not Civilizations, What?" *Foreign Affairs* 72, no. 4, September–October 1993.

Husain, Mir Zohair, *Global Islamic Politics,* New York: Harper Collins, 1995.

al-Jabri, Mohammed Abed, "Clash of Civilizations: The Relations of the Future?" in Gema Martin Munoz, ed., *Islam, Modernism, and the West:*

Cultural and Political Relations at the End of the Millennium, London: I. B. Tauris, 1999, pp. 65–70.

Jervis, Robert, Book Review of *Clash of Civilizations* by Samuel Huntington, *Political Science Quarterly* 112, no. 2, 1997, pp. 307–308.

Joffé, George, "Algeria in Crisis," Royal Institute of International Affairs Briefing Paper, London, no. 48, June 1998.

———, "Relations Between the Middle East and the West," *Middle East Journal* 48, no. 2, Spring 1994, pp. 251–267.

Joseph, Robert, "Proliferation, Counter-Proliferation and NATO," *Survival* 38, no. 1, Spring 1996, pp. 111–130.

Julius, Deanne, "Globalization and Stakeholder Conflicts: A Corporate Perspective," *International Affairs* 73, no. 3, 1997, pp. 453–468.

Kadioğlu, Ayse, "Women's Subordination in Turkey: Is Islam Really the Villain?" *Middle East Journal* 48, no. 4, Autumn 1994, pp. 645–660.

Kalicki, Jan H., "A Vision for the U.S.-Saudi and U.S.-Gulf Commercial Relationship," *Middle East Policy* 5, no. 2, May 1997, pp. 73–78.

Kamrava, Mehran, "Conceptualising Third World Politics: The State-Society See-saw," *Third World Quarterly* 14, no. 4, 1993, pp. 703–716.

———, "Non-democratic States and Political Liberalisation in the Middle East: A Structural Analysis," *Third World Quarterly* 19, no. 1, 1998, pp. 63–85.

———, *Politics and Society in the Developing World*, London: Routledge, 2000, 2nd ed.

Karawan, Ibrahim A., "Arab Dilemmas in the 1990s: Breaking Taboos and Searching for Signposts," *Middle East Journal* 48, no. 3, Summer 1994, pp. 433–454.

Karshenas, Massoud, and M. Hashem Pesaran, "Economic Reform and the Reconstruction of the Iranian Economy," *Middle East Journal* 49, no. 1, Winter 1995, pp. 89–111.

Katouzian, Homa, "Islamic Government and Politics: The Practice and Theory of the Absolute Guardianship of Jurisconsult," paper delivered to the Symposium on the Postwar Arab Gulf, 12–14 July 1989, Centre for Arab Gulf Studies, University of Exeter, pp. 14–17.

Kedourie, Elie, "Feature Article: Islam Resurgent," *Encyclopaedia Britannia Book of the Year 1980: Events of 1979,* Chicago: Encyclopaedia Britannica, 1980, pp. 58–63.

Kemp, Geoffrey, "Iran: Can the United States Do a Deal?" *Washington Quarterly* 24, no. 1, Winter 2001, pp. 109–124.

———, "The Persian Gulf Remains the Strategic Prize," *Survival* 40, no. 4, Winter 1998–1999, pp. 132–149.

Kennedy, Paul, *The Rise and Fall of Great Powers: Economic Change and Military Conflict from 1500 to 2000*, London: Fontana Press, 1989.

Khalilizad, Zalmay, "The United States and the Persian Gulf: Preventing Regional Hegemony," *Survival* 37, no. 2, Summer 1995, pp. 95–120.

Khalizad, Zalmay, and David Ochmanek, "Rethinking U.S. Defence Planning," *Survival* 39, no. 1, Spring 1997, pp. 43–64.

Khasan, Hilal, "The New World Order and the Tempo of Militant Islam," *British Journal of Middle Eastern Studies* 24, no. 1, May 1997, pp. 5–24.

Kienle, Eberhard, "More Than a Response to Islam: The Political Deliberalization of Egypt in the 1990s," *Middle East Journal* 52, no. 2, Spring 1s998, pp. 220–235.

Kratochwil, Friedrich V., "Politics, Norms and Peaceful Change," *Review of International Studies* 24, Special Issue, December 1998, pp. 193–218.

Krause, Joachim, "Proliferation Risks and Their Strategic Relevance: What Role for NATO?" *Survival* 37, no. 2, pp. 135–148.

Lake, Anthony, "Confronting the Backlash States," *Foreign Affairs* 73, no. 2, March–April 1994, pp. 45–55.

Latham, Robert, "History, Theory, and International Order: Some Lessons from the Nineteenth Century," *Review of International Studies* 23, no. 4, October 1997, pp. 419–443.

Lewis, Bernard, *The Political Language of Islam,* Chicago: University of Chicago Press, 1988.

Luck, Steve, et al., eds., *Philips Millennium Illustrated Encyclopedia,* London: George Philip, 1999.

Maddy-Weitzman, Bruce, and Efraim Inbar, eds., *Religious Radicalism in the Greater Middle East,* London: Frank Cass, 1997.

Mahdi, Fadhil A., "Responses to Globalization in the Gulf Countries," paper presented to the Conference on Globalisation and the Gulf, 2–4 July 2001, Institute of Arab and Islamic Studies, University of Exeter, United Kingdom.

Marr, Phebe, "The United States, Europe and the Middle East: An Uneasy Triangle," *Middle East Journal* 48, no. 2, Spring 1994, pp. 211–225.

Marshall, Don D., "National Development and the Globalisation Discourse: Confronting 'Imperative' and 'Convergence' Notions," *Third World Quarterly* 17, no. 5, 1996, pp. 875–901.

Maynes, Charles William, "The Middle East in the Twenty-first Century," *Middle East Journal* 52, no. 1, Winter 1998, pp. 9–16.

Mazrui, Ali A., "Islamic and Western Values," *Foreign Affairs* 76, no. 5, September–October 1997, pp. 118–132.

McGrew, Anthony G., and Paul G. Lewis, eds., *Global Politics: Globalization and the Nation-State,* Cambridge: Polity Press, 1992.

Merza, A. K., "Economic Reforms in Major Arab Oil-Producing Countries," paper presented to the Conference on Globalization and the Gulf, 2–4 July 2001, Institute of Arab and Islamic Studies, University of Exeter, United Kingdom.

Miller, Judith. "The Challenge of Radical Islam," *Foreign Affairs* 72, no. 2, Spring 1993, pp. 43–56.

Morales, Waltrund Queiser, "U.S. Intervention and the New World Order: Lessons from Cold War and Post–Cold War Cases," *Third World Quarterly* 15, no. 1, 1994, pp. 77–98.

Munoz, Gema Martin, ed., *Islam, Modernism, and the West: Cultural and Political Relations at the End of the Millennium,* London: I. B. Tauris, 1999.

Murden, Simon, *Emergent Regional Powers and International Relations in the Gulf: 1988–1991,* Reading: Ithaca Press, 1995.

———, "Review Article: Huntington and His Critics," *Political Geography* 18, 1999, pp. 1017–1022.

Murphy, Richard W., and F. Gregory Gause III, "Democracy and U.S. Policy in the Muslim Middle East," *Middle East Policy* 5, no. 1, January 1997, pp. 58–67.

Norton, Augustus Richard, "The Future of Civil Society in the Middle East," *Middle East Journal* 47, no. 2, Spring 1993, pp. 205–216.

O'Hagan, Jacinta, "Civilisational Conflict? Looking for Cultural Enemies," *Third World Quarterly* 16, no. 1, March 1995, pp. 19–38.

O'Sullivan, Meghan L., "The Politics of Dismantling Containment," *The Washington Quarterly* 24, no. 1, Winter 2001, pp. 67–76.

Owen, Roger, *State, Power and Politics in the Making of the Modern Middle East,* London: Routledge, 2000, 2nd ed.

Pamir, Peri, "Peace-building Scenarios After the Gulf War," *Third World Quarterly* 13, no. 2, 1992, pp. 283–300.

Parekh, Bhikhu, "When Religion Meets Politics," *Demos,* no. 11 (Quarterly), 1997, pp. 5–7.

Parker, Geoffrey, "Globalization and Geopolitical World Orders," Chapter 5 in Gillings Young and Eleonore Kofman, eds., *Globalization: Theory and Practice,* London: Pinter, 1996, pp. 73–80.

Peterson, J. E., "The Political Status of Women in the Arab Gulf States," *Middle East Journal* 43, no. 1, Winter 1989, pp. 35–50.

Pfaff, William, "The Reality of Human Affairs," *World Policy Journal* 14, no. 2, 1997, pp. 89–96.

Pinto, Maria do Céu, *Political Islam and the United States: A Study of U.S. Policy Towards Islamist Movements in the Middle East,* foreword by James Piscatori, Reading: Ithaca Press, 1999.

Piscatori, James, "Islam and World Politics," Chapter 12 in John Baylis and N. J. Rengger, eds., *Dilemmas of World Politics: International Issues in a Changing World,* Oxford: Oxford University Press, 1992.

———, "The Rushdie Affair and the Politics of Ambiguity," *International Affairs* 66, no. 4, 1990, pp. 767–789.

Pratt, Nicola, "Conceptualizing Globalization: Some Political Implications for the Arab World," paper presented to the Conference on Globalization and the Gulf, 2–4 July 2001, Institute of Arab and Islamic Studies, University of Exeter, United Kingdom.

Quandt, William, "The Middle East on the Brink: Prospects for Change in the 21st Century," *Middle East Journal* 50, no. 1, Winter 1996, pp. 9–17 (adapted from his address to the Middle East Institute's forty-ninth annual conference in Washington, 29–30 September 1995).

Ramazani, Nesta, "Women in Iran: The Revolutionary Ebb and Flow," *Middle East Journal* 47, no. 3, Summer 1993, pp. 407–428.

Ramazani, R. K, "The Shifting Premise of Iran's Foreign Policy: Towards a Democratic Peace?" *Middle East Journal* 52, no. 2, Spring 1998, pp. 177–187.

Al-Rasheed, Madawi, "Saudi Arabia's Islamic Opposition," *Current History* 95, no. 597, January 1996, pp. 16–21.

———, "God, the King and the Nation: Political Rhetoric in Saudi Arabia in the 1990s," *Middle East Journal* 50, no. 3, Summer 1996, pp. 360–371.

Ravenhill, John, "The North-South Balance of Power," *International Affairs* 66, no. 4, 1990, pp. 731–748.

Reeves, Julie, "Culture, Civilization and IR Theory," paper presented at the

Annual Conference of the British International Studies Association, Brighton, 14–16 December 1998.

Richards, Alan, "Economic Imperatives and Political Systems," *Middle East Journal* 47, no. 2, Spring 1993, pp. 217–227.

Robinson, Glenn E., "Can Islamists Be Democrats? The Case of Jordan," *Middle East Journal* 51, no. 3, Summer 1997, pp. 373–387.

Roy, Olivier, *The Failure of Political Islam*, London: I. B. Tauris, 1994.

Rugh, William A., "Time to Modify Our Gulf Policy," *Middle East Policy* 5, no. 1, January 1997, pp. 46–57.

Said, Edward W., "A Devil Theory of Islam," *The Nation,* 12–19 August 1996, pp. 28–32.

———, *Orientalism: Western Conceptions of the Orient,* London: Penguin Books, reprint of 1978 edition with new afterword, 1995.

Salamé, Ghassan, "Torn Between the Atlantic and the Mediterranean: Europe and the Middle East in the Post–Cold War Era," *Middle East Journal* 48, no. 2, Spring 1994, pp. 226–249.

Salinger, Pierre, "The United States, the United Nations, and the Gulf War," *Middle East Journal* 49, no. 4, Autumn 1995, pp. 595–613.

Sayigh, Yezid, "The Gulf Crisis: Why the Arab Regional Order Failed," *International Affairs* 67, no. 3, July 1991, pp. 487–507.

Schama, Simon, *A History of Britain: At the Edge of the World? 3000BC–AD1603,* London: BBC Worldwide, 2000.

Scholte, Jan Aart, "Global Capitalism and the State," *International Affairs* 73, no. 3, July 1997, pp. 427–452.

Serfaty, Simon, "Bridging the Gulf Across the Atlantic: Europe and the United States in the Persian Gulf," *Middle East Journal* 52, no. 3, Summer 1998, pp. 337–350.

Al-Shayeji, Abdullah, "Dangerous Perceptions: Gulf Views of the U.S. Role in the Region," *Middle East Policy* 5, no. 3, September 1997, pp. 1–13.

Sidahmed, Abdel Salam, and Anourshiravan Ehteshami, eds., *Islamic Fundamentalism,* Boulder, Colo.: Westview Press, 1996.

Sidaway, James Derrick, "What Is in a Gulf? From 'Arc of Crisis' to the Gulf War," Chapter 10 in Gearóid Ó Tuahail and Simon Dalby, eds., *Rethinking Geopolitics,* London: Routledge, 1998.

Simon, Steven, "U.S. Strategy in the Persian Gulf," *Survival* 34, no. 3, Autumn 1992, pp. 81–97.

Sivan, Emmanuel, "Sunni Radicalism in the Middle East and the Iranian Revolution," *International Journal of Middle Eastern Studies* 21, no. 1, February 1989, pp. 1–30.

Spector, Leonard, "Neo-Nonproliferation," *Survival* 37, no. 1, Spring 1995, pp. 66–85.

Sridharan, Kripa, "G-15 and South-South Cooperation: Promise and Performance," *Third World Quarterly* 19, no. 3, 1998, pp. 357–373.

Tahi, Mohand Salah, "Algeria's Democratisation Process: A Frustrated Hope," *Third World Quarterly* 16, no. 2, June 1995, pp. 197–220.

Tal, Lawrence, "Dealing with Radical Islam: The Case of Jordan," *Survival* 37, no. 3, Autumn 1995, pp. 139–156.

Tarock, Adam, "Civilisational Conflict? Fighting the Enemy Under a New Banner," *Third World Quarterly* 16, no. 1, March 1995, pp. 5–18.

Tehran Declaration on Dialogue Among Civilizations, adopted by the Islamic Symposium on Dialogue Among Civilizations, Tehran, 3–5 May 1999. Text reproduced on the Homepage of the Permanent Delegation of the OIC to the UN Offices in Geneva and Vienna, http://www.oic-un.org/8/tehdec. stm.

Tétreault, Mary Ann, "Individualism, Secularism, and Fundamentalism," paper presented at the Annual Conference of the British Society for Middle Eastern Studies, Birmingham, 5–8 July 1998.

Tétreault, Mary Ann, and Haya al-Mughni, "Modernization and Its Discontents: State and Gender in Kuwait," *Middle East Journal* 49, no. 3, Summer 1995, pp. 403–417.

Thomas, Caroline, "Where Is the Third World Now?" *Review of International Studies* 25, Special Issue: The Interregnum: Controversies in World Politics 1989–1999, December 1999, pp. 225–244.

Turner, Bryan S., *Orientalism, Postmodernism and Globalism,* London: Routledge, 1994.

Weiss, Linda, "Globalization and National Governance: Antinomy or Interdependence," *Review of International Studies* 25, Special Issue: The Interregnum: Controversies in World Politics 1989–1999, December 1999, pp. 59–88.

Welch, David, "The Clash of Civilizations Thesis as an Argument and as a Phenomenon," *Security Studies* 6, no. 4, 1997, pp. 197–216.

Wilkin, Peter, "New Myths for the South: Globalisation and the Conflict Between Private Power and Freedom," *Third World Quarterly* 17, no. 2, 1996, pp. 227–238.

Wilson, Rodney, "The Contribution of Muhammad Baqir Al Sadar to Contemporary Islamic Economic Thought," paper presented at the Annual Conference of the British Society for Middle Eastern Studies, St. Catherine's College, Oxford, 6–9 July 1997.

———, "The Economic Relations of the Middle East: Toward Europe or Within the Region?" *Middle East Journal* 48, no. 2, Spring 1994, pp. 268–287.

———, "Markets Without Capitalism: An Islamic Economic System?" Paper presented at the British Society of Middle Eastern Studies Annual Lecture, London, 1998.

Yaphe, Judith S., "Iraq: The Exception to the Rule," *The Washington Quarterly* 24, no. 1, Winter 2001, pp. 125–137.

Zunes, Stephen, "The Function of Rogue States in U.S. Middle East Policy," *Middle East Policy* 5, no. 2, May 1997, pp. 150–165.

———, "Hazardous Hegemony: The United States in the Middle East," *Current History* 96, no. 606, January 1997, pp. 20–24.

Index

Abdullah, Crown Prince of Saudi
  Arabia, 73, 113
Abdullah, King of Jordan, 83
Afghanistan-Pakistan-Kashmir
  Islamic milieu, 76, 77, 78, 81, 202,
  203
Afghan *mujahidin,* 76
Ahmed, Akbar S., 123
Ajami, Fouad, 35, 151, 206
Al-Aqsa mosque (Jerusalem), 52,
  189, 200, 207
Al-Azhar mosque and university
  (Cairo), 143
Albright, Madeline, 63, 71, 74
Algerian economic reform, 107
Anglo-American model of liberalism,
  2, 3, 100, 104–105
Arab nationalism, 96, 97, 134, 135,
  189
Arafat, Yasser, 50–53
Asad, Hafiz al-, 142
Asian economic crisis (1997–1998),
  103–104, 107
Atlantic Charter, 2, 212
Ayodhya mosque (India), 11

Bani-Sadr, Abolhassan, 138, 176
Banna, Hasan al-, 140, 162, 214
Barak, Ehud, 51
Barber, Benjamin, 10, 12, 36,
  121–122, 207
Bashir, Umar al-, 170

Bazargan, Mehdi, 174
Belhadj, Ali, 171
Ben 'Ali, Zayn al-'Abidin, 171
Benjedid, Chadli, 107, 136, 146
Berlusconi, Silvio, 38
Bin Laden, Usama, 17, 77–79, 81, 84,
  85, 140
Bonyads (Islamic foundations in
  Iran), 108, 109, 124
Bosnia, 35, 44, 196
Boudief, Muhammad, 146
Bouteflika, Abdelaziz, 147
Bush, George, 5, 45, 47, 49
Bush, George W., 6, 46, 54, 75, 80,
  82, 86
Buzan, Barry, 33, 39

Campaign for the Defense of
  Legitimate Rights (CDLR) (Saudi
  Arabia), 163
Camp David talks (July–August
  2000), 51
China: long-term interests in the Gulf,
  86, 206; nuclear assistance to Iran,
  69; UN Security Council member,
  45, 64
Clash of Civilizations, The. See
  Huntington, Samuel
Clinton, Bill: administration's attitude
  toward Iran, 70–71, 74, 75; Camp
  David talks (July–August 2000),
  51, 58; sympathy for Israel, 54, 74

Cosmopolitan consumer culture, 10,
16, 94–95, 119–123
Council for the Determination of
Exigencies *(Shura-i Mashlahat-I
Nezam)* (Expediency Council)
(Iran), 66, 119, 173, 177
Counter-Proliferation Initiative (U.S.
Department of Defense), 46
Crony capitalism, 104–106
Cultural revivalism, 10, 23–24, 28

Dar al-Islam/dar al-Harb (realm of
Islam or peace/realm of War), 187
Dar al-sulh (realm of truce), 187
Declaration of Principles (Israel-
Palestinian agreement 1993), 48, 50
Djerejian, Edward, U.S. assistant sec-
retary of state for Near Eastern and
South Asian affairs, 37
Dual containment policy, 57–58, 74

East African embassy bombings
(August 1998), 79
Egyptian economic reform, 106–107
End of History. See Fukuyama,
Francis
European Union (EU), 7; constructive
engagement with Iran, 47, 71, 72,
75; long-term interests in the
Middle East, 86–87, 206; supervi-
sion of global markets, 7, 99

Fahd, King of Saudi Arabia, 83, 164
Front de Libération Nationale (FLN;
National Liberation Front)
(Algeria), 135, 146
Front Islamique du Salut (FIS;
Islamic Salvation Front) (Algeria),
76, 146, 147, 162, 194
Fuda, Farag, 143
Fukuyama, Francis, 1, 12, 17, 24–29,
39, 158, 212

Gama'a al-Islamiyya (Egypt), 140,
141, 149, 150, 194
Ganji, Akbar, 176, 178
General Agreement on Tariffs and
Trade (GATT), 5, 100–102

Ghali, Yousseff Boutros, 107
Al-Ghannoushi, Rachid, 171
GIA. *See* Group Islamique Armé
Globalization, 3, 4, 9, 25, 93, 95, 97,
98, 114, 119, 120, 126, 127, 205,
208
"Glocalization," 3, 36
Grand Mosque (Mecca), 77, 142
Groupe Islamique Armé (GIA; Armed
Islamic Group) (Algeria), 146,
147, 149
Group of Seven (G7), 70, 93–94

Halliday, Fred, 34, 37, 126, 206
Hamas (Palestinian), 51, 52, 65, 194
Hijab (veiling), 125, 137, 139, 161,
172, 174, 193
Historical and post-historical worlds,
25, 39–40
Hizballah (Party of God) (Lebanon),
65, 192, 201
Hizb al-Nahda (Renaissance Party),
171
Homo economicus, 115, 116
Huntington, Samuel, 12, 17, 29–31,
34–37, 39, 186, 201, 207
Hussein, King of Jordan, 145
Hussein, Saddam, 45, 49, 58–63, 65,
76, 83, 108, 142, 158, 192, 195, 196

IAEA. *See* International Atomic
Energy Agency
IDF. *See* Israel Defense Forces
IMF. *See* International Monetary
Fund
Infitah (opening), 96, 97, 135–137
International Atomic Energy Agency
(IAEA), 59, 69
International Monetary Fund (IMF), 5,
93, 99, 100, 104, 106, 107, 110, 111
Internet, 120, 121
Inter-Service Intelligence (ISI)
(Pakistan), 76
Intifadah (Palestinian uprising), 50;
al-Aqsa (from September 2000),
52–55, 63
Iran and Libya Sanctions Act (1996)
(U.S.), 71, 75

Iraq: economic reform prior to 1990, 108; invasion of Kuwait, 45
Iraq Liberation Act (1998) (U.S.), 61
IRI. *See* Islamic Republic of Iran
Islamic fundamentalism, 11, 138, 139, 141, 167, 192, 206, 207
Islamic modernists, 14, 138, 139, 174, 176
Islamic Republic of Iran (IRI): ban on satellite television, 121; economic reform, 108–110; hostility to U.S., 65–66; military development, 68–70; political reform, 157, 173–180, 209; revolution of 1978–1979, 14, 32, 65, 67, 141; theocratic system, 172–173
Islamic revival, 11, 12, 14, 17, 133, 137, 138, 142, 150, 156, 186
Islamic Welfare Party (Turkey), 170
Israel Defense Forces (IDF), 52, 53
Israeli settlement of the Occupied Territories, 48, 51, 54

Jamaat-i-Islami (Pakistan), 76, 167, 202
Jazeera, Al- (satellite television network), 165
Jerusalem, 51–55, 83, 135, 189, 200, 208, 214
Jihad (holy struggle), 78, 139
Jihad, Al- (Egypt), 140, 192, 194

Karbaschi, Gholamhossain, 177
Karzai, Hamid, 81
Kashmir conflict, 197, 198
Kemel, Mustafa (Ataturk), 96, 162
Kennedy, Paul, 5
Khalifa, Shaikh Hamad bin Issa al-, Emir of Bahrain, 166
Khameini, Ayatollah Ali, 66, 75, 173, 175, 177–179
Khatami, Mohammad: CNN interview (January 1998), 67–68; dialogue among civilizations, 38, 67, 201; diplomatic progress, 72–73, 193; economic reforms, 109; electoral victories, 72, 175, 178, 179; opposition of conservatives,

176–180; political reform agenda, 152, 176, 177, 180; views on U.S., 67–68
Khobar Towers bombing (Dhahran, Saudi Arabia) (June 1996), 77
Khomeini, Grand Ayatollah Ruhollah, 69, 119, 139, 141, 168, 172–175, 192, 193, 214
Kramer, Gudrun, 168, 169

Lake, Anthony, 57
Liberalism, 1, 4, 25, 28, 29, 38, 48, 155, 158, 160, 161, 211–212

Madani, Abbasi, 146
Madrid peace conference (October–November 1991), 49, 86
Mashlaha (common good), 169, 173
Mawdudi, Abu al-Ala al-, 139, 166–168, 170, 214
McWorld. See Barber, Benjamin
Miller, Judith, 33
Mitchell Commission, 48, 54
MNCs. *See* Multinational corporations
Mojahedin-e Khalq (People's Combatants), 174
Mohammad, Prophet of Islam, 139, 142, 162, 187, 213
Mubarak, Hosni, 76, 83, 84, 106, 107, 144
Multinational corporations (MNCs), 9–10, 93, 98–99, 117
Muslim Brotherhood, 140, 144, 145, 149, 167, 202
Muslim migration, 12, 30, 181, 206

Nasser, Gamal Abdul, 96, 135
National Democratic Party (NDP) (Egypt), 144
NATO. *See* North Atlantic Treaty Organization
Neofundamentalism, 148–149
New world order, 45–47
No-fly zones (over Iraq), 59, 61
Non-Proliferation Treaty (NPT), 46, 69; Iranian commitment to, 69–70
North Atlantic Treaty Organization

(NATO), 6, 44, 46, 58, 70
Nuri, Abdollah, 177

OIC. *See* Organization of the Islamic
Conference
Omar, Mullah Mohammad, 78, 162
Ontology, 4, 14
Organization of Petroleum Exporting
Countries (OPEC), 73, 100
Organization of the Islamic
Conference (OIC), 18, 189–191;
opposition to Islamic terrorism,
199, 203; potential for collective
action, 197–200; position on
human rights, 156–157; rejection
of Iran and Libya Sanctions Act,
71
Ottoman Empire, 95, 188, 204, 214

Pahlavi, Mohammad Reza, 141
Palestinian National Authority (PNA),
50–53, 55
Palestinian suicide bombings, 50–52,
53
Peres, Shimon, 50
Piscatori, James, 168
PNA. *See* Palestinian National
Authority
Popular Arab and Islamic Conference,
202

Qaeda, al- (the base), 78–81, 148,
194, 199, 202, 203
Quran, 139, 159, 213
Qutb, Sayyid, 139, 140, 167, 168,
170, 191, 192, 213

Rabin, Yitzhak, 50
Rafsanjani, Ali Akbar Hashemi, 66,
67, 69, 73, 108, 109, 152, 175,
177, 193
Rahman, Shaikh Omar Abdel, 34, 78,
79
Reagan, Ronald, 2, 3, 5, 32, 98
Riba (unearned income, interest),
116–118
Rogue states, 46–47, 57, 75, 87
Roy, Olivier, 119, 148, 149, 206

Rushdie, Salman, 160, 193

Sadat, Anwar, 96, 135, 136, 140
SAP. *See* Structural adjustment program
Saudi Arabia: economic reform,
111–113; influence in the Muslim
world, 76; political reform, 159,
163–165, 208; *Shura* Council, 164;
supply of U.S. arms, 56; U.S. basing, 47, 58, 76–77, 82, 202
September 2001 attacks (New York
and Washington), 11, 17, 32, 38,
79–80, 82, 84–86, 148, 186, 199,
201–204
Sharia (Islamic law), 14, 138, 139,
142, 143, 149, 159–163, 166–169,
172, 213
Sharon, Ariel, 52, 53, 83
Shura (consultation), 161–163, 169,
170
Soroush, Abdol-Karim, 176
Structural adjustment program (SAP),
100, 103, 104, 106, 114, 127

Taha, Mahmud Mohammad, 138
Takfir (to excommunicate as an apos-
tate), 143
Taliban movement, 44, 78, 80, 81,
147, 162, 199, 202
Tehran Declaration on Dialogue
Among Civilizations, 38
Tenet, George, Director of the CIA,
52
Thatcher-Reagan capitalist revival, 2,
3, 98, 115, 212
Tri-islands dispute (Iran–United Arab
Emirates), 73
Turabi, Hasan al-, 78, 170, 202

Umma (Islamic people), 187–189,
191, 195, 196, 200
United Nations (UN), 2, 54, 188, 196,
197
UN control regime on Iraq: British
and U.S. bombing, 59–61, 64;
decay of sanctions regime, 63–
65; human cost of sanctions,

61–62; weapons inspector, 63
United States: alliance system in the
   Middle East, 37, 43, 47, 83–84,
   198–199; alliance with Israel, 48,
   49, 83; military power, 5–7; oil
   interests, 44; provision of hege-
   monic services, 5, 6, 43, 44, 84–86;
   war on terrorism, 80–82, 84
Universal Declaration on Human
   Rights (1948), 33, 156, 160, 212
UN Security Council, 2, 45
UN Security Council Resolution 687
   (1991), 59
UN Security Council Resolution 1284
   (1999), 63
UN Special Commission (UNSCOM),
   59–61, 63
UN Year of Dialogue Among
   Civilizations, 38
U.S.S. *Cole* bombing in Aden
   Harbour, Yemen (October 2000),
   79
Utaiba, Juhayman al-, 142

Velayat-e faqih (guardianship of the
   jurisconsult), 67, 141, 162,
   174–176, 215

War in Afghanistan (2001), 80–81
War in Bosnia, 196
Western hegemony, 4, 7–8, 28, 44, 49,
   156, 198, 200, 204, 211
Wilson, Woodrow, 2, 45
World Bank, 5, 99, 100, 104, 111
World Economic Forum, 8
World Trade Center bombing
   (February 1993), 34, 78–79
World Trade Organization (WTO), 93,
   99, 101–103, 111–113

Yazdi, Ayatollah Mohammad, 66
Yazdi, Ebrahim, 174

Zawahiri al-, Ayman, 78, 140
Zinni, Anthony, 83
Zionism, 48, 49, 55
Zones of peace and conflict, 39, 44

About the Book

S imon Murden investigates how Muslim societies in the Middle East are being affected by globalized politics and economics and how they are adapting to them.

Murden describes how a Western-designed set of economic and political norms, institutions, and regimes has come to be a hegemonic system. His focus is on the encounter between the Islamic vision of society, with its emphasis on community and social control, and the Western liberal vision of economic liberation and individual choice. Attempting to make sense of the various political purposes to which Islam is being put in Middle Eastern states, he explores the response of the Islamic world to the penetration of the liberal political agenda.

Moving the debate beyond the polarization engendered by the "clash of civilizations" thesis, Murden reveals the complex interactions between Islam and the West that are shaping Middle Eastern politics.

Simon Murden is senior lecturer in the Department of Strategic Studies and International Affairs at Britannia Royal Naval College in Dartmouth. He is author of *Emergent Regional Powers and International Relations in the Gulf, 1988–1991*.